Intellectual Property - Global Perspective Advances and Challenges

Edited by Sakthivel Lakshmana Prabu and Appavoo Umamaheswari

Published in London, United Kingdom

Intellectual Property - Global Perspective Advances and Challenges
http://dx.doi.org/10.5772/intechopen.104193
Edited by Sakthivel Lakshmana Prabu and Appavoo Umamaheswari

Contributors
Appavoo Umamaheswari, Sakthivel Lakshmana Prabu, I. Gede Agus Kurniawan, Taufik H. Simatupang, Si-Yeol Kim, Yue Xu, Yumao Wang, Sentosa Sembiring, Vladlena Lisenco, Pavel Svačina, Tatiana Ertner, Diericon Cordeiro, Ramon Miranda, Lucas Aguiar, Yu Uny Cao, Hu Wang, Eva R. Porras

First published in London, United Kingdom, 2023 by IntechOpen
IntechOpen is the global imprint of INTECHOPEN LIMITED, registered in England and Wales, registration number: 11086078, 5 Princes Gate Court, London, SW7 2QJ, United Kingdom

British Library Cataloguing-in-Publication Data
A catalogue record for this book is available from the British Library

Additional hard and PDF copies can be obtained from orders@intechopen.com

Intellectual Property - Global Perspective Advances and Challenges
Edited by Sakthivel Lakshmana Prabu and Appavoo Umamaheswari
p. cm.
Print ISBN 978-1-83769-502-7
Online ISBN 978-1-83769-501-0
eBook (PDF) ISBN 978-1-83769-503-4

Meet the editors

Dr. Sakthivel Lakshmana Prabu obtained Ph.D. in Pharmaceutical Sciences from Manipal University, India, and a postgraduate degree in Intellectual Property Right Law from the National Law School of India University. At present, he is working as Assistant Professor (S. Gr) at Anna University, BIT Campus, India since 2009. He has more than 20 years of experience in academia and pharmaceuticals. Dr. Lakshmana Prabu has published 114 peer-reviewed papers in international and national journals and 30 book chapters and has 4 patents to his credit. He has also edited six books. He serves as a reviewer and editorial board member for several journals. He has organized numerous national and international conferences, trainings, workshops, and symposiums. Dr. Lakshmana Prabu has worked on projects funded by the Department of Biotechnology, New Delhi, India; Tamil Nadu State Council for Science and Technology, India; and the Centre for Sponsored Research and Consultancy, Anna University, India.

Dr. Appavoo Umamaheswari obtained a B.Pharm from The Tamil Nadu Dr.M.G.R. Medical University, Chennai, India. She is a recipient of the Thiru Gnana Sebastian Endowment Award in M.Pharmacy, and was offered the Management Gold Medal award as Best Outgoing Student for the Year 2006 by Periyar College of Pharmaceutical Sciences, India. She obtained a Ph.D. in Pharmaceutical Technology from Anna University, India, where she is an Assistant professor (S. Gr) at the University College of Engineering. Her responsibilities include teaching undergraduate and graduate students in biopharmaceutical technology. She has numerous research publications to her credit. Dr. Umamaheswari is an editor for *Computer Applications in Drug Discovery and Development* and a referee for various other journals. She has also authored fifteen book chapters. She has one patent to her credit. She has given multiple presentations at national and international conferences and is an active member of many professional and academic bodies. She serves as a referee for various reputed journals. Dr. Umamaheswari has worked on projects funded by the Department of Biotechnology, New Delhi, India, and the Centre for Sponsored Research and Consultancy, Anna University.

Contents

Preface

Intellectual property (IP) helps to support the development of wide-ranging technologies in different fields. In the evolution of company models, IP is a key component of value and its prospective growth has driven changes in the global economic status. Therefore, IP has become one of the largest and fastest-growing legal disciplines worldwide, thus requiring IP specialists who are knowledgeable in this field to handle IP rights (IPR) across national and international borders.

Two key components for every country's long-term development and progress are creativity and innovation. Our educational system needs to aggressively integrate both creativity and innovation. The development of concrete economic value and the ownership of new information has recently led to an "IPR divide" between the West and other nations of the world.

Intellectual Property – Global Perspective Advances and Challenges highlights the concerns and disputes in IP, focusing on copyright and traditional knowledge issues. In this book, we share developments in IPR at the global level, thanks to the diversity of our contributors.

Chapter 1, "Introductory Chapter: A Fundamental Conception on Copyright and Related Rights" by Appavoo Umamaheswari and Sakthivel Lakshmana Prabu, focuses on the genesis of copyright and its related rights.

Chapter 2, "The Existence of Copyrights on Traditional Cultural Expressions Held by the State: Implications and Orientations" by I. Gede Agus Kurniawan, examines existing copyright laws with respect to the expression of traditional culture and suggests harmonizing the law on various existing regulations with respect to traditional knowledge and traditional cultural expressions in Indonesia.

Chapter 3, "Inspired or Plagiarism: Application of Substantial Similarity in the Protection of Architectural Works towards Renewal of Indonesia's Copyright Law" by Taufik H Simatupang, discusses the substantial similarity of architectural work as plagiarism and suggests making some amendments and technically regulating existing copyrights law in Indonesia.

Chapter 4, "A Deriving Quantitative Similarities to Computer Programs and Determining Copyright Infringement in South Korea" by Kim Si-Yeol, focuses on determining the substantial similarity in computer program works and proposes to utilize the expert testimony system and substantial similarity with appropriate responses to limit copyright infringement.

Chapter 5, "IP Protection of Traditional Knowledge: A Dilemma Faced by the Chinese Traditional Medicine in Global Competition" by Yue Xu and Yumao Wang, describes the impasse faced by Traditional Chinese Medicine in global market competition under traditional knowledge and its protection.

Chapter 6, "The Utilization of the Economic Value of Geographic Indications as a Communal Right in Increasing Community Welfare (In the Perspective of Indonesian Trademark Law and Geographical Indications)" by Sentosa Sembiring, discusses the importance of geographical indications as a material right to improve the economic value of a community and obtain communal rights as exclusive rights for their geographical indications.

Chapter 7, "Intellectual Property in the Innovative Development of the World Economy" by Vladlena Lisenco, analyzes IP as a factor influencing the innovative development of economies and outlines IP as the main instrument of innovative transformation in the present global scenario.

Chapter 8, "Remuneration of Employee Inventions: Building a Typology of Existing Approaches" by Pavel Svacina, discusses the remuneration of employees for their inventions.

Chapter 9, "The Role of Intellectual Property in Assuring Cultural and Gender Diversity in Labor Force in an Internationalized World" by Tatiana Ertner, Diericon Cordeiro, Ramon Miranda and Lucas Aguiar, studies the role of IP as a tool in assuring cultural and gender diversity.

Chapter 10, "New IP and Standardization Practices in China's Data-Centric Digital Economy" by Yu Uny Cao and Hu Wang, examines the importance of a data-centric digital economy and its policies, practices, and innovations in data, IP, and standardization.

Chapter 11, "Intellectual Property and the Blockchain Sector, a World of Potential Economic Growth and Conflict" by Eva R. Porras, discusses the development of Blockchain technologies and their management under IPR.

This book provides a greater understanding of the role of IP and its related challenges and concerns. It is a recommended resource for research scholars, students, industrial experts, technologists, and scientists.

We acknowledge the full support of all the contributing authors. We also give special thanks to the staff at IntechOpen for their help and support throughout the publication process.

Dr. Sakthivel Lakshmana Prabu and Dr. Appavoo Umamaheswari
Department of Pharmaceutical Technology,
University College of Engineering (BIT Campus),
Anna University,
Tiruchirappalli, Tamil Nadu, India

Section 1

Introduction

Chapter 1

Introductory Chapter: A Fundamental Conception on Copyright and Related Rights

Appavoo Umamaheswari and Sakthivel Lakshmana Prabu

1. Introduction

Intellectual Property Rights (IPR) are the rights granted to persons as ownership for the works of their imagination and to provide exclusive right to exploit their ideas for a definite period [1, 2].

1.1 Development of international intellectual property regulations

During nineteenth century, successive congresses were held in Vienna and other parts of Europe, which laid the basis for International Intellectual Property Protection. Paris Convention in the year 1883, the protection of industrial property was established. The three principal types of property such as Trade Mark, Patents and Industrial designs were protected by this convention. During 1886, based on Berne Convention the International Copyright Act was adopted for the protection of literary and artistic works.

In 1949, The General Agreement on Tariffs and Trade (GATT) was established, but it was last until 1993; however, in 1995 World Trade Organization replaced the GATT. World Intellectual Property Organization was formed in 1960; it manages both Berne and Paris convention. Through these conventions WIPO was established in 1967. World Trade Organization (WTO) is an International Organization was created in 1977 for improvement and understanding of IPR.

From January 1, 1995, Trade Related Aspects of Intellectual Property Rights (TRIPS) has come into force. It establishes the basic requirements for the protection and enforcement of IPR in member nations, which are essential to encourage appropriate and effective protection of IPR in order to reduced trade distortions and barriers. The requirements under TRIPS agreement concern with minimal requirements for protection within the legal frameworks and customs of the member nations [3].

Norms and standards are provided under TRIPS agreement for the following Intellectual Property. They are Patents, Copyrights and related rights, Trade Marks, Geographical Indications, Industrial Designs, Layout Designs of Integrated Circuits, Protection of Undisclosed Information (Trade Secrets) and Plant varieties [4].

IPR are broadly divided into two main categories. They are

1. Copyright and related rights

2. Industrial property

2. Copyright and related rights

Copyright and related rights are a type of rights under Intellectual Property which protect the ownership/authorship of their original works in a tangible form of expression. In simple it is called the Principle of Inherency. Under Copyright law different types works like literary works, dramatic works, musical composition, artistic works, cinematograph film (movie), sound recording, computer program, photograph, painting, poems and architectural works. Generally the duration of copyright lasts for 60 years, for original dramatic, literary, artistic and musical works, and the 60-year window is measured starting from the year after the author's passing.

The rights under copyrights are categorized into

1. Economic rights

2. Moral rights.

Economic Rights—These rights bring the economic benefits to the owner/author of copyright.

Moral Rights—These are special rights given to the owner/author.

3. Economic rights

3.1 Literary works, dramatic works and musical work

i. Literary works include computer program and compilation of computer databases

ii. Dramatic works include choreographic work, scenic arrangement and entertainment in dumb show

iii. Musical works include music of work with any graphical representation.

The rights under this category are

a. Replicating the work in different material form

b. Distributing the work as copies to the public

c. Execution of the work in public

d. Creating any cinematograph film

e. Doing some any translation of the work

f. Making any adaptation for the work.

3.2 Artistic work

Artistic work includes painting, drawing, sculpture, engraving, photograph and architecture.

The rights under this category are

a. To replicate the work in any sensible form

b. To inform the public about the work.

c. To circulate the copies into the public

d. To make any revision of the work

e. To use the work in a cinematic project.

3.3 Cinematograph work

Any visual recording on a medium that is made by a procedure that allows a moving image to be formed is considered a cinematograph work.

The rights under this category are

a. To make a reproduction of the film

b. To vend or give on hire

c. To inform the public about the film.

3.4 Sound recording

Recording the sound from which it is possible to reproduce the sound, independent of the media used to do so is called sound recording.

The rights under this category are

a. To create a sound recording that captures it.

b. To sell or give on hire or offer for sale

c. To communicate the sound recording to the public.

The composer is the sole owner of the music's copyright, whereas the sound recording's producer is the sole owner of the music's recorded copyright. Live performances are not protected by copyright in the same way that recording of music performance or sporting events.

3.5 Computer program

Computer program are literary works that are written, recorded, or reduced to tangible form.

The rights under this category are

a. To carry out any act that a person who owns the copyright of music, literature, or dramatic may carry out provided that the work is not a computer program regardless of whether the copy has been sold or rented.

b. To vend or give on hire or offer for hire of sale.

4. Moral Rights

These are special rights given to the owner/author, and these rights are parallel and independent to the author's economic rights.

Different types of moral rights are

i. Paternity right or right of authorship—right to claim the authorship of the work.

ii. Integrity rights or rights against distortion—rights to protect his honour and reputation

iii. General right—not to have a work falsely attributed to him

4.1 Transfer of copyright

A licence may be issued by the owner of a copyright to a third party. The licence may only apply to a certain interest or to the full copyright. A licence might be exclusive or nonexclusive and typically just some rights, not all, are subject to it.

Licence and assignment

An assignment is distinct from a licence. In the licencing procedure, the licencee obtains the right to exercise specified rights subject to be condition of the licence and does not become owner of the rights. While in an assignment, the assignee takes ownership of the interest that was given to them.

Licence and consent

Consent is distinct from licence, which does not necessarily need one but is required for any specific use or purpose of the copyright work.

5. Duration of a licence

A licence may be granted indefinitely or it may be limited for a specific period of time. The publisher cannot be prevented from selling any unsold copies of a work that was printed within the licence period after the licence expires in the case of a licence to publish a work of literature or another type for a specific period of time.

Different types of licence are

i. Exclusive and non-exclusive licence

A licence that only applies to the licensee or the person authorized by him is known as an exclusive licence. Non-exclusive licences allow the copyright holder to grant licences to more than one person or to exercise the right alone.

ii. Non-voluntary or compulsory licence

These provisions are proposed when there is any issue for the enforcement of copyright [5–10].

DOI: http://dx.doi.org/10.5772/intechopen.1001447

6. Conclusion

Our introductory chapter mainly sheds light on the International Intellectual Property Regulations. In particular, copyrights and related rights are described in brief with economic as well as moral rights. The Intellectual Property Rights are rights which provide protection of ideas which inspire to create an innovative technology with modernization in different arenas. In this modern era, protection of rights for a certain invention is considered as a major concern due to the increased risk of infringements. Owing to potential economic benefits associated with these intellectual assets which are intangible in nature when they laid into the market. Furthermore, among different IPR rights, copyright and related rights are exclusive rights as they are automatically protected once the expression of idea has been completed in a definite form and it is not compulsory to get registered. IPR is a key element which aids in attaining both economic as well as social advancement. Hence, the owner/author registers their expression of idea as innovative work under copyrights, and then they can gain more benefits economically as well as in the societal status.

Author details

Appavoo Umamaheswari and Sakthivel Lakshmana Prabu*
Department of Pharmaceutical Technology, University College of Engineering, BIT Campus, Anna University, Tiruchirrappalli, India

*Address all correspondence to: slaxmanvel@gmail.com

References

[1] What is intellectual property? Available from: https://www.wipo.int/about-ip/en/ [Accessed on 10.02.2023]

[2] What are intellectual property rights? Available from: https://www.wto.org/english/tratop_e/trips_e/intel1_e.htm [Accessed on 10.02.2023]

[3] WIPO-A brief history. Available from: https://www.wipo.int/about-wipo/en/history.html [Accessed on 10.02.2023]

[4] Overview: the TRIPS agreement Available from: https://www.wto.org/english/tratop_e/trips_e/intel2_e.htm [Accessed on 12.02.2023]

[5] Intellectual property: protection and enforcement. Available from: https://www.wto.org/english/thewto_e/whatis_e/tif_e/agrm7_e.htm [Accessed on 12.02.2023]

[6] Copyright. https://www.wipo.int/copyright/en/ [Accessed on 12.02.2023]

[7] Understanding of copyright and related rights. Available from: https://www.wipo.int/edocs/pubdocs/en/wipo_pub_909_2016.pdf [Accessed on 12.02.2023]

[8] Basic notions of copyright and related rights Available from: https://www.wipo.int/edocs/mdocs/sme/en/wipo_wasme_ipr_ge_03/wipo_wasme_ipr_ge_03_4.pdf [Accessed on 14.02.2023]

[9] Copyright and related rights. Available from: https://www.wipo.int/export/sites/www/sme/en/documents/pdf/ip_panorama_5_learning_points.pdf [Accessed on 14.02.2023]

[10] Copyright in the digital world. Available from: https://www.wipo.int/ip-outreach/en/ipday/2016/ip_digital.html [Accessed on 14.02.2023]

Section 2

Copyright and Its Related Issues

Chapter 2

The Existence of Copyrights on Traditional Cultural Expressions Held by the State: Implications and Orientations

I. Gede Agus Kurniawan

Abstract

Expression of traditional culture is an intellectual property with a communal character. In this case, as a multicultural country, of course there are many aspects of culture in Indonesia that meet the aspects to be registered as part of intellectual property. The legal issue in this research is that there is no Government Regulation as mandated in Article 38 paragraph (4) of the Copyright Law. This study aims to understand the implications as well as to suggest future arrangements regarding copyright regulation on traditional cultural expressions. This research is normative legal research. The primary legal materials in this study include: the 1945 Constitution of the Republic of Indonesia, the Copyright Law, and the Regulation of The Minister Of Law and Human Rights of Communal Intellectual Property. Secondary legal materials include the draft of Traditional Knowledge and Traditional Cultural Expressions law and studies on intellectual property rights for traditional cultural expressions. Non-legal materials include language dictionaries. This research uses a statutory and conceptual approach. The results of the study confirm that the implication of the absence of a Government Regulation as mandated by Article 38 paragraph (4) of the Copyright Law is a legal ambiguity in the phrase "held by the state". This also includes the unregulated potential for inter-regional disputes that claim each other over a culture, including disputes between countries over cultural claims, especially in countries belonging to the same family. Apart from that, the future orientation that can be carried out is to form Government Regulations as mandated by Article 38 paragraph (4) of the Copyright Law, of course by harmonizing the law on various existing regulations. In addition, to make it more optimal, it is necessary to pass the Bill on Traditional Knowledge and Traditional Cultural Expressions to guarantee legal certainty for cultural arrangements in Indonesia.

Keywords: traditional cultural expressions, intellectual property rights, culture, copyright law, traditional knowledge

1. Introduction

Culture is one of the essential aspects of the establishment of a nation and state [1]. In this case, culture can become an identity as well as a unifying spirit for the existence of a nation or state [2]. Indonesia is a country with a variety of cultures. Indonesia deserves the nickname, the house of cultural diversity or a home for various existing cultures [3]. That is because almost all regions in Indonesia have their style and cultural system, which are distinctive and of various kinds. The UNESCO World Heritage Convention in 2022 places Indonesia with the most world heritage in Southeast Asia, surpassing Vietnam and Thailand in second and third place [4]. Furthermore, until the end of 2021, Indonesia has 1239 intangible cultural heritages recorded by UNESCO [5]. That is reinforced by the Ministry of Education and Culture release, which has determined as many as 289 Indonesian intangible cultural heritages by the end of 2021 [6]. That shows that almost every year, there are hundreds of additions regarding releasing the amount of Indonesia's intangible cultural heritage. This number is relatively large compared to other countries, especially in Asia and Southeast Asia.

Furthermore, at the end of 2022, Indonesia's intangible cultural heritage will be number two in Southeast Asia after Vietnam. The following table shows the number of countries with intangible cultural heritage in Southeast Asia.

From **Table 1** above, it can be concluded that Indonesia occupies the second position in terms of the amount of intangible heritage in 2022 that has been recognized by UNESCO. Indonesia is in second place after Vietnam, with 14 intangible cultural heritages.

The data shows that the Indonesian nation's cultural wealth is so varied that it needs to be preserved and recorded. In this context, the state plays a role in facilitating and establishing appropriate regulations to preserve and record the cultural heritage of the Indonesian nation. Indonesia has Law no. 28 of 2014 concerning Copyright (hereinafter referred to as the Copyright Law) which facilitates aspects of intellectual property regarding Indonesian cultural heritage. That is as stated in Article 38 of the Copyright Law, which emphasizes traditional cultural expressions whose creators are unknown (communal) to be made part of the communal intellectual property of the Indonesian nation. In addition, the struggle to accommodate traditional cultural expressions and knowledge in laws was also fought in the National Legislation

No	Country Name	Total Intangible Cultural Heritage
1.	Filipina	4
2.	Laos	1
3.	Thailand	3
4.	Singapura	1
5.	Timor Leste	1
6.	Malaysia	6
7.	Kamboja	5
8.	Vietnam	14
9.	Indonesia	12
10.	Myanmar	0
11.	Brunei Darussalam	0

(Source: UNESCO Intangible Cultural Heritage).

Table 1.
Countries with intangible cultural heritage in Southeast Asia.

Program 2010-2014 which included the Draft Law on Traditional Knowledge and Traditional Cultural Expressions (hereinafter referred to as the Draft Law concerning Traditional Knowledge) to be ratified as a separate law [7]. Even so, until 2022, the legislators have not ratified the Draft Law concerning Traditional Knowledge.

The legal issue in guaranteeing intellectual property rights for traditional cultural expressions is the provision of Article 38 paragraph (4) of the Copyright Law which mandates through delegation regulations or further regulations the regulation of copyrights on traditional cultural expressions held by the state through the establishment of Government Regulations. However, until 2022, a Government Regulation as a delegation regulation on Article 38 paragraph (4) of the Copyright Law has yet to be formed. The government only regulates communal traditional cultural expressions in the Minister of Law and Human Rights Regulation No. 13 of 2017 Concerning Communal Intellectual Property Data. In fact, with the mandate of Article 38 paragraph (4) of the Copyright Law, there should be a Government Regulation that specifically regulates copyrights on traditional cultural expressions held by the state.

Moreover, the Minister of Law and Human Rights on Communal Intellectual Property only has the character of an inventory or merely assists in recording and does not explicitly regulate copyright arrangements for traditional cultural expressions as mandated by Article 38 paragraph (4) of the Copyright Law. This study aims to understand the implications and initiate future arrangements regarding regulating copyrights on traditional cultural expressions. Research on traditional cultural expressions in the context of intellectual property was conducted by Yenny Eta Widyanti (2020) on the Protection of Indonesian Traditional Cultural Expressions in the Yang Sui Generis System, which focuses on efforts to establish special regulations regarding traditional cultural expressions [8]. Furthermore, research conducted by Nuzulia Kumala Sari and Dinda Agnis Mawardah [9] on the Alternative Integrated Cultural Data Collection System for Legal Protection of Traditional Cultural Expressions focuses on the orientation of legal policy ideas regarding an integrated data collection system for traditional culture [9]. Furthermore, Purnama Hadi Kusuma and Kholis Roisah (2022) research on the Protection of Traditional Cultural Expressions and Geographical Indications: An Intellectual Property with Communal Ownership focuses on aspects of strengthening communal ownership in the intellectual property of traditional cultural expressions [10].

Of the three previous studies, research on copyrights for traditional cultural expressions held by the state as stipulated in Article 38 paragraph (4) of the Copyright Law has never been carried out. Thus, this research is original. This study seeks to answer two formulations of the problem, namely: (i) What are the implications of copyright for traditional cultural expressions that have not been regulated in Government Regulations as mandated in Article 38 paragraph (4) of the Copyright Law, and (ii) What is the future orientation of rights regulation on traditional cultural expressions to protect the intellectual property rights of traditional cultural expressions in Indonesia?.

This research is a normative legal research that discusses the unregulated normative provisions in Article 38 paragraph (4) of the Copyright Law which require the establishment of a Government Regulation concerning copyrights for traditional cultural expressions held by the state [11]. The primary legal materials in this study include: the 1945 Constitution of the Republic of Indonesia, the Copyright Law, and the Minister of Law and Human Rights of Communal Intellectual Property. Secondary legal material includes the Draft Law concerning Traditional Knowledge and studies on intellectual property rights over traditional cultural expressions.

Non-legal materials include language dictionaries. This study uses a statutory and conceptual approach [11].

2. The copyright implications for traditional cultural expressions in copyright law: What and how?

Intellectual property is various types of intellectual works that originate from human thought and have economic value. Intellectual property emphasizes that humans can only do intellectual work. This is because humans can think and have the logical capacity to produce intellectual work. That confirms that humans can only make intellectual property and cannot be made by creatures other than humans or not due to natural factors [12]. The characteristics of intellectual property that humans can only make emphasize that every human intellectual work is intellectual property, one of which is a cultural expression. Cultural expression as part of culture itself is part of intellectual property because culture manifests human taste, creativity, and intention through specific processes [13]. That makes culture and its expressions an intellectual work with moral and economic values. In this case, the state is essential in providing arrangements and formulating policies to facilitate and preserve the culture that exists and develops in society.

The state's role in making legal products is likely to provide facilities and guarantees for culture and its expressions. That is also an effort to guarantee the existence of a culture and its expressions. In Indonesia, arrangements regarding guarantees for the existence of culture within the intellectual property framework are contained in the Copyright Law [14]. Although, in general, Copyright Law facilitates every general human intellectual creation, until 2022, Copyright Law is the only law that facilitates cultural expression in the context of intellectual property rights. Attempts to form a different law regarding cultural aspects and their expression in the context of intellectual property rights have been rolled out in the 2010–2014 National Legislation Program by forming the Draft Law concerning Traditional Knowledge [15]. In the Copyright Law, it is emphasized that the name of the law formed is Traditional Knowledge and Traditional Cultural Expressions. Referring to the name of the bill, in the opinion of the author, there are three orientations of the legislators regarding the name of the bill.

First, the legislators specifically (*lex specialis*) seek to listen to the aspirations of the people regarding the need for separate arrangements for cultural expressions in the context of intellectual. Of course, the intellectual property of cultural expressions is more oriented as a collective cultural work which is undoubtedly different from various other aspects of intellectual property rights, which are more individual [16]. *Second*, the Draft Law concerning Traditional Knowledge, as its name implies, is oriented towards regulating specific copyrights in knowledge and traditional cultural expressions. The affirmation between knowledge and traditional cultural expressions confirms an affirmation of orientation between traditional knowledge and traditional cultural expressions. Traditional knowledge is more of a system and specific procedures that shape the dimensions of knowledge or people's beliefs about something [17]. In this context, traditional knowledge is an alternative to modern science, which tends to have a logical-methodological dimension, so it marginalizes traditional knowledge, which has unique characteristics. One of the urgency of the importance of extracting traditional knowledge is the phenomenon of post-modernism, which has revolutionized the paradigm and mindset of modern science, which tends to the Cartesian-Newtonian paradigm, which has an empirical dimension and is value of traditional knowledge is expected to add new treasures as well as efforts to explore and preserve traditional knowledge in Indonesia. In this context, the Draft Law concerning Traditional Knowledge is urgent for the preservation of traditional knowledge [18].

Third, the Draft Law concerning Traditional Knowledge also emphasizes the importance of inventorying and preserving traditional cultural expressions. Expressions of traditional culture can vary, such as traditional ceremonies, and dances, to various traditional arts unique to the community, such as regional songs. Because Indonesia is a multicultural country with several similarities with neighboring countries that tend to be allied, mutual claims on cultural expressions are necessary and often even become a cultural problem between Indonesia and the surrounding countries. That is, for example, mutual claims regarding *Batik* motifs and fabrics, claims regarding *Reog Ponorogo* art, as well as several regional songs that occurred between Indonesia and Malaysia. That happens because the countries that claim to each other are allied countries with similarities in culture, customs, and traditions. In this case, the importance of the Draft Law concerning Traditional Knowledge is to facilitate the inventory, determination, and efforts to preserve various cultural expressions in Indonesia so that they are not easily claimed by other countries, especially countries with cultural similarities with Indonesia, such as Malaysia [19] (**Table 2**).

Referring to the three orientations in the Draft Law concerning Traditional Knowledge, it is relevant to ratifying the Draft Law concerning Traditional Knowledge to become a Law [20]. However, as is commonly known, the formation of laws is not a process that is impervious to non-legal influence [21]. In this case, the formation and ratification of law always require actors who have social-personal solid strength to make a law pass. Even though it is a legal process and procedure, the non-legal dimension also has a strong orientation in ratifying laws [22]. In this context, even though he has been included in the National Legislation Program, the Draft Law concerning Traditional Knowledge still needs to be passed, which remains a separate note in the lack of maximum legal protection for traditional knowledge

No	Culture Name	Origin
1.	*Pencak Silat* (Martial Arts)	Almost all over Indonesia
2.	Rasa Sayange' Song	Maluku
3.	Pendet Dance	Bali
4.	*Reog Ponorogo*	Ponorogo, East Java
5.	Rendang	West Sumatra
6.	*Tari Piring* or Plate Dance	Solok, West Sumatra
7.	Tor-Tor Dance	North Sumatra
8.	*Batik*	Dominant in Java and Several Other Regions in Indonesia
9.	*Kuda Lumping*	Ponorogo, East Java
10.	Makanan Lumpia	Semarang, Central Java

Table 2.
List of Indonesian intangible culture claimed by Malaysia.

and expressions of traditional culture. Even so, in fact, regarding legal protection for traditional cultural expressions, especially regarding copyright, in passing, it has also been regulated in Article 38 of the Copyright Law [23].

Article 38, paragraph (1) of the Copyright Law explains copyright on traditional cultural expressions held by the state. Regarding the phrase "held by the state," this is an exciting thing to study more deeply [24]. This is because the phrase held by the state in elucidating the Copyright Law needs to contain a comprehensive explanation [25]. The term "hold" in Great *Indonesian Dictionary* means "holding on, attached to, and guided by". In the context of Article 38, paragraph (1) of the Copyright Law, the term held by the state must be interpreted grammatically based on the state. This means that copyrights on traditional cultural expressions are recorded or registered based on provisions made by the state. That is a systematic interpretation relevant to Article 38, paragraph (4) of the Copyright Law stipulating that it is necessary to establish a government regulation regarding copyrights for traditional cultural expressions held by the state. Even so, until 2022, there is no Government Regulation as mandated by Article 38 paragraph (4) of the Copyright Law. Article 125 of the Copyright Law has emphasized that all implementing regulations mandated by the Copyright Law must be formed by 2 years after the Copyright Law is enacted. The Copyright Law was passed in 2014, which means that it should be by 2016. As mandated by Article 38 paragraph (4) of the Copyright Law, the Government Regulation has been ratified.

In other provisions, the Minister of Law and Human Rights of Communal Intellectual Property has provided arrangements for recording or inventory of communal intellectual property, such as cultural expressions [26]. Of course, because it is not a direct delegated regulation from the Copyright Law, the Communal Intellectual Property Ministerial Regulation has several weaknesses related to copyrights on traditional cultural expressions held by the state as mandated by Article 38 paragraph (4) of the Copyright Law. There are three aspects of weakness in the regulation of copyrights on traditional cultural expressions held by the state in the Minister of Law and Human Rights of Communal Intellectual Property. *First*, the Minister of Law and Human Rights of Communal Intellectual Property is only limited to an inventory of traditional cultural expressions. In this context, the Minister of Law and Human Rights on Communal Intellectual Property is limited to providing facilities for the community to take an inventory of traditional cultural expressions. *Second*, the Minister of Law and Human Rights of Communal Intellectual Property is a regulation that is an executive act. In this case, as a regulation, the Minister of Law and Human Rights for Communal Intellectual Property only stipulates the policy, and its substance only implements the law as a regulation above it. Provisions regarding rights and obligations to the substance of legal protection regarding traditional cultural expressions have yet to be explained in the Minister of Law and Human Rights of Communal Intellectual Property.

Third, the Minister of Law and Human Rights of Communal Intellectual Property is not a delegation regulation on Article 38 paragraph (4) of the Copyright Law. That is simultaneously confirms that the Minister of Law and Human Rights of Communal Intellectual Property certainly cannot substantively and optimally regulate further provisions as stipulated in Article 38 paragraph (4) of the Copyright Law. Based on the weaknesses of the Minister of Law and Human Rights of the Communal Intellectual Property above, this has implications for the regulation of copyrights on traditional cultural expressions held by the state, including (i) regulation and legal protection regarding the regulation of copyrights on traditional cultural expressions held by the state are not yet optimal because the Government Regulation has not yet been formed as mandated by Article 38 paragraph (4) of the Copyright Law, (ii) the meaning "held by the state" in Article 38 paragraph (4) of the Copyright Law still creates legal obscurity because the Copyright Law does not provide further explanation regarding the meaning of "held by the state," and (iii) arrangements regarding legal remedies for potential disputes related to copyrights on traditional cultural expressions held by the state. The potential for such disputes can include disputes between regions that claim each other over a culture, including disputes between countries that claim culture, especially in countries belonging to the same family.

3. The *Ius Constituendum* regarding copyrights of traditional cultural expressions: an orientation

Although, on the one hand, the Minister of Law and Human Rights for Communal Intellectual Property has provided a brief and simple arrangement, however, this clearly has not met the demands and expectations regarding the regulation of copyrights on traditional cultural expressions held by the state in a comprehensive manner. This is because the Minister of Law and Human Rights of Communal Intellectual Property is not a delegation regulation on the provisions in Article 38 paragraph (4) of the Copyright Law. In this case, Article 38 paragraph (4) of the Copyright Law mandates the establishment of a Government Regulation. Constitutionally, in the 1945 Constitution of the Republic of Indonesia, as in Article 5 paragraph (2) it is emphasized that Government Regulations are legal products whose orientation is to implement the provisions of the Law [27]. According to Ni'matul Huda, the provisions in this Government Regulation emphasize that a Government Regulation in its preamble must include a Law as the basis for forming a Government Regulation [28]. The function of government regulations is to implement laws, so it can be concluded that without government regulations, laws are complicated to implement or implement in social-community realities [29].

Article 38, paragraph (4) of the Copyright Law actually contains an order to form delegation regulations in the form of forming government regulations. Delegation regulations, according to Moh. Fadli is actually regulations that are in the realm of executive authority to regulate further provisions regulated by laws originating from legislative authority [30]. Because it is an order of authority from the legislative power, the formulation of delegation regulations must be limited and clear to minimize the existence of blank delegation regulations [31]. Delegation regulations that are unclear and do not provide clear boundaries can potentially expand and widen the provisions of the Act, which can be regulated at will by the executive power [32]. Therefore, the formulation of delegation regulations must be firm, directed, and clear.

Referring to the formulation in Article 38 paragraph (4) of the Copyright Law, in the context of the formulation of delegation regulations, at least the author believes of two aspects. *First*, in general, the provisions of Article 38 paragraph (4) of the Copyright Law are already relevant to the formulation of delegation regulations that at least explain the types of regulations and the substance of the regulation [33]. The type of regulation ordered by Article 38 paragraph (4) of the Copyright Law is a Government Regulation, while the substance of the regulation is related to copyrights on traditional cultural expressions held by the state. Fundamentally, the actual formulation of Article 38 paragraph (4) of the Copyright Law is in line with the introductory provisions for drafting delegation regulations. *Second*, the potential for arbitrariness in delegation regulations in the form of Government Regulations regarding copyrights on traditional cultural expressions held by the state has the potential to occur in the formulation of Government Regulations because of the ambiguity in the meaning "held by the state." That is because the phrase "held by the state" can lead to multiple interpretations, especially with regard to whether the state actually holds the intention. Is held by the state the same as owned by the state?, does the state facilitate it, or does it have another meaning. In this context, it is appropriate that before a Government Regulation is issued regarding copyrights to traditional cultural expressions held by the state, it is necessary to clarify the meaning held by the state in the formulation of the Copyright Law [34]. This is to provide guarantees of legal certainty for Government Regulations, which are orders from Article 38 paragraph (4) of the Copyright Law.

Legal ambiguity in interpreting the phrase "held by the state" can have a big impact, for example, whether it is permissible for the regions to take part in or make claims on the rights of traditional cultural expression. This is, for example, *Reog Ponorogo*, which has a regional identity pattern. Is it permissible for the regions to also hold intellectual property rights regarding traditional cultural expressions [35]. This legal issue occurred because there was no authentic interpretation in the Copyright Law regarding the authentic meaning of the phrase "held by the state." In addition, there is also no Government Regulation which is an order from Article 38 paragraph (4) of the Copyright Law so that further provisions regarding "held by the state" in any form and mechanism. That confirms that the absence of a Government Regulation, an order from Article 38 paragraph (4) of the Copyright Law, has created legal obscurity. In jurisprudence, legal obscurity is a "disease" of written Law or positive Law [36]. Text-based positive Law sometimes cannot holistically and comprehensively explain a particular term [37]. This makes positive Law full of ambiguities and requires interpretation to solve it [38].

In the case that occurred in Article 38 paragraph (4) of the Copyright Law, the interpretation of the meaning "held by the state" alone is not enough. This happened because the Law's order to form a Government Regulation still needs to be implemented. According to the author's opinion, the orientation that can be carried out in overcoming legal problems, primarily related to the absence of a Government Regulation as mandated in Article 38 paragraph (4) of the Copyright Law, namely: (i) establishing a Government Regulation concerning copyright on traditional cultural expressions held by state including providing an authentic interpretation of the meaning of "held by the state" along with its criteria and provisions, (ii) the establishment of a Government Regulation as mandated in Article 38 paragraph (4) of the Copyright Law can be carried out by first harmonizing it with various laws and regulations such as the Law Culture and the Minister of Law and Human Rights of Communal Intellectual Property, as well as the urgency to include the Draft Law concerning Traditional Knowledge to be included in the National Legislation Program and ratified as a law so that the protection and guarantee of legal certainty for the expression of traditional culture and traditional knowledge can be optimally enforced.

4. Conclusions

The implications for regulation of copyrights for traditional cultural expressions held by the state are: regulation and legal protection regarding the regulation of copyrights for traditional cultural expressions held by the state is not yet optimal because a Government Regulation has not been formed as mandated by Article 38 paragraph (4) of the Copyright Law, the meaning of "held by the state" in Article 38 paragraph (4) of the Copyright Law still creates legal obscurity. After all, the Copyright Law does not provide further explanation regarding the meaning of "held by the state" and arrangements regarding legal remedies for potential disputes related to rights copyright over traditional cultural expressions held by the state. The potential for such disputes can include disputes between regions that claim each other over a culture, including disputes between countries that claim culture, especially in countries belonging to the same family. Orientations that can be carried out in overcoming legal issues, especially related to the absence of Government Regulations as mandated in Article 38 paragraph (4) of the Copyright Law, namely establishing Government Regulations regarding copyright on traditional cultural expressions held by the state, including providing an authentic interpretation of the meaning of "held by the state" along with the criteria and provisions and the formation of Government Regulations as mandated in Article 38 paragraph (4) of the Copyright Law can be carried out by first harmonizing various laws and regulations such as the Culture Law and the Minister of Law and Human Rights of Communal Intellectual Property. In order to be more optimal, in future arrangements there is an urgency to include the Draft Law concerning Traditional Knowledge to be included in the National Legislation Program and passed into law so that the protection and guarantee of legal certainty for the expression of traditional culture and traditional knowledge can be optimally enforced.

Author details

I. Gede Agus Kurniawan
National Education University (Undiknas), Denpasar, Indonesia

*Address all correspondence to: gedeaguskurniawan@undiknas.ac.id

References

[1] Firdaus DW. Pewarisan Nilai-Nilai Historis Dan Kearifan Lokal Masyarakat Kampung Adat Dalam Pembelajaran Sejarah. Jurnal Artefak. 2017;**4**(2):129. DOI: 10.25157/ja.v4i2.906

[2] Asshiddiqie J. Konstitusi Kebudayaan dan Kebudayaan Konstitusi. 1st ed. Malang: Intrans Publishing; 2017

[3] Khobir A, Jaeni M, Basith A. Multikulturalisme dalam Karya Ulama Nusantara, IBDA. Jurnal Kajian Islam dan Budaya. 2019;**17**(2):319-344. DOI: 10.24090/ibda.v17i2.2983

[4] Sadya S. Indonesia Miliki Warisan Dunia UNESCO Terbanyak di Asia Tenggara. Available from: dataindonesia.id. 2022

[5] Arnani M. Ini 11 Warisan Budaya Tak Benda Indonesia yang Diakui Dunia. Available from: www.kompas.com. 2021

[6] Kemendikbudristek. Kemendikbudristek Tetapkan 289 Warisan Budaya Takbenda Indonesia Tahun 2021. Jakarta; 2021 Available from: www.kemdikbud.go.id

[7] Herzani AP. Peran Pemerintah Dalam Menginventarisasi Ekspresi Budaya Tradisional Indonesia. Jurnal Hukum & Pembangunan. 2021;**50**(4):954. DOI: 10.21143/jhp.vol50.no4.2865

[8] Widyanti YE. Perlindungan Ekspresi Budaya Tradisional Indonesia Dalam Sistem Yang Sui Generis. Arena Huk. 2020;**13**(3):389

[9] Sari DAMNK. Sistem Pendataan Kebudayaan Terpadu Alternatif Perlindungan Hukum Ekspresi Budaya Tradisonal. Legislasi Indonesia. 2021;**18**(3):406

[10] Kusuma KRPH. Perlindungan Ekspresi Budaya Tradisional dan Indikasi Geografis: Suatu Kekayaan Intelektual Dengan Kepemilikan Komunal. Jurnal Pembangunan Hukum Indonesia. 2022;**4**(1):110

[11] Al Amaren EM, Hamad AMA, Al Mashhour OF, Al Mashni MI. An introduction to the legal research method: To clear the blurred image on how students understand the method of the legal science research. International Journal of Multidisciplinary Sciences and Advanced Technology. 2020;**1**(9):50-55

[12] Kadek Sukadana I, Ayu G, Nia P. Perlindungan Hak Cipta Terhadap Ekspresi Budaya Tradisional Geguritan Bali Di Indonesia. Jurnal Media Komunikasi Pendidikan Pancasila Dan Kewarganegaraan. 2021;**3**(2):108-120

[13] Ramadhan GD. Ruang Lingkup Perlindungan Hak Kekayaan Intelektual Terhadap Video Game. Journal of Intellectual Property. 2021;**4**(2):1-14

[14] Setiawan D. Dampak Perkembangan Teknologi Informasi dan Komunikasi Terhadap Budaya. Jurnal SIMBOLIKA: Research and Learning in Communication Study (e-journal). 2018;**4**(1):62. DOI: 10.31289/simbollika.v4i1.1474

[15] Mahmuzar. Model Negara Kesatuan Republik Indonesia Di Era Reformasi. Huk. dan Pembang. 2020;**50**(2):303. DOI: 10.21143/jhp.vol50.no2.2590

[16] Oka MAA. Harmonisasi Peraturan Perundang-Undangan. In: Artikel Hukum Tata Negara Dan Peraturan Perundang-Undangan. 2021

[17] Rizky Syahputra ZA, Kridasaksana D. Perlindungan Hukum

Bagi Musisi Atas Hak Cipta Dalam Pembayaran Royalti. Semarang Law Review. 2022;**3**(1):85

[18] Perangin-angin RBB, Nababan R, Siahaan PG. Perlindungan Pengetahuan Tradisional sebagai Hak Konstitusional di Indonesia. Jurnal Konstitusi. 2020;**17**(1):178. DOI: 10.31078/jk1718

[19] Lee J, Suh T, Roy D, Baucus M. Emerging technology and business model innovation: The case of artificial intelligence. Journal of Open Innovation Technology Market and Complexity. 2019;**5**(3). DOI: 10.3390/joitmc5030044

[20] Rauta U, Siswanto A. Revitalization of Adat Law as an instrument of social engineering in Central Sumba. Jurnal Dinamika Hukum. 2018;**18**(3):347-356

[21] Lestari S. Peran Teknologi dalam Pendidikan di Era Globalisasi. Edureligia Jurnal Pendidikan Agama Islam. 2018;**2**(2):94-100. DOI: 10.33650/edureligia.v2i2.459

[22] Ormerod R. The history and ideas of sociological functionalism: Talcott Parsons, modern sociological theory, and the relevance for OR. Journal of the Operational Research Society. 2020;**71**(12):1873-1899. DOI: 10.1080/01605682.2019.1640590

[23] Hastangka H, Tjahyadi S, Djalu Sembada A, Sinaga YT. Education for sustainable develoment (ESD) – Pancasila di Desa Towangsan: Paradigma Pembangunan yang Berkelanjutan. Jurnal Pengabdian Kepada Masyarakat. (Indonesian Journal of Community Engagement). 2019;**4**(2):159. DOI: 10.22146/jpkm.30134

[24] Ali A. Menguak Teori Hukum & Teori Peradilan Termasuk Interpretasi Undang-Undang (Legisprudence). In: Pemahaman Awal. 7th ed. Vol. 1. Jakarta: Kencana; 2017

[25] Wiratraman HP. Perkembangan Politik Hukum Peradilan Adat. Mimb. Huk. - Fak. Huk. Univ. Gadjah Mada. 2018;**30**(3):488. DOI: 10.22146/jmh.38241

[26] Yunus A, Muddin AA. Penyelesaian Sengketa Tanah Ulayat Yang Telah Bersertifikat Berdasarkan Hukum Adat Malind-Anim. Journal of Kertha Patrika. 2019;**41**(3):206. DOI: 10.24843/KP.2019.v41.i03.p0

[27] Anggono BD, Firdaus FR. Omnibus Law in Indonesia: A comparison to the United States and Ireland. Lentera Hukum. 2020;**7**(3):319-336. DOI: 10.19184/ejlh.v7i3.19895

[28] Huda RNN'M. Teori dan Pengujian Peraturan Perundang-Undangan, Digital. Bandung: Nusamedia; 2020

[29] Redi A. Hukum Pembentukan Peraturan Perundang-Undangan. 1st ed. Jakarta: Sinar Grafika; 2018

[30] Fadli M. Peraturan Delegasi di Indonesia: Ide Untuk Membangun Kontrol Preventif Terhadap Peraturan Pemerintah. Malang: Universitas Brawijaya; 2020

[31] Hikmah M. Delegasi Wewenang Dalam Undang-Undang Perpajakan. In: Simposium Nasional Keuangan Negara. Vol. 3. 2018. pp. 320-335

[32] Widodo H, Prasetio DE, Disantara FP. Relasi Kekuasaan Antar Presiden dan Wakil Presiden dalam Sistem Ketatanegaraan Republik Indonesia. Pandecta Research Law Journal. 2020;**15**(1):13-25. DOI: 10.15294/pandecta.v15i1.24554

[33] Whittington KE, Iuliano J. The myth of the nondelegation doctrine. University of Pennsylvania Law Review. 2017;**165**(2):379-431

[34] Suwarni W. Obstacles to enforcement of book copyright law in Indonesia based on the legal structure, legal substance, and legal culture. International Journal of Advanced Research and Publications. 2019;**3**(3):153-157

[35] Ade V, Affandi I. Implementasi Nilai-Nilai Kearifan Lokal Dalam Mengembangkan Keterampilan Kewarganegaraan (Studi Deskriptif Analitik Pada Masyarakat Talang Mamak Kec. Rakit Kulim, Kab. Indragiri Hulu Provinsi Riau). Jurnal Pendidikan Ilmu Sosial. 2016;**25**(1):77. DOI: 10.17509/jpis.v25i1.3671

[36] Christianto H. Norma Persatuan Sebagai Batasan Perbuatan Pidana Penyebaran Ujaran Kebencian Melalui Internet. Verit. Justitia. 2020;**6**(1):94-126. DOI: 10.25123/vej.3501

[37] Nany Suryawati MDS. Harmonization of the application of customary law and positive law in village communities of malang regency. International Journal of Applied Business and International Management. 2021;**6**(2):6

[38] Bedke M. What normativity cannot be. Journal of Ethics and Social Philosophy. 2020;**18**(2):211-227. DOI: 10.26556/jesp.v18i2.1020

Chapter 3

Inspired or Plagiarism: Application of Substantial Similarity in the Protection of Architectural Works towards Renewal of Indonesia's Copyright Law

Taufik H. Simatupang

Abstract

Architecture is a work of art of high value. An architect who produces architectural works not only masters the technicalities of making them but is also an artist. In historical records there are not a few architectural works that have similarities to each other, for example, the Eiffel Tower in Paris and the Golden Gate Bridge in San Francisco, similar works are often found in various countries. Then how to measure whether the work that was born later is an independent work and not the result of plagiarism? To prove that an architectural work is an original work, the concept of substantial similarity can be used. Self-creation is a proven formula that has been carried out in the United States of America. Indonesia itself does not yet have clear formulations and qualitative measurement tools to determine whether similar architectural works that are born later are original works of art and not works of plagiarism. Therefore, Indonesia needs to technically regulate acts of imitation that are considered to substantively violate the entire form, spatial arrangement, and design of architectural works through amendments and updates to the Copyright Law in the future.

Keywords: copyright law, architectural works, substantial similarity, independent creation, plagiarism

1. Introduction

Intellectual Property Rights (IPR) are rights that arise from the brain's thought processes that produce a product or process that is useful to humans. In general, it can be said that objects regulated in IPR are works that arise or are born because of human intellectual abilities. But in a lot of literature, there are also those who use the term Intellectual Property Rights.

Philosophically, the rationale for providing legal protection to individuals for their creations cannot be separated from the domination of the natural law school of thought which emphasizes the human factor and the use of reason. The origin of the conception of natural law can be traced back to the ancient Greeks, which is about +2500 years ago. According to this theory, natural law is seen as a universal and eternal law [1].

One of the ancient Greek philosophers, Aristoteles, argued that natural law has a universal scope and is based on the idea that natural law is independent of all human desires. Later in the middle ages, Thomas Aquinas stated that natural law is part of the nature of life and through natural law humans participate as rational beings. Natural law is part of God's law. Humans as intelligent beings apply part of God's law to human life, so that he can distinguish between good and bad [2]. Therefore, basically, IPR is recognized as the work of a person based on his intellectual ability, and the person who creates and produces it will get natural ownership rights.

In principle, justice will give someone what is his right, meaning that the law guarantees that something that someone gets is his right. In the next stage, the law will also provide guarantees for each person to enjoy exclusively the material objects created by him, with the help of the state.

Apart from that, it is also interesting to disclose the property theory of John Locke in his famous work: Two Treaties of Government, which basically states that humans from birth have the right to inherit the world given by God. Furthermore, he also stated that: "Every man has a 'property' in his own "person". The labor of his body and the work of his hands, we may say, are his proper." This theory became known as "Labor Theory" which, according to Justin Hughes, although incomplete, was very strong in providing a foundation for intellectual property protection.

One of the influences of this natural law thinking is that apart from being seen as economic or commercial rights, IPRs are also seen as political rights or human rights [3]. From the point of view of economic rights, the protection of IPR is essentially the protection of the economic rights of a human intellectual creativity. Arranged objects are works arising from human intellectual abilities. According to W.R Cornish, intellectual property protects the use of ideas and information that has commercial or economic value. David I Bainbridge also argues that: "Intellectual Property" is the collective name given to legal rights which protect the product of the available to cover that body of legal rights which arise from mental artistic endeavor.

In Article 27 of the DUHAM, it has been stated that.

1. Everyone has the freedom to participate in the life and culture of society, enjoy the arts and be involved in the advancement of science;

2. Everyone has the right to the protection of the moral and material interests resulting from any scientific, literary, or artistic production produced and created by him.

In Indonesia itself, in the context of the implementation of human rights, IPR can also be seen as property rights, which are rights that cannot be taken arbitrarily by anyone. Thus, the government is obliged to provide protection for the implementation of this human right. This is important because the provisions that provide constitutional guarantees for human rights are considered one of the main characteristics of the principle of rule of law in a country, including Indonesia.

IPR can also be classified as rights over intangible goods. This is because a protected object is an idea generated by someone. The classification of these rights into the law of property is because the nature of these rights is close to the nature of material rights and is an absolute right. The analogy is that if these ideas come out of the human mind and are incarnated in a creation of literature, science, etc., then they become tangible objects and can be a source of profit. The IPR system is basically an exclusive right granted by the state privately to every creator, inventor, designer, and so on, to get appreciation and reward for their work and creative process to produce something useful for mankind. Through these awards and rewards, it is hoped that it will encourage others to do the same thing.

Intellectual property rights are the same as objects that have value to be transferred. Objects that have value certainly need to be regulated legally. The law of objects, regarding objects in general states the broadest meaning of the word "object", is everything that can be owned by people. Here, object means object as opposed to subject or "person" in law. There are also words that nouns are used in a narrow sense, namely as things that can only be seen. There is also used, if one's wealth is meant [4].

Objects regulated in IPR are works that arise or are born because of human intellectual abilities. As an intellectual work that is born from the ability of the human brain, IPR contains the following principles [5]:

1. Economic principles;
2. The principle of justice;
3. Principles of culture (the development of science, literature, and art to improve human life);
4. Social principles (regulating human interests as citizens).

IPR is divided into two major parts, namely Copyright and Industrial Property Rights, which include industrial property rights including.

1. Patents;
2. Marks and Geographical Indications;
3. Trade Secret;
4. Industrial Design;
5. Integrated Circuit Layout Design;
6. Plant Variations.

In its development, the argument that states that developed countries are countries that have abundant natural wealth is now not very appropriate. Mastery of science and technology that produces intellectual works that have economic value is now a measuring tool for a country's progress.

In its development, IPR has changed from being a part of business law that was not overlooked, and now it has become one of the business fields that encourages the development of the world economy. Universities and research institutes in developing countries no longer carry out research solely for science, but far more how research results can then benefit markets and industry. Collaboration between universities, research institutes, and industry has become a promising new phenomenon. This collaboration, with the support of experts and specialists, will continue to develop by creating new inventions that are useful for society at large [6].

Within this framework, technology transfer is needed. Technology Transfer [7] as an application of technology originating from developed countries to be implemented in Indonesia in an effort to spur industrialization. If related to the nature of technology, then the issue of technology transfer is not limited to technical mastery of the transferred technology, but also includes managerial mastery, and must even be supported with certain values. Entering the new millennium, IPR is an important issue that always receives attention, both in national and international forums.

The development, renewal, and development of technology in general is the work of the community, because of the craftsmanship, perseverance, ability to think, and work of its members. Activities among researchers, scientists, and people with certain qualifications with high creativity are also works of humanity. The results of persistence, creativity, and the resulting ability are basically able to change, improve, and accommodate the various needs of humanity, for the present and for the future [8].

According to Robert C Sherwood as quoted by Ranti Fauza Mayana in the book Protection of Industrial Designs in Indonesia in the Era of Free Trade in Intellectual Property Rights Understanding the Basic Principles, Scope and Applicable Laws, it is stated that there are five basic theories of intellectual property protection, namely.

a. Reward Theory: This theory means that recognition of intellectual work is needed produced by creators/inventors/designers by giving awards as a counterweight to their creative efforts to find/create an intellectual work.

b. Recovery Theory: In this theory, it is explained that creators/inventors/designers who have spent time, money, and energy to produce intellectual works must get back what they have spent.

c. Incentive Theory: Based on this theory, incentives need to be given to seek the acceleration of useful research activities.

d. Risk Theory: In Risk Theory, it is stated that work contains risks. Intellectual property which is the result of research carries the risk of allowing other people to first discover the method or improve it. Thus, it is reasonable to provide a form of legal protection for efforts or activities that contain these risks.

e. Economic Growth Stimulus Theory: Protection of IPR is a tool for economic development. A country with an IPR protection system running well, then its economic growth will also be good.

2. Method

The writing of this part of the book is the result of a literature study that utilizes documents and literature related to indications of plagiarism of architectural works on the pretext of being inspired by previous architectural works. Research data was obtained from various books and journals, both national and international by utilizing Internet media. The data obtained is narrated and then analyzed using the Indonesian Copyright Law and the principle of originality which has been widely applied in developed countries, especially in the United States.

The purpose of this research is to review how to prove architectural works that were born later are indeed inspired by previous works and are not the result of plagiarism. It is in this context that it is important to adopt the principle of originality of architectural works in the Indonesian Copyright Law, as has been done in many developed countries. The principle of originality is actually the assessment that the works that appear later do not substantially imitate previous works, meaning that in new architectural works it must be proven that there is an independent creative process carried out as a form of creativity from the creator.

3. Legal arrangements concerning copyright

3.1 Definition

One indicator of the level of progress and intelligence of a nation can be seen from the many discoveries in science and technology. A discovery certainly not only gives pride to the inventor and his country but can also be economically profitable. The exploitation of science and technology through a series of research, so as to produce findings that are beneficial to society, has a place that is highly valued, especially in developed countries.

In order to support the growing interest of community members to create and innovate, the state must provide facilities. One of these conveniences is the issue of legalization by law. As a developing country, of course we must proactively provide understanding to members of the public about the importance of rights in the IPR dimension. One aspect of IPR that is often in the spotlight is copyright. It should be a creation that has economic value should be given an award. One of the awards referred to is a reward for the creator.

Law Number 28 of 2014 Concerning Copyright has explained that copyright consists of three fields, namely science, art, and literature. Each of these sections has quite a lot of types of copyrighted works. Compared to other intellectual works such as patents, brands, industrial designs, and trade secrets, copyright is part of the intellectual property rights that govern the most protected objects.

Copyright as part of IPR also has a close relationship with the creative economy and information technology that is currently being developed in Indonesia. The development of the creative economy and information technology is believed to be able to improve the country's economy. Therefore, legal protection is needed for copyrights that arise, especially in terms of protection of related rights. IPR itself can generally be divided into two parts, namely copyright and industrial property rights, as can be seen in the **Figure 1**.

Information and communication technology is an important aspect of the current changes to the Copyright Law. The potential for copyright infringement by utilizing information technology through Internet media has recently shown quite high numbers. Proportional arrangements are necessary, so that positive functions can be optimized and negative impacts can be minimized. New matters regulated in Law Number 28 of 2014 which were not previously regulated in Law Number 19 of 2002 Concerning Copyright are as follows:

a. A longer period of time as implemented in many countries, such as certain copyright protection is enforced for the lifetime of the creator plus 70 (seventy) years after the creator's death.

b. Restrictions on sales and transfer of economic rights.

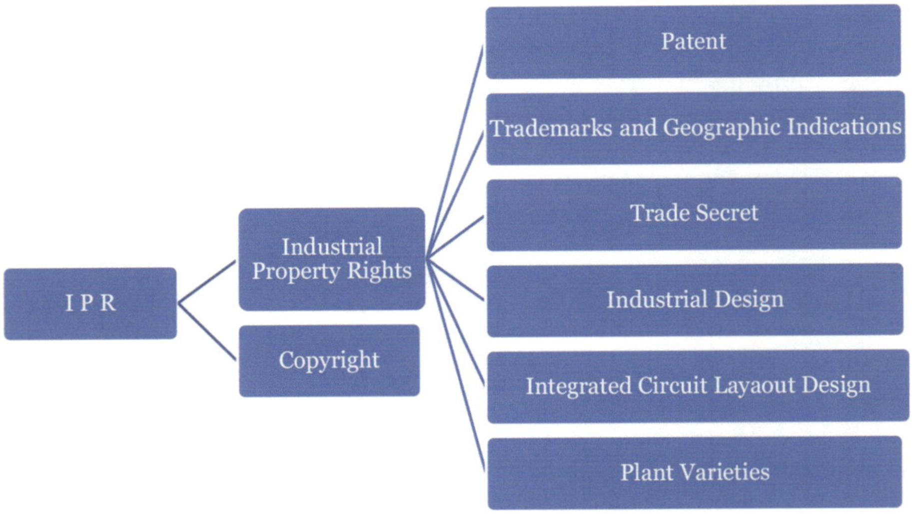

Figure 1.
Distribution of types of IPR. Source: Simatupang [9].

c. Settlement of disputes through mediation, arbitration or court processes, as well as application of complaint offenses for criminal prosecution.

d. Seller's responsibility for goods resulting from copyright infringement and related rights it sells.

e. Copyright can be used as a fiduciary guarantee object.

f. The minister has the authority to delete works that violate.

g. Creators, copyright holders, and related rights owners become members of the collective governing body to collect royalties.

h. Authors and related rights owners receive royalties for works or related rights products created in a legal relationship and used commercially.

i. Collective management institutions whose function is to collect and manage the economic rights of creators and owners of related rights are required to submit an application for an operating permit to the Minister.

j. Use of copyright and related rights in multimedia devices.

Legally, according to the declarative principle, the special rights and privileges granted by the state to the creator are born when the copyrighted work can be realized in a tangible form without the need to be registered. According to Copyright Law, an author is a person or several people who individually or jointly produce a creation that is unique and personal. Whereas what is meant by work is any copyrighted work within the scope of science, art, and literature that is produced based on inspiration, ability, thought, imagination, dexterity, skills, and expertise as outlined in a tangible form.

3.2 Scope

In the Copyright Law, it is stated that the copyright holder is the creator as the owner of the copyright, the party who received the rights legally from the creator, or other parties who received further rights from the party who received the rights legally. The scope of copyright covers the fields of science, art, and literature. Further classification and types of copyrighted works from each protected field in the Copyright Law can be seen in the **Figure 2** and **Table 1**.

3.3 Recording procedure

Unlike the case with Law Number 19 of 2002 which recognizes the term registration, Law Number 28 of 2014 no longer recognizes the term registration but records. As stipulated in Law Number 28 of 2014 Concerning Copyrights, the recording of creations and related rights products is not a requirement for obtaining copyrights and related rights. Registration of creations cannot be carried out on paintings in the form of logos or distinctive marks used as brands in trade in goods/services or used as symbols of organizations, business entities, or legal entities.

Registration of works and related rights products shall be submitted with a written application in Indonesian by the creator, copyright holder, owner of related rights, or their proxy to the Minister. Applications can be made electronically or manually by attaching examples of works, related rights products, or substitutes for them. Then attach a statement of ownership of the creation and related rights and pay a fee. If an application is filed by several people who are jointly entitled to a work or related rights product, the application must be accompanied by a written statement. Meanwhile, if the ownership is from a legal entity, then the application must be accompanied by an official copy of the deed of establishment of the legal entity which has been legalized by the competent authority. If the application is submitted by several people, the applicant's name must be written including one of the applicant's selected addresses. In the event that the application is submitted by an applicant originating from outside

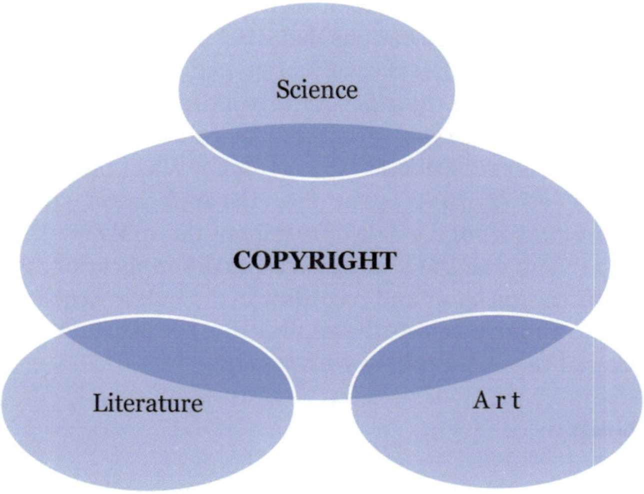

Figure 2.
Scope of copyright. Source: Law Number 28 of 2014 Concerning Copyright.

Science	Art	Literature
Books, pamphlets, published versions of works, and all other scientific/non-fictional written works)	Songs and/or music with or without subtitles	Fiction publications (poems, short stories, and novels)
Lectures, speeches, and other similar creations	Drama, musical drama, dance, choreography, wayang, and pantomime	
Props made for the benefit of education and science	Fine art in all forms such as paintings, drawings, carvings, calligraphy, sculptures, sculptures, or collages	
Architectural work	Applied arts	
Map	Architectural work	
Translations, interpretations, adaptations, anthologies, databases, adaptations, arrangements, modifications, and other works resulting from the transformation	Batik artwork or other motif art	
Translation, adaptation, arrangement, transformation, or modification of traditional cultural expressions	Photographic works	
Compilation of works or data, either in a format that can be read with a computer program or other media	Portrait	
Video game	Cinematographic work	
Computer program	Compilations of traditional cultural expressions as long as they are original works	

Source: Law Number 28 of 2014 Concerning Copyright.

Table 1.
Field and type of copyright.

the territory of the Unitary State of the Republic of Indonesia, it must be made through an intellectual property consultant registered as a proxy.

The Minister will examine applications that meet the requirements. Examination is carried out to determine whether the work or related rights product being applied for is essentially the same or not the same as the work recorded in the General Register of Works or other intellectual property objects. The results of the inspection are used as material for the Minister's consideration to accept or reject the application. The Minister shall make a decision to accept or reject the application within a maximum period of 9 (nine) months from the date of receipt of the application that meets the requirements. In the event that the Minister accepts the application, the Minister issues a creation registration letter and records it in the Public Register of Works. On the other hand, if the Minister rejects the application, the Minister shall notify the applicant in writing of the refusal along with reasons.

3.4 Dispute resolution

Dispute settlement as stipulated in the Copyright Law can be resolved through alternative dispute resolution, arbitration, or the Commercial Court. All copyright infringement lawsuits must be filed with the Commercial Court. The Commercial

Court is the only institution that has the authority to do so, as long as the parties are located in Indonesian territory. The Commercial Court must first seek settlement of disputes through mediation before filing criminal charges. Authors, copyright holders, and related rights holders or their heirs who suffer economic losses are entitled to receive compensation as stated in court decisions regarding criminal cases of copyright and related rights. Compensation payments to creators, copyright holders, and/or owners of related rights are paid no later than 6 (six) months after the court decision has permanent legal force.

In the event that a work has been recorded, other interested parties can file a claim for cancelation of the registration of a work in the Public Register of Works through the Commercial Court addressed to the registered creator and/or copyright holder. The transfer of copyright on all works to other parties does not reduce the rights of the creator or his heirs to sue anyone who deliberately and without rights and without the consent of the creator violates the moral rights of the creator. The transfer of the performers' economic rights to another party does not reduce the rights of the performers or their heirs to sue anyone who deliberately and without rights and without the consent of the performers violates the moral rights of the performers.

The creator, copyright holder, or owner of related rights have the right to file a claim for compensation to the Commercial Court for infringement of copyright or related product rights, in the form of a request to surrender all or part of the income derived from holding lectures, scientific meetings, performances or exhibitions of work which constitute result of copyright infringement or product-related rights. In addition, the plaintiff can also apply for a temporary injunction or interlocutory decision to the Commercial Court to request confiscation of works that have been published or reproduced, and the copying tools used to produce works resulting from copyright infringement and related rights. The Commercial Court can also order copyrighted products and related rights to stop publishing, distributing, communicating, and duplicating works because they are the result of copyright infringement and related product rights.

3.5 Criminal provisions

Actions that are considered criminal acts according to the provisions of Law Number 28 of 2014 Concerning Copyrights are any acts that violate the economic rights of copyright owners and holders and related rights for commercial purposes. The actions referred to are as follows:

1. Eliminate, change, or destroy information about: methods or systems that can identify the originality of the substance of creation and its creators and information codes and access codes. Including copyright electronic information which includes information about a work, which appears and attaches electronically in connection with the activity of announcing a work, the author's name, alias or pseudonym, the creator as the copyright holder, the period and conditions of use of the work, information number and code;

2. Destroy, destroy, remove, or render non-functional means of controlling technology used to protect creations or related rights products as well as safeguards for copyrights or related rights, except for the interests of state defense and security, as well as other reasons in accordance with the provisions of laws and regulations, or otherwise agreed;

3. Renting of works without the permission of the creator or copyright holder;
4. Translation of works without the permission of the creator or copyright holder;
5. Adaptation, arrangement, or transformation of works without the permission of the creator or copyright holder;
6. Performance of works without the permission of the creator or copyright holder;
7. Communication of works without the permission of the creator or copyright holder;
8. Publishing works without the permission of the creator or copyright holder;
9. Reproduction of works in all its forms without the permission of the creator or copyright holder;
10. Distribution of works or copies thereof without the permission of the creator or copyright holder;
11. Publication of works without the permission of the creator or copyright holder;
12. Trade place managers allow the sale and/or duplication of goods resulting from copyright infringement and/or related rights at the trading place they manage.
13. Commercial use, reproduction, announcement, distribution, and/or communication of portraits made for the purpose of commercial advertising or billboards without the written consent of the person being photographed or their heirs.
14. Broadcasting or communicating performances by performers, fixing shows that have not been fixed, duplicating fixing shows in any way or form, distributing fixing shows or copies thereof, renting fixing shows or copies to the public, and providing fixing shows that can be accessed by the public without the permission of the performer.
15. Reproduction of the phonogram in any manner or form, distribution of the original or a copy of the phonogram, rental of copies of the phonogram to the public, and provision of the phonogram by wire or wirelessly accessible to the public without permission from the phonogram producer;
16. Broadcast rebroadcast, broadcast communication, broadcast fixation, and/or duplicating broadcast fixation without a broadcasting institution's license.

In fact, every intellectual work produced by everyone cannot stop as a result of scientific development. More than that the development of science in question must be useful for the life of mankind. This means that intellectual works that require energy, time and money must be utilized by many people, while at the same time bringing economic benefits to the owner.

However, in Indonesia, creators, inventors, and designers have not received proper benefits for their intellectual works because there are still many piracy and plagiarism. This is because every time an original registered intellectual work is born, and at the same time, there are already counterfeit products that are "created" by unscrupulous business actors who are not responsible. Imitation of this original product was carried out massively. In general, it is also known that counterfeit products are sold cheaper than the original product. The issue of the relatively large price difference between genuine and imitation products should receive attention from all parties involved. Especially in the tax and licensing sector, it should be made easier so that genuine products can be purchased at more affordable prices by consumers.

One of the creative works that still gets a little attention in Indonesia is an architectural work. Architectural work is basically a work of art from an architect. An architect in his creative process cannot be separated from the influence of previous architectural works that inspired him. The question of whether an architectural work that was born later is included in the area of inspiration or plagiarism is a question that is not easy to answer. However, protection of a copyrighted work that must be protected by moral rights and economic rights is a mandatory thing that must be provided by the rule of law.

4. Architectural works: inspired vs. plagiarized

Architectural works have experienced rapid development from time to time, and the amount of information available in various media has facilitated irresponsible acts of plagiarism. The lack of awareness to respect copyrighted works and the unclear arrangement between actions that include plagiarism or are indeed inspired by previous works have contributed to exacerbating the existing problems [10]. The early presence of architecture began because of the need for a building which was expressed by an architect through working drawings [11]. In addition, architecture is also part of art, because architecture cannot be separated from taste. This causes the understanding of architecture to continue to evolve and is influenced by ways of thinking, ways of making, ways of viewing, and culture [12].

Historically, architecture as a science has provided masterpieces for human life and civilization. The science of architecture that produces architectural works is a marker of identity and pride of a country. There are so many famous architectural masterpieces to this day, such as the Eiffel Tower by architect Gustave Eiffel which was built in 1889 or the Golden Gate bridge masterpiece by Joseph B. Strauss in 1930 in San Francisco which has always been a backdrop that also embellishes Hollywood films.

Architect Zaha Mohammad Hadi (Zaha Hadid), a woman born in Baghdad, Iraq, October 31, 1950, also contributed to the world's architectural treasures today. Zaha Hadid's works are indeed unusual, even quite special. Some of them even trigger pros and cons. For example, the Al Warkah football stadium in Qatar, which will host the 2022 World Pilala in Qatar, is said to have killed many workers during construction. Other notable architectural works by Zaha Hadid include the Aquatic Center for the 2012 London Olympics, the Heydar Aliyev Center in Baku, Azerbaijan, and the MAXXI Museum in Rome, Italy [13].

Indonesian architects are no less great, for example, the DPR/MPR building, the masterpiece of architect Soejoedi Wirjoatmodjo, born in Surakarta, December 27, 1928, which was built in 1965. Or the Itiqlal Mosque, the National Monument and Gelora Bung Karno, the masterpiece of architect Friedrich Silaban, born in Bonandolok, Sumatra North, December 16, 1912.

According to Zaha Hadid, at first glance there are similarities between one architectural work and another. This is something that is natural because every architect is always influenced by what he sees [14]. Architectural works that appear later, whether consciously or not, are inspired by previous architectural works, and this is something that is reasonable and can be legally justified. The problem is what happens when an architect's work is an imitation, both as a whole and as an imitation of the most substantive part of an architectural work.

Not all imitation processes can be justified, for example, the case of Zaha Hadid in China. Even though Zaha Hadid justifies imitation, she never brought a plagiarism case against her work to court. An article titled Never Meant To Copy, Only To Surpass: Plagiarism Versus Innovation In Architectural Imitation, tells about a case of plagiarism committed by a developer from China, Chongqing Meiquan, who made a building called Meiquan twenty-second century. In the design process, Chongqing copied the work of Zaha Hadid in Beijing, China, namely Wangjing SOHO. Zaha Hadid was accused of plagiarism because the Meiquan Chongqing building had begun its construction process at the same time as the Wanjing SOHO building, so Zaha Hadid suspected that there had been an abuse of blueprints belonging to Wanjing SOHO. In addition, with this simultaneous development, it is feared that the construction of the twenty-second century Meiquan will be completed earlier than the original building, namely Wanjing SOHO. This of course will be detrimental to many parties, including the project owner and Zaha Hadid herself [15].

5. Copyright protection for architectural works in Indonesia

The new Copyright Law has protected various aspects of copyright and related rights that have a close relationship with the dimensions of technology and information, especially copyrighted works born of their contact with the Internet world. In the future, Copyright Law needs to accommodate more aspects of the legal protection of architectural works by looking at technical understandings related to architecture as stipulated in Law Number 6 of 2017 concerning Architects (Architect Law). According to the Act on architects, what is meant by architecture is actually a combination of science, technology, and art.

Legal protection for architectural works must be able to cover aspects of copyright as a combination of science and art born of human intellectual abilities. The application of architectural copyright protection, which has received little attention so far due to the difficulty in determining the uniqueness of architectural work, must find a way out [16]. In the Copyright Law, architectural works are physical buildings, building design drawings, building technical drawings, and building models or mockups. In other parts of the Copyright Law, it stipulates that the use, retrieval, duplication and/or modification of a creation, and/or related rights product, either in whole or in large part, is not considered to violate copyright if the source is stated.

The formal norms contained in Article 44 paragraph (1) of the Copyright Law are norms of contradiction, which according to Bruggink are legal norms conflicts between prohibition norms and permissive norms or permit norms [17]. This means that the limitations and/or exclusions as referred to in Article 44 paragraph (1) of the Copyright Law are certainly a "violation" of the law, if the source is not stated, for commercial purposes, using, retrieving, duplicating, and/or modifying a work and/

or product-related rights in whole or in substantial part. The elucidation of Article 44 Paragraph (1) of the Copyright Law states that what is meant by "substantial portions" is the most important and distinctive part that distinguishes a work.

6. Comparison of arrangements for the protection of architectural works in the United States and Indonesia

The United States implemented the protection of architectural works after passing the Architectural Works Copyright Protection Act (AWCPA). Under Section 102 (a) Title 17 of the United States Code, works protected under the USA Copyright Act are literary works, musical and lyrical works, dramatic works and accompanying music, pantomime and choreography, pictorial works, moving images and audiovisuals, sound recordings, and architectural works. Furthermore, in Section 101, it is stated that what is meant by an architectural work is a building design embodied in a concrete form of expression, including architectural plans and building drawings. It also includes the overall form of the arrangement, the composition of the space, and the elements in the design, but does not include the individual standard features. Standard features that are not included in protected parts include windows, doors, and various functional elements whose placement is in accordance with their use. To determine whether architectural works that appear later are original architectural works and not the result of plagiarism from earlier architectural works, the United States has applied the principle of originality after the emergence of cases decided by courts, which will be explained in the next section.

Indonesia itself regulates the protection of architectural works in the Copyright Law, which defines architectural works as works in the form of physical buildings, building arrangements, model drawings, or building markets. Meanwhile, those included in the violation of architectural works, the Indonesian Copyright Law has not regulated it explicitly. However, referring to the limitations of copyright infringement that are regulated in general, which states that the use of works and related

	USA	Indonesia
Definition	Architectural work includes building plans that are embodied in a tangible form, including architectural plans and building drawings. It also includes the overall form of arrangement, spatial composition, and elements in the design, but does not include standard features such as windows, doors, and various functional elements whose placement is in accordance with their use.	Architectural works include works in the form of physical buildings, building arrangements, drawings, and building models.
Size of Plagiarism	The panel of judges in the USA has applied the principle of originality to the alleged plagiarism of architectural works. This principle is to prove that architectural works that appear later can be said to be inspired and not plagiarized if the creator does independent creativity and does not take a distinctive/important part of the previous work.	Not yet set specifically the dimensions of plagiarism of architectural works.

Source: Title 17 of the United States Code and Indonesian Copyright Act.

Table 2.
Comparison of definitions and measures of architectural work violations in the USA and Indonesia.

rights products in whole or in substantial part is an infringement. It is further regulated that the meaning of a substantial portion is the most distinctive and important part and characterizes a work. To clarify the comparison of arrangements for the protection of architectural works in the USA and Indonesia, it will be described in two aspects, namely definition and size of plagiarism, as shown in the **Table 2**.

7. Application of the concept of substantial similarity in the protection of architectural works

Every country will feel proud if it has a beautiful building icon; moreover, it can attract tourists to visit it. On the other hand, countries in the world are also competing to make buildings with high architectural art. At the beginning of its history, architectural works with high artistic value were dominated by religious buildings, developing into other functional buildings such as hospitals, markets, museums, and so on. An architectural work is actually a work that combines two aspects at once, namely technical and esthetic aspects (**Figures 3–7**) [20].

Referring to famous architectural masterpieces that recently appeared "copy" in various places, then can it be said that architectural works that have appeared recently have imitated architectural works that have appeared for the first time? This question is certainly not easy to answer, because most architects are basically "artists" who are always influenced by works of architecture they have seen before, perhaps even influencing their creative process in creating.

Assessing allegations of plagiarism in an architectural work according to the Copyright Act is not an easy job. Alleged plagiarism of architectural works should be assessed through criticism from an architect, and even one of the studies [21] introduced that the discourse of discussing the plagiarism of architectural works is actually more interesting than judging it by copyright law. The ease of access to various resources on the Web on Internet media has made it possible to democratize access to information, but at the same time, it also raises huge plagiarism problems [22]. Acts of plagiarism of architectural works through Internet media show extraordinary numbers, and detection engines such as plagiarisma.net and viper are felt to

Figure 3.
The Eiffel tower [18].

Figure 4.
The Tokyo tower [18].

Figure 5.
The Golden gate bridge [18].

be insufficient so that other developments are needed that can detect plagiarism of architectural works [23]. One of the discourses offered is to detect the plagiarism of architectural works in the form of text, by categorizing six different topics, namely prototype, archetype, motif, expression of ideas, modification, and modernization, and some of these topics can be considered together in certain cases. This is the first step in objective guidelines for assessing acts of architectural plagiarism [24].

One of the architectural violation cases that occurred in New York, United States of America, was between Thomas Shine and David Childs. Shine sued Childs for infringement of rights in the form of plagiarism in building design, because Childs' building design, namely "Freedom Tower", was considered to have similarities with Shine's building design, namely "Shine 99" and "Olympic Tower" [25]. Considering that an architect is an artist who is definitely influenced and inspired by the

Figure 6.
The Ponte de 25 Abril [18].

Figure 7.
Design of the new DPR building [19].

architectural works of other people he has seen and admired, the boundary between being inspired and copying is a question that is not easy to answer.

However, bearing in mind that an architectural work is a copyright that must receive respect and legal protection, violations, both imitation and plagiarism, cannot be justified. To prove that architectural works in the future are copies and plagiarism of previous works, one of the principles that can be used is the principle of originality.

In the United States, the application of the principle of originality uses the substantial similarity approach and the independent creation approach. If there are similarities between the two architectural works created, then the principle of independent creation can be used to prove that one architectural work is not a copy of another architectural work, and vice versa. This concept can actually be applied in Indonesia because indirectly the Indonesian Copyright Law also recognizes that the independent creative process carried out by the creator, by not taking things that are substantive in nature from previous works, is not a copyright infringement.

The application of the principle of originality in Indonesia has never been carried out because there is no court to handle cases related to the similarity of architectural works. The Indonesian Copyright Law does not yet stipulate in detail what can and cannot be protected from an architectural work, so that in the future the application of the principle of originality can be formulated using several approaches. In the United States, the principle of originality has been applied in the case of Shine vs. Childs through proving substantial similarity or taking substantial part. The protection of architectural works in the Copyright Law in the United States very detailed regulates what is protected as stated in Article 10 of the United States Copyright Law (title 17 United State Code) that the protection of architectural works includes all forms and arrangements, spatial composition and elements in the design as well as the arrangement of things that are not protected from architectural works, such as standard features, in the form of windows, doors, and functional elements [26].

8. Conclusion

The results of this study conclude that the principle of originality with a substantial equality approach and an independent creation approach can be used to prove that an architectural work that appears later is not the result of a copy of an earlier architectural work, and vice versa, as has been implemented in several countries, especially in the United States. Therefore, Indonesia needs to technically regulate acts of imitation that are deemed to substantively violate the entire form, spatial composition, and design of architectural works through amendments and updates to the Copyright Law in the future.

Author details

Taufik H. Simatupang
Research Center for Law, Institute of Social Science and Humanities, National Research and Innovation Agency (BRIN), Jakarta, Indonesia

*Address all correspondence to: th_tupang@yahoo.co.id

References

[1] dan Sidharta DD. Pokok-pokok Filsafat Hukum: Apa dan Bagaimana Filsafat Hukum Indonesia. Jakarta: Gramedia Pustaka Utama; 1995

[2] M. Djumhana dan R. Djubaedillah. Hak Milik Intelektual: Sejarah, Teori, dan Praktek. Bandung: Citra Aditya Bakti; 1993

[3] Cita Citrawinda Priapantja. Hak Kekayaan Intelektual: Tantangan Masa Depan. Jakarta: Badan Penerbit FH Universitas Indonesia; 2003

[4] Subekti R. Pokok-Pokok Hukum Perdata. Jakarta: Intermasa; 2003

[5] Elsi Kartika Sari dan Advendi Simangunsong. Hukum dalam Ekonomi. Jakarta: Gramedia Widiasarana Indonesia; 2005

[6] Idris K. Pedoman Pengembangan Kebijakan Kekayaan Intelektual Bagi Perguruan Tinggi dan Lembaga Penelitian dan Pengembangan. Jenewa: World Intellectual Property Organization;

[7] Zudan Arif Fakrulloh dan Hadi Wuryan. Hukum Ekonomi. Surabaya: Karya Abditama; 1997

[8] Husni Syawali dan Neni Sri Imaniyati. Kapita Selekta Hukum Ekonomi. Bandung: Mandar Maju; 2000

[9] Simatupang TH. Intellectual Property Law (An Introduction). Jakarta, Indonesia: Attahiryah Islamic University; 2017

[10] Mosafa M. Inspiration versus plagiarism: Academic integrity in architectural education. International Journal of Construction Environmet. 2011;**1**(3):85-99

[11] Fikriarini Y, Putrie E. Membaca Konsep Arsitektur Vitruvius dalam Al Quran. Malang: UIN Malang Press; 2006

[12] Fikriarini A. Arsitektur Islam: Seni Ruang dalam Peradaban Islam. El-Harakah. 2011. DOI: 10.18860/EL

[13] Hilda BA. Mengenang Zaha Hadid Arsitek Kontroversial yang Berpengaruh. Kompas. 2017. Available from: https://properti.kompas.com/read/2017/05/31/112735221/google.mengenang.zaha.hadid.arsitek.kontroversial.yang.berpengaruh.?page=all. [Accessed: February 26, 2021]

[14] DW.Com. Bangunan-bangunan Tiruan. DW.Com. https://www.dw.com/id/bangunan-bangunan-tiruan/g-17804737. [Accessed: January 26, 2021]

[15] Septianna Puteri MBS. Imitasi dan Disain Berulang: Apakah Suatu Pelanggaran, Seminar Nasional Cendekiawan Ke 4, Buku 1 Teknik, Kedokteran Hewan, Kesehatan. Lingkungan dan Lanskap; 2018

[16] Miranti RNMM, Santoso B. Perlindungan Hukum Terhadap Karya Arsitektur Kolonial Melalui Sistem HKI (Studi Pada Arsitektur Kolonial di Kota Bandung). Diponegoro Law Journal. 2017;**6**(2):1-14

[17] Suhartono S. Hukum Positif Problematik Penerapan dan Solusi Teoritiknya. Jurnal Ilmu Hukum. 2020;**15**(2):201-211

[18] Available from: https://www.dw.com/id/bangunan-bangunan-tiruan/g-17804737. [Accessed: March 1, 2021]

[19] Available from: https://nasional.tempo.co/read/323998/

meniru-desain-arsitektur-bisa-dipidana. [Accessed: March 1, 2021]

[20] Prihastomo B. Pergeseran Paradigma dan Persepsi Karya Arsitektur Bagi Arsitek di Era Informasi. Jurnal Arsitektur dan Perencaan. 2018;**1**(1):81-96

[21] Kim Y, Choi J. The applicability of aesthetics of appropriation for the Disscussion on architectural plagiarism. Journal of Architectural Institute of Korea Planning Design. 2020;**36**(5):11-22

[22] Hambi EM, Benabbou F. A deep learning based technique for plagiarism detection: A comparative study. IAES International Journal of Artificial Intelligence. 2020;**9**(1):81-90. DOI: 10.11591/ijai.v9.i1.pp81-90

[23] Ovhal P. Detecting plagiarism in images. In: International Conference on Information Processing (ICIP). India. 2015. pp. 85-89. DOI: 10.1109/INFOP.2015.7489356

[24] Kim Y, Choi J. Addressing the issues on architectural Palgiarism through the analysis of discourses. Journal of Architectural Institute of Korea Planning Design. 2019;**35**(12):3-12

[25] Taufik H. Simatupang and friends. Study on the application of the concept of substantial similarity for the protection of architectural works towards renewal of the copyright law in Indonesia. In: Proceedings of the 2nd International Conference on Law and Human Rights 2021 (ICLHR 2021). Netherlands: AtlantisPress; 2021. Available from: https://casetext.com/case/shine-v-childs

[26] Elfia Rahma Cindy Rizky Wardani Hanny. Perlindungan Terhadap Karya Arsitektur yang Memiliki Kemiripan dengan Ciptaan Lain Berdasarkan Prinsip Originalitas Berdasarkan UU Nomor 28 tahun 2014 tentang Hak Cipta. Brawijaya: Universitas Brawijaya; 2019. Availanble from: https://casetext.com/case/shine-v-childs

Chapter 4

A Deriving Quantitative Similarities to Computer Programs and Determining Copyright Infringement in South Korea

Si-Yeol Kim

Abstract

A substantial similarity is one of the factors for recognizing copyright infringement. Determining whether there is a substantial similarity is a hard work. For computer program works, judging the substantial similarity is even more difficult, because professional ability is required to measure. In Korea, this problem is solved through the expert testimony system in the trial process. In trial practice, quantitative similarity is mainly used as a method for determining substantial similarity. However, there are several limitations in two methods taken here, namely the use of the expert testimony system and the use of substantial similarity. Appropriate responses are required to overcome this limitation.

Keywords: software forensics, copyright, civil procedure, quantitative similarity, computer program works

1. Introduction

When a trial is conducted because of copyright infringement of a computer program, a problem has arisen. The problem is that judges cannot easily understand the expression of computer programs, which are the subjects of a lawsuit. In order to judge whether copyright is infringed, the determination of facts must be preceded. But the judgment for this is bound to be limited because of the judge's ability of perception. This phenomenon is also a characteristic of modern lawsuits that are increasingly complex and specialized. The recent expansion of modern lawsuits has caused a change in the role of judges in the trial process. There are some limitations of the lack of judges' knowledge in the professional field. So, in particular, the systems of utilizing experts for trials are gradually developing to overcome the limitations. In addition, this change is actively shown in intellectual property disputes, especially in the lawsuit of copyright infringement with the aim of computer programs.

In the Republic of Korea, the appraisal system [1] as a judge's order appraisal is widely used in litigation procedures. The system reflects the ex officio principle. Therefore, in using this procedure, several discussions on how to utilize experts and how judges accept the results are taking place in practice. There is a method used in the case of the copyright disputes of computer programs in Korea. It is deriving a degree of similarity with numerical values is broadly used to determine whether the copyright is infringed. Also, judgments based on the derived similarity is used either.

In general case, experts only analyze and identify objective facts without the intervention of subjective values. However, computer program copyright infringement lawsuits are characterized by experts requiring a value judgment to determine the facts. Separate from the judgment of 'same' or 'different,' the concept of 'similar' is bound to be reflected in the above numerical values indicating the degree of similarity. It inevitably involves subjective judgment to some extent by the subject who judges it. At this moment, this subjective judgment is fully based on the experts' discretion. But the important thing is that it should be handled under the theoretical limitations perceived by copyright law.

Such software forensics plays a critical role in copyright litigation in Korea. Therefore, many discussions have taken place regarding copyright law or litigation procedures. Hereinafter, we will examine the overview of the appraisal process, which is a system where software forensics can be utilized in copyright infringement lawsuits in Korea. So, we'll see how software forensics are being used.

2. Copyright infringement in computer programs and judging practical similarity

2.1 Types of copyright infringement in computer programs

Disputes over copyright infringement on computer programs occur because of various causes, such as transaction relationships of computer programs, turnover of computer program producers, contractual relationships, etc. After analyzing various cases, copyright infringement in which practical similarity becomes an issue can be classified into the following four types.

Type 1. One unfairly acquired a computer program and used it to create the same kind of new program.

This case is the most basic types of disputes over copyright infringement on computer programs. In this case, the infringer defends himself/herself by mainly arguing that the computer program developed by the infringer is completely different from the one owned by a victim of the infringement. Another case is that if the victim of the infringement developed the program by referring to the technology of external third-party company. The infringer argues that the program was developed by referring not to the victim's but to the same third-party company's technology [2].

Type 2. One moved to another company and created the same kind of new program using source code from the previous company.

This case is also a very distinctive type of dispute. However, there are various reasons why the infringer possesses the original copyright company's source code. One of the main types of leakages is duplicating the source code during the development process to work outside the office, especially at home. Another one is the case of directly duplicating and taking the source code when leaving the company [3].

Type 3. While one was legitimately using the computer program, he reversely engineered it and created the same kind of new program.

Though it is not relatively common, this type mainly occurs in web-based software that can easily reverse-engineer the original program and requires a quick business response. It happens wherein a user uses the program by paying a certain cost first. Later, the user creates and uses a new computer program with the purpose of avoiding usage fee payment. Since, it would be easier to create another program by modifying the original one [4].

Type 4. One created the same kind of new program using computer programs from other companies while he acquired in the course of his work.

This type corresponds to a large-scale and complex computer program compared to Type 3. It starts with a relationship that helps copyright owners based on a professional level of understanding of the original program. But after that, the infringer takes away the market of copyright owners by engaging in unfair copying [5].

2.2 The structure of judging the copyright infringement

The Copyright Act does not specifically stipulate principles capable of judging acts of copyright infringement by law. But considering the basic principles of copyright law, certain standards by theories and precedents are formed and used. Even if they are the criteria for determining whether copyright infringement occurs, opinions on it are not fully consistent. In general, three criteria are applied to the precedents and theories in Korea. First, the plaintiff has valid copyright; second, the defendant created the work of infringement after seeing the plaintiff's work with copyright; and third, an identity or substantial similarity exists between the defendant's work of infringement and the plaintiff's work with copyright. Copyright infringement can be recognized when the above conditions are all met. Of the three criteria above, the third issue of substantial similarity is the most important. Compared to issues wherein a relatively clear conclusion can be made according to specific facts, the question of similarity is inevitably a value judgment made by a judge. In other words, in a state that they are not completely the same or different, the question of how similar two works can be viewed as similar to each other. The criterion for making a judgment is that the degree of similarity that confirms copyright infringement must be substantial. Deciding upon that degree is a very abstract and difficult matter. It sets a boundary somewhere on a straight line connecting the two ends of similarity, completely different and completely identical.

It is difficult to judge whether there is substantial similarity because it cannot be easily judged because of the abstraction and uncertainty of the degree of similarity. In practice, therefore, the judgment on whether copyright is infringed often depends on whether substantial similarity can be recognized.

2.3 Limitations of substantial similarity judgment and calculation of similarity (%)

It is indeed practically impossible to set clear and objective criteria for determining how similar works must be to be said they are substantially similar. Because of this point, it is believed that the process of determining whether a copyright is infringed inevitably connotes ambiguity.

However, the purpose of the trial in a copyright infringement lawsuit is not to reveal to what extent the two subjects of comparison must be similar to be regarded as substantially similar relationships. But it is to determine whether they are substantially similar when there are specific similarities between them. Because it is virtually impossible to find the point, judges do not find a point of criterion to judge that they are substantially similar in a specific case. The issue can only be solved to the extent that it determines whether a certain 'degree of similarity' belongs to the right or left of the point of criterion that would be somewhere [6].

In the process of determining whether practical similarity can be recognized in the copyright infringement dispute over computer programs, in the trial practice in Korea, the degree of similarity is mainly used. The degree of similarity between the two programs is expressed as figures (%). Although this method has some limitations, it is used by supplementing them in practice because of its high efficiency in problem-solving.

3. A judicial procedure for determining substantial similarity: expert testimony

3.1 The concept of appraisal

An appraisal is an investigation of evidence to supplement the judge's judgment ability. It requires a person with professional knowledge and experience to report to the court. The court gets the regulations and empirical rules, or the fact judgment derived by applying them to specific facts from experts. The Korean litigation law system stipulates expert testimony in Article 335 of the Civil Procedure Act. The expert testimony stipulated in the legal procedure laws means to perform an appraisal by a judge's appraisal order.

3.2 Procedures of Expert Testimony under the Civil Procedure Act

3.2.1 Overview

The expert testimony of the specialized field, a type of evidence supplied by expert witnesses, the contents are more professional and complicated than judges look. In this case, it is subject to practical limitations in applying the principle of free evaluation of evidence [7]. In some cases, it has led to problems hindering the procedural processes, such as high expert testimony fees, poor and insincere expert testimony, delays in reporting the results of expert testimony, moral hazard, as well as preventing quickness and economic efficiency. Therefore, there has been an ongoing debate on the need to improve the procedures at the level of judicial reform.

3.2.2 Duty of Expert Witness

This regulation considers serious problems such as poor expert testimony and outsourcing — blanket subcontracts — from the expert testimony of construction appraisal in the past. It can be seen as responding more strictly to poor expert testimony. Also, it would be seen as trying to increase the reliability and level of expertise by explicitly stipulating the regulation, which had not been explicitly recognized in the law [7]. It also embodies the application of the multiple appraisal system. In general, it is common for one expert to be designated as an expert witness. But Article 339 of the Civil Procedure Act regulates that multiple expert witnesses shall state their opinions together when they receive the request for expert testimony. Considering that, the multiple appraisal system is recognized under the existing regulation. In addition, when multiple appraisers conduct an appraisal, all of them shall be designated by the court when conducting an appraisal jointly to prevent the entrustment of expert testimony.

3.2.3 Methods of Stating Expert Testimony and Examining Expert Witness

The revision originated from the problem that the process of verifying the contents of the results of expert testimony submitted by expert witnesses is not properly carried out in practice. The parties are allowed to state their opinions on the results of expert testimony through dates for pleadings or fact inquiries in practice. However, the revision is intended to guarantee the process more clearly and procedural.

Expert witness examination can be divided into two cases: (1) the court requires expert witnesses to attend for the first time to take an oath, informs matters for expert testimony, and orders them to make expert testimony, and (2) expert witnesses make supplementary statements to the court after submitting the results of expert testimony in writing. In Article 339–2 of the Civil Procedure Act, expert witness examination can correspond with the latter. When the methods of examining expert witnesses were not separately stipulated, examining expert witnesses and the examination of expert witnesses under Article 340 of the Civil Procedure Act seemed not to be clearly distinguished in practice. However, those two are now clearly classified, and the examination of witnesses is defined differently by the revised regulation. In relation to examining expert witnesses, the method of witness examination by cross-examination does not apply mutatis mutandis to ease the burden on the parties. It follows the ex officio examination in principle, but the right to supplementary examination of the parties is guaranteed.

3.2.4 Examination of Expert Witness through Video or Other Transmission Systems

This regulation considers the burden on expert witnesses, such as the fact that they must argue with the parties and representatives face-to-face. And in case of they receive a small amount of fees because of the characteristic of public interest, the fact that they must appear in court as out-of-hours can be another burden. So, the regulation reflects that it is more reasonable to prepare the procedure wherein the court can hear statements without expert witnesses' appearance in court. It would be better than to force them to serve summons. Unlike witness examination, which adopts the method of cross-examination, the expert witness examination follows the ex officio examination in principle. And it is also legally valid in relation to Article 339–2, which guarantees the right to the supplementary examination of the parties.

For expert witnesses, it is common to feel pressured by the questioning of the court and the parties about the results of the expert testimony. As a result, there is a situation where the court seems not to choose the expert witness examination to avoid the expert witness testimony [8]. Some pointed out that it eventually acts as the factor that hinders the acquisition of high-quality appraisal results and the effective end of disputes through it in practice. However, the court seemed to expect the effect of improving the phenomenon of avoiding expert testimony by allowing expert witnesses not to feel too much pressure during expert witness examination.

3.2.5 Entrustment for Expert Testimony

Entrustment for expert testimony means that a court may, if deemed necessary, entrust an expert testimony to a public agency, school, other organizations having adequate equipment, or a foreign public agency. The court may, also, have the person designated by a public agency, school, other organizations, or a foreign public agency make a supplementary explanation on a written expert testimony if the submitted statement is unclear or inconclusive (Article 341–2). The regulation applies mutatis mutandis to the examination of expert witnesses through video or other transmission systems during the examination of expert witnesses when the examination of the entrusted institutions for expert testimony is conducted. By this, it expects an improvement in the phenomenon of avoiding expert testimony of specialized institutions which can conduct entrusted expert testimony. In the case of the copyright appraisal under Article 119 of the Copyright Act, there was controversy over who should respond to an examination between an appraisal institution and an expert who actually conducted an appraisal. It was the case that showed the burden on the examination of expert witnesses. Also, it was expected that faithful and efficient evidence investigation could be conducted depending on the case.

3.3 System of the Procedures of Copyright Expert Testimony

Article 119 ① 1 of the Copyright Act allows the Korea Copyright Commission (KCC) to conduct an appraisal in which a court requests for an appraisal of infringement of copyright or other rights for a trial or investigation. In this case, the subject of the appraisal is the KCC. It conducts the appraisal in the manner of entrustment prescribed in Article 341 of the Civil Procedure Act, not as an appraiser as a natural person under the Civil Procedure Act.

Specific procedures or methods of the appraisal system under this Act are delegated to the Presidential Decree. Article 64 of the Enforcement Decree of the Copyright Act regulates the submission of the materials to deal with the duty. These materials are such as original copy or duplicate of a work subject for the appraisal, materials by which it can compare the similarity of related works in the case of a request for the appraisal on infringement. Other materials that the KCC requests as it judges necessary for the appraisal to the KCC and the organization of the Expert Appraisal Committee (EAC) could be the material too. Specific procedures of the appraisal system are delegated to the KCC. Moreover, under the principle of payment by the beneficiary, the KCC may request a copyright appraisal fee from a client, and the amount can be determined by the KCC. In civil cases, plaintiffs and defendants in the lawsuit are those who actually requested appraisals. So, they shall pay appraisal fees notified by the KCC to the competent court in advance. After appraisals are completed, the court pays the fees to the KCC. In criminal cases, appraisals are conducted after the state institutions, such as the court, prosecution, and police. So, they pay fees to the KCC, as the state is responsible for proving guilt [9].

Currently, the procedures of the copyright appraisal under the Copyright Act are divided into six stages: (1) application of appraisal and submission of appraisal materials (2) analysis of appraisal materials (3) estimate and notification of appraisal cost (4) appointment of professional appraiser (5) deliberation from EAC and (6) notification of appraisal result. In addition, additional materials may be requested if it is insufficient or inappropriate to conduct an appraisal after analyzing the submitted materials. Moreover, if it is necessary to revise the deliberation results of the EAC after the appraisal is conducted, it shall be corrected [10].

To request an appraisal, the court or investigation agency's request for an official appraisal is required. Those who intend to request for appraisal shall submit applications of appraisal and materials to the KCC (Article 64 ① of the Enforcement Decree of the Copyright Act). It is necessary to analyze the appraisal at a certain level to calculate an appropriate appraisal fee and plan the appraisal following the request. Next, to conduct a full-fledged appraisal, the estimated appraisal fee calculated through an appraisal analysis must be notified, and the fee must be paid. In the case of a civil lawsuit, the person who actually requests an appraisal shall pay an appraisal fee notified by the KCC to the competent court in advance. In the case of a criminal lawsuit, an appraisal shall be conducted after an investigation institution pays a fee to the KCC. After the estimated appraisal fee is paid, a professional appraiser with the most appropriate professional ability conducts an appraisal. Multiple experts can be required to cooperate if necessary. An appraisal result is evaluated by the EAC, and the fairness, appropriateness, and reliability of the written appraisal are assessed so that they can provide a substantially and legally high-quality appraisal result. The appraisal result is then notified to the requesting institution, and follow-up actions such as the settlement of the appraisal fee, return of appraisal materials, and response to the questioning about the appraisal are made.

Such an appraisal procedure is sometimes problematic in that it somewhat conflicts with the court's appraisal procedure under the Civil Procedure Act. A typical example is the procedural problems related to the provision of appraisal materials and the calculation of expected appraisal fees. The copyright appraisal under the Copyright Act proceeds with the procedures such as receiving materials and calculating estimated appraisal fees based on the entrustment for appraisal in practice. But the appraisal procedure of the court is to designate appraisers or entrust appraisals after confirming the estimated appraisal fees. In particular, it is very limited to provide materials for calculating estimated appraisal fees as appraisals have not been entrusted to the court yet. Moreover, there are certain problems including omitting important considerations for the selection of appraisers in practical appraisals under the Copyright Act. These problems arise as the court cannot confirm estimated appraisal fees before conducting appraisals based on the consent of the litigants.

Meanwhile, it is also worth considering that other institutions are not prohibited from conducting the same kinds of appraisals. Even though the appraisal procedure under the Copyright Act is institutionalized, it could be if the court may entrust the appraisals to them. The reason is that they seem to have similar practical issues in general.

3.4 Problems caused by using of these systems in intellectual property litigation

First, it is a matter regarding the difficulty of securing fairness. This represents a phenomenon in which the importance of the stage of appraisal in the trial process is linked to personal interests. A typical case for this is the construction appraisal corruption case in 2015. In March 2015, a builder and an owner filed a lawsuit over the cost of the new hotel construction in Geoje, Gyeongsangnam-do. In this lawsuit, the court appointed A as an appraiser, and he secretly offered both builders and builders to give an advantage. Knowing the importance of appraisal to the outcome of the trial, both parties each handed A KRW 10.8 million and KRW 8.5 million. In addition, B, the representative of the company to which A belongs, gave 'subcontract' to other technicians for the appraisal that A should take. Moreover, he submitted an appraisal under A's name to the court. At this time, there is a mention that there is a practice that B usually receives about 10% of the appraisal cost as a fee. In particular, when an employee who left the company was selected as a litigation appraiser, B conducted an appraisal without the employee's recognition and submitted it to the court [11]. This type of case was also the main cause of the revision of the appraisal regulations when the Civil Procedure Act was revised in 2016 [12].

The second problem is that the de facto binding phenomenon for appraisal results is increasing. As mentioned previously regarding the change in the type of appraisal, complex and highly professional litigation often occurs that judges cannot have various expertise corresponding to facts. So, a phenomenon in which judges are bound to the appraisal results may occur. In this regard, the Supreme Court prohibits judges from rejecting the appraisal results without clear grounds. The court said, "If the scientific evidence method proves that all the facts on the premise are true and the method of inference is scientifically justified, so the possibility of an error is regarded to be negligible or minimal since judges are quite binding in acknowledging facts, rejecting them without any reasonable grounds is prohibited as it is beyond the limits of the principle of free evaluation of evidence even if the fact acknowledgment is of the trial court's full authority" [13]. In other words, it is acknowledged that the judge is bound to the appraisal result to a certain extent. If a judge has no choice but to be bound to the appraisal result beyond a certain level, the appraisal system is not simply constructed on the premise of assisting judges. But it must be reorganized to make the institutional system more advanced [14].

Third, it is a problem in accordance with the specificity of the use of appraisal procedures in the process of intellectual property trial. While the appraisal procedure is widely used in trials related to various professional fields, there are differences in using appraisal procedures. In intellectual property rights–related trials and other trials, the biggest difference is that the individuality of each case is considered in the trials related to intellectual property rights. When using the appraisal procedure in the trial process in general, an appraiser's designation can be made based on certain rules. Replacing an appraiser with another expert also does not matter much. However, in trials in the field of intellectual property rights, factors such as expertise in the case and diversity of fields exist. Therefore, there is a big difference in that the process of investigating and designating appraisers suitable for solving each case should be dealt respectively. This characteristic leads to a problem in that the process of finding an appropriate appraiser. Also, selecting him/her as an appraiser imposes considerable difficulty and burden on the court in the course of individual cases would be a problem in trial practice.

Fourth, a problem is also pointed out that the closeness between appraisal results and judgment is very high. In reality, if the appraisal results are presented in a trial related to intellectual property rights, in reality, the appraisal results will inevitably have a very close impact on the trial's final judgment. Accordingly, the court carefully addresses conducting the appraisal in the process of intellectual property rights–related trials. Unlike other fields, when an appraisal is performed in a trial related to intellectual property rights, it is common that the appraisal contents are basically connected to the matter of rights. For this reason, the reliability of the subject performing the appraisal plays a very important role. It is because that the judgment of the right to some extent is inevitably accompanied in some form in performing the appraisal [15]. Originally, judgments on facts and norms should be clearly distinguished into appraisers and judges. But these distinctions are not clear and somewhat mixed in the intellectual property rights–related trials. Thus, the reliability for appraisers has a higher demand compared to other fields. Furthermore, appraisals conducted by the appraisers with secured reliability — public confidence — are also important for the efficiency of the trial process as they can prevent unnecessary disputes during the trial.

Fifth, the high cost of an appraisal is also pointed out as a problem. In civil litigation, either or both parties in the case pay for the appraisal. However, even if it is a litigation appraisal, this point of cost becomes a problem in the case of criminal litigation. In the criminal procedure, the government bears the appraisal cost, inevitably resulting in considerable limitations to using the financial resources because it comes from the national budget. As a result, the high cost of appraisal becomes a burden, so it may be expected that courts will be unable to utilize necessary and appropriate appraisal. However, even in the case of civil litigation, the high appraisal cost can also lower the use of the appraisal. Moreover, since there cannot be a standard of appropriate appraisal cost, it is necessary to establish a series of standards of the appraisal cost calculated by reputable appraisers.

4. A method of determining the substantial similarity of a computer program using software forensics

4.1 The nature of the calculated similarity of a computer program

For a computer program work, quantitative similarity is used as a factual premise to determine whether there is substantial similarity.

Quantitative similarity refers to a numerical value (ratio) expressing the result of analyzing the source code of the two computer programs and comparing them by applying a certain standard. To calculate the quantitative similarity, the part expressed in the form of characters are the basic targets; for computer programs, the source code and the purpose code are the main targets [16]. This method shows the degree of similarity between the two computer programs, that is, the extent to which the infringer copied and used the copyright owner's program in an objective figure. In addition, the presentation of such objective grounds is widely used as a basis to determine substantial similarity because of some advantages. For example, there are advantages of reducing unnecessary disputes in determining copyright infringement and deriving some generalized quantitative standards to promote legal stability. From a software engineering point of view, there can be various methods of calculating quantitative similarity. However, in order to determine practical similarity, it is necessary to establish standards and methods and calculate quantitative figures by reflecting the legal concepts and requirements contained therein. The quantitative similarity calculated without properly reflecting them is not appropriate for use as a basis for determining substantial similarity [17]. Therefore, in this case, it can be used as a basis for figuring out similarity, which is a requirement to prove whether it is based on the plaintiff's material among the copyright infringement requirements. But it cannot be used as a basis for practical similarity.

4.2 Characteristics of quantitative similarity

First, it expresses the qualitative value of substantial similarity as the quantitative value by using numbers as a means of expression. It cannot be considered that the meaning of similarity is limited to the quantitative. It is because what is similar inevitably depends on the subjective intention of the person who determines it. In addition, the meaning of substantial itself is not drawn from specific quantitative standards as a qualitative value. But rather, it shows that the infringement of technology and effort through reproduction reaches the substantial degree to protect the value of technology and effort input by the creator to produce the work. It can be said that expressing these qualitative values in quantitative values through the numerical medium is a characteristic of calculating quantitative similarity.

Second, the calculation result of quantitative similarity is utilized as the basis for determining substantial similarity. Eventually, it not only plays a role of the basis for determining copyright infringement but is also used with expansion to the basis for stealing business secrets or calculating compensation for damages. In this case, it should be utilized with the recognition that there is a significant difference in concepts between the types of similarity for different purposes. It needs to be distinguished the similarity used as the basis for determining substantial similarity under the copyright law and the similarity used for other purposes. This is because, for example, if the similarity is used as the basis for stealing business secrets, it does not necessarily reach a significant degree but is meaningful for detecting that others use the content specified as business secrets. It is different from the area of copyright law, in which there should be something similar to a substantial extent.

Third, quantitative similarity represents similarity to both literal and nonliteral expressions. The literal expressions include an infringement on the character itself, that is, the literal expression, which appears on the source code line. Nonliteral expressions, on the other hand, include the structure, sequence, and organization of computer programs —source code [18]. Although they would all differ in extent depending on their functionality, they have a similar meaning to literary works. Also, the expression of similarity can be considered including both literal and nonliteral expressions [19]. In the case of nonliteral expressions, however, there are several controversies over various issues, such as to what extent copyright currently must be protected and how to calculate the quantified similarity. The stance of precedents also seems to be inconsistent.

Fourth, the value from the copyright law is reflected in the technical calculation method. This is due to the reality that the domain of judges intersects with that of experts in computer program copyright disputes that have the nature of professional litigation. It allows expert analysis and judgment to have an appropriate effect on the judgment. In practice, it seems that the protected scope of expression and the limitation of the concept of similarity are physically considered when quantitative similarity is calculated.

4.3 A method of calculating quantitative similarity

4.3.1 Overview

Looking at quantitative similarity from the perspective of technology, the methods for calculating a specific ratio can be widely varied. As mentioned, however, if this is not limited to the technical perspective but viewed as a value as close as possible to determine the substantial similarity under the copyright law conditions differs. There are restrictions in the calculation method arising. It can be seen that there are two major restrictions. First, similarity calculation should be conducted only by using the expressions protected by copyright law as a comparison target; second, the criteria for similarity determination should be established. This is because what is completely the same or different has no room for the intervention of subjective value. But similarity can yield significantly different results depending on what criteria determine whether they are similar or not. Of them, the latter case has relative difficulties. In practice, when comparing such as source codes, physical standards are applied to determine them as similar. These standards are mostly based on empirical rules. This is because specific consideration is insufficient on how to express the criteria for similarity determination as a physical standard.

4.3.2 Classification based on the expression method of similarity

Method 1 is a form that divides source codes and databases into file pairs to calculate the similarity of each and presents the results as they are. It can be used in cases where similarity is difficult to derive by applying one criterion because of different expression forms such as source code and database [20]. Method 2 is a form that derives the degree of similarity for each component (comparison element) and calculates and presents a single overall similarity by adding all of them. This method is mainly used to identify the clear degree of product unit infringement since a specific computer program is composed of a single product. While weighted value is sometimes applied to similarity calculation, the similarity is calculated by adding a certain weighted value in consideration of the significance of each component of a computer program [21]. However, some criticize that this is only a value calculated by a specific formula. They argue that it cannot be recognized as a value presented as close as possible to the actual similarity by calculating the weight problem or the comprehensive similarity forcefully.

4.3.3 Classification based on the calculation method of similarity

Method 3 is a way to calculate by comparing the degree of similar lines of the source code constituting a computer program with the entire line. It is to calculate the similarity faithfully to the literal expression of a computer program even if the functional part is slightly less considered [22]. Method 4 is a way that classifies computer programs by components (modules, files, etc.), determines whether each element is similar or not, and calculates the overall similarity by synthesizing them (**Table 1**) [23].

4.4 Limitations

First, it is the limitation of the calculated value close to the legal meaning. Upon examining precedents, it was commonly found that the basic concepts of copyright law are physically reflected for calculating quantitative similarity. Also, the two are

Classification based on the expression method of similarity		**Classification based on the calculation method of similarity**	
Method 1	**Method 2**	**Method 3**	**Method 4**
Divide source codes and databases into file pairs to calculate the similarity of each and present the results as they are	Derive the degree of similarity for each component (comparison element);	Calculate by comparing the degree of similar lines of the source code constituting a computer program with the entire line	Classify computer programs by components (modules, files, etc.);
	Calculate and present a single overall similarity by adding all of them		Determine whether each element is similar or not;
			Calculate overall similarity by synthesizing them

Table 1.
Quantitative similarity calculation scheme type.

compromised through comparison and analysis based on this. Nevertheless, no matter how precisely the quantitative similarity is calculated in consideration of the value of copyright law, there is a limitation in essence, that the actual similarity cannot be directly expressed. In this regard, the essence is the characteristic that the quantitative similarity is a technical analysis value. And thus, the process of its interpretation in terms of legal value must ensue.

Second, it is a limitation that the substantial meaning of quantitative similarity can be reduced. Changes on the computer program development environment are increasing the use of copyright non-protection targets. Therefore, there is a risk that the actual meaning of the quantitative similarity calculated may be distorted. It happens if this is excluded from the comparison according to the basic principles of the copyright law, compared and analyzed only with the remaining source codes. For example, if there is a source code of 100 lines and all of them were directly created, 60% of the quantitative similarity may be regarded as duplicating 60 lines out of 100. However, if 50 lines must be removed from the comparison target, such as automatic generation code and open source, the actual duplicated source code is 30 lines if there is the same 60% of similarity. In other words, it means that even though the quantitative similarity is the same, the actual amount of duplicated source code may vary. Therefore, even if both quantitative similarities are the same at 60% in a computer program with the same size of 100 lines, these two cases cannot be equally determined.

Third, it is a limitation caused by the distortion phenomenon because of the quantitative scale of the source code. The mistake that is most likely to be made in practice is to try to establish a quantitative standard for what percent of similarity is substantially similar. Quantitative similarity does not indicate the amount of source code judged to be similar in a computer program but simply presents its ratio. The actual amount of source code duplicated by the infringer cannot be identified only by the similarity expressed quantitatively. It is a matter that should be examined through a separate review.

Fourth, it is a limitation on the application of weighted value. Substantial similarity is the result of the determination of whether the quantity and quality of similar parts are substantial when comparing the comparison targets. Since the quality of similarity should be considered, the similarity may be calculated by reflecting the importance of the part that appears to be reproduced throughout the whole program. There is a case in which such qualitative importance is expressed as a weighted value and reflected in the process of similarity calculation in precedents and practices. However, applying the weighted value in comparing computer programs is controversial. It is because the question of how the appropriate the value assigned as a weight can be secured. In case law and practice, such qualitative importance is sometimes expressed as a weight and reflected in the similarity calculation process. However, it is somewhat questionable whether the weighted value can be applied so precisely in proportion to the difference brought by a minor change in figures. Finally, it is believed that applying the weighted value to consider the qualitative aspect in determining substantial similarity should be carefully approached [24].

Fifth, there are various methods of calculating the quantitative similarity of computer programs found in precedents. Despite the comparison under the same conditions, various results can be derived, because there are various methods of similarity calculation. This will act as the cause of a significant reduction of the predictability of each issue of copyright disputes over a computer program. In the end, a limitation arises that the inefficiency of dispute resolution is inevitably increased because of this. The **Figure 1** is an example of deriving similarities when Method 3 and Method

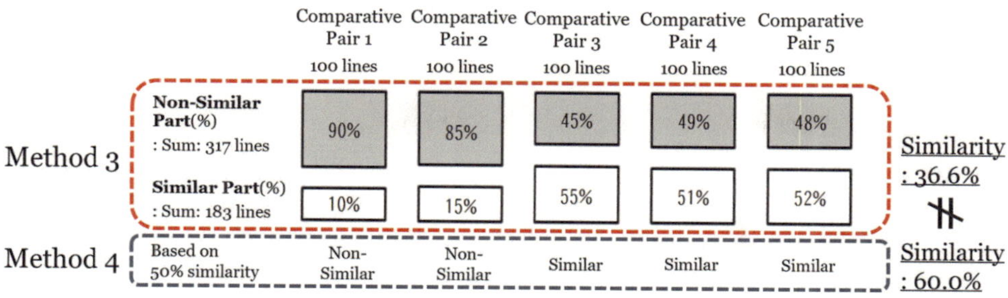

Figure 1.
Example of different calculated similarity by comparison method.

4 are applied to two programs with a total of 500 lines and 5 comparison pairs. Although it is the same target, the result is 36.6% when Method 3 is applied, and 60.0% when Method 4 is applied, which shows a significant difference.

Sixth, it is a limitation of the difficulty in the clear establishment of the criteria for similarity. The establishment of the physical extent of the criteria for similarity are the most difficult problem in putting quantitative similarity close to substantial similarity. As discussed previously, the quantitative similarity of computer programs is basically calculated with text as a target. When comparing text, knowledge of how to set the criteria for similarity are very important as it affects the final degree of similarity.

5. Conclusions

Korean courts use the appraisal procedure under the litigation law. It is based on the ex officio principle to determine whether the copyright of computer programs is infringed. In this process, the quantitative similarity is derived to secure objective information on the degree of similarity, which is used as a basis for judgment of substantial similarity. Although several inherent limitations exist in this method, it is difficult to resolve them structurally. In practice, a method that secures reasonable methodology for each case is being used by fully considering these problems in the software forensics process. The result is shown differently depending on the method chosen to calculate the quantitative similarity. In other words, determining the method of calculating the similarity is critical in the trial outcome. However, depending entirely on experts' goodwill is deemed to be inappropriate. Active discussions on not only a range of methodologies but also ways to improve the litigation procedures for the use of experts must be carried out.

Author details

Si-Yeol Kim
Korea Institute of Intellectual Property, Seoul, Republic of Korea

*Address all correspondence to: sykimlaw@hanmail.net

References

[1] Civil Procedure Act Articles 333 to 342; Criminal Procedure Act Articles 169 to 179-2

[2] Cases include Seoul Southern District Court Decision 2002Kahap2277 Decided May 12, 2004; Seoul Southern District Court Judgment 2005Gahap3367 Sentenced November 18, 2005; Seoul Central District Court Judgment 2006Gahap76502 Sentenced December 7, 2007; Seoul Central District Court Decision 2006Kahap2827 Decided April 13, 2007, etc

[3] Cases of this include Seoul Central District Court Decision 2004Kahap2396 Decided March 16, 2005; Seoul Southern District Court Decision 2004Kahap3090 Decided January 4, 2006; Seoul Central District Court Judgment 2004Gahap76119 Sentenced September 7, 2006; Seoul Central District Court Judgment 2006Gahap40343 Sentenced February 8, 2007; Seoul Central District Court Judgment 2007Gahap82740 Sentenced June 18, 2009; Seoul High Court Judgment 2009Na60413 Sentenced May 25, 2011, etc

[4] Cases of this include Seoul Central District Court Decision 2004Kahap3789 Decided October 13, 2005, etc

[5] Cases of this include Seoul High Court 2011La457 Decided June 23, 2011; Seoul High Court Judgment 2002Na35586 Sentenced October 6, 2004; Seoul High Court Judgment 2006Na113835, 2006Na113842 (Merged) Sentenced May 27, 2009, etc

[6] Si-Yeol K. Computer Program Copyright Similarity Theory. Seoul South Korea: Sechang Publish; 2018. p. 13

[7] Sung-Soo K. Research on Improvement Plans of the Appraisal System and the Expert Commissioner System. Seoul South Korea: Judicial Policy Research Institute; 2016. p. 33

[8] Jae Yun Yun. Legislative Study: Appraisal and Assessment Process on Special Litigation. Journal of Bupjo. 2002;**51**(11):262

[9] Si-Yeol K. A Study of Appraisal System on Copyright: The Effect and the Improvement. Seoul South Korea: Korea Copyright Commission; 2013. pp. 12-13

[10] Korea Copyright Commission. 2011 A Withe Paper. 2012. p. 263

[11] Chosun Media. "I'll give you an advantage"... Court appraisal falters. 2015. Available from: https://www.chosun.com/site/data/html_dir/2015/10/27/2015102700231.html

[12] The Supreme Court Press Release (3.23.2015)

[13] Supreme Court Judgment 2007Do1950 Sentenced May 10. 2007

[14] LawReview. The Supreme Court & Korean Bar Association's "Trial System Improvement Council" promotes the expansion of physical appraisal agencies. 2016. Available from: http://lawreview.co.kr/archives/30300

[15] Chaho JUNG, Hye SHIN, Eun. A Study on Introduction of the American Amicus Curiae System to Korean Patent Litigation System. Journal of Korea Information Law. 2019;**23**(2):157

[16] Supreme Court Judgment 2009Da 52304,52311 Sentenced June 6. 2011

[17] Seoul High Court Decision 2008Ra1199 Decided August 5. 2009

[18] Osterberg RC, Osterberg EC. Substantial similarity in copyright Law. Vol. 8-3. New York, US: Practising Law Institute; 2005

[19] Supreme Court Judgment 2009Da52304 Sentenced June 6. 2011

[20] Seoul High Court Decision 2011Ra457 Decided June 23. 2011

[21] Seoul Southern District Court Judgment 2005Gahap3367 Sentenced November 18. 2005

[22] Seoul High Court Judgment 2009Na71420 Sentenced. 17 Aug 2011. Seoul High Court Judgment 2006Na113835, 2006Na113842 (Merged) Sentenced. 27 May 2009

[23] Si-Yeol K. Computer Program Copyright Similarity Theory. Seoul South Korea: Sechang Publish; 2018. pp. 133-140

[24] Si-Yeol K. A Study on the Relationship between Weighted Value and Qualitative Standard in Substantial Similarity. Journal of Software Assessment and Valuation. 2019;**15**(1):29-30. DOI: 10.29056/jsav.2019.06.03

Section 3

Traditional Knowledge and Geographical Indications

Chapter 5

IP Protection of Traditional Knowledge: A Dilemma Faced by the Chinese Traditional Medicine in Global Competition

Yue Xu and Yumao Wang

Abstract

Traditional Chinese medicine (TCM) refers to medicine extracted from natural material, such as plants, animals, and minerals. The invention of TCM follows unique principles and methods inherited from ancient China. This chapter discusses a dilemma faced by TCM in global market competition. On one hand, based on the extensive Chinese medicine literature, practices, and therapies, TCM enjoys traditional knowledge-based advantages. On the other hand, in facing underdeveloped intellectual property (IP) protection both at home and abroad, TCM suffers from institutional disadvantages in global competition. It seems difficult for TCM to maintain traditional knowledge-based advantages and to push global integration without IP protection at the same time—a dilemma that needs to be resolved for the development of TCM. Building on a case study of a famous Chinese herbal medicine, Lianhua Qingwen, we explain the nature of the dilemma and provide advice for the future of TCM in global competition.

Keywords: traditional Chinese medicine (TCM), Chinese herbal medicine (CHM), traditional knowledge (TK), intellectual property (IP), Lianhua Qingwen (LHQW)

1. Introduction

Debate on the importance and contributions of traditional Chinese medicine (TCM) to health has never stopped. However, TCM has been treated as an "informal therapy" for years, and its intellectual property (IP) has not received global recognition. Till today, exporting TCM to most developed countries is restricted through standard control due to suspicion of toxic substances, pesticide residues, and heavy metals in it. However, worldwide attention to TCM has been upsurged by its impressive treatment of COVID-19 since the breakout of pandemic in early 2020. In February 2022, the World Health Organization (WHO) held a virtual meeting of 21 international experts from six WHO regions to evaluate and understand how to effectively enhance the contribution of TCM in global pandemics [1].

TCM dates more than 2000 years ago, representing one of world's oldest medical systems. Before the introduction of Western medicine in the Qing dynasty (1644–1911), TCM therapies played a crucial role in maintaining the Chinese people's health and nourishing their lives so that serious diseases would not recur. The official meaning of TCM can be found in Article 2 of the TCM Law of P.R. China.[1] Accordingly, TMC is a collective term of medicine of all Chinese ethnic groups including the Han and minority ethnic groups. TCM represents the Chinese perception of life, health, and disease. TCM reflects the Chinese pharmacology system developed with a long historical tradition, unique theories, and technical methods.

The market potential of TCM is impressive due to TCM's unique value to a large population. For example, TCM helps cancer patients recuperate from chemotherapy's side effects. It demonstrates the effective treatment of influenza epidemics in recent decades. It also works to boost the immune system of a body. WHO ([2]: p. v) noted that TCM is "one of the most popular forms" of traditional, complementary, and integrative medicine (TCIM) worldwide. About 60% of the world's population directly or indirectly uses TCM to treat diseases. By 2020, a total of 2711 TCM products have been included in the Chinese Pharmacopeia 2020 Edition.[2] The TCM market size reached USD 18.8 Billion in 2021, showing rising demand from developing economies in particular.[3]

However, TCM industry in China is facing seemingly doomed technical bottlenecks. Take Chinese Herbal Medicine (CHM), the main part of TCM, as an example. Its R&D development is seriously hampered by lack of defined criteria and measurement. Furthermore, poor clinical trial data often make CHM and its formulation not technically evidenced to international standards, thus not eligible to secure intellectual property (IP) protection when joining the global competition. Compared with the fast development of the Japanese Han-prescription medicine [3–6], CHM is far lagged and rather detached from global innovation competition.

Starting from Shang Dynasty (1600–1046 BC), CHM has been deeply rooted and widely thrived, especially in Asian countries including China, Japan, and South Korea where people trust TCM as the mode of health care [7]. But China still stays downstream of the global herbal medicine industry[4] for decades. Acting as a key herbal material supplier rather than a competitive herbal medicine inventor, China is seeing a shrinking growth rate in the global herbal medicine market. According to China Pharmaceutical Enterprises Association (CPEA),[5] from 2013 to 2016, CHM showed a year-on-year growth trend; however, it began to fluctuate and decline in

[1] "The TCM Law of the PRC" was promulgated by National Administration of Traditional Chinese Medicine on July 1, 2017. The content is publicly available from: http://www.natcm.gov.cn/fajiansi/zhengce-wenjian/2018-03-24/2249.html [Accessed: February 5, 2023].

[2] Mode TCM industry information can be found from "Chinese Pharmacopeia 2020 Edition: Key Points" at https://www.accestra.com/chinese-pharmacopoeia-2020-edition-key-points/ [Accessed: February 14, 2022].

[3] More information can be referred to "Traditional Chinese Medicine Market Size Worth USD 50.27 Billion in 2030" at https://www.emergenresearch.com/press-release/global-traditional-chinese-medicine-market [Accessed: February 14, 2023].

[4] The segment information can be referred "Herbal Medicine Markets" at https://www.insightslice.com/herbal-medicine-market [Accessed: February 6, 2023].

[5] More information about CHM market and TCM industry report can be referred to CPEA website at http://m.cpema.org/index.php?m=content&c=index&a=show&catid=26&id=7625 [Accessed: February 14, 2023].

DOI: http://dx.doi.org/10.5772/intechopen.1001820

2017. In 2019, the main business income reached 458.7 billion yuan, a year-on-year decrease of 1.47%.

We argue CHM is currently facing a serious dilemma that needs to be resolved in a timely manner. On one hand, CHM stands with competitive advantages because of its traditional knowledge (TK) base rooted in unique Chinese medicine culture. On the other hand, CHM's underdeveloped innovation has been deterred by poor IP institutions both at home and abroad. This study aims to understand the formation of this dilemma and provide our suggestions.

2. The development of CHM

Although CHM and botanic medicine share some similarities, they could be fundamentally different. Both refer to drugs that are wholly or partially extracted from plant material. However, botanic medicine theories focus on how to identify a single function through plant extraction to get chemical substances. In comparison, CHM theories aim to identify multiple functions via plant extraction to create a synergized substance. In other words, CHM follows certain principles derived from the Chinese TK that are not followed in the development of botanic drug. Below we highlight the status of CHM by three segments, namely, crude herbal, herbal piece, and herbal drug market, respectively.

2.1 Crude herbal

Crude herbal refers to the raw material of herbal plants ready to be used for treatment. Over the years, herbal materials with the best clinical effect have been identified and publicly acknowledged as genuine material. As shown in **Figure 1**, the annual changes in planting areas of Chinese herbal medicine have been increasing steadily over the years. In 2014, the total planting area was 2638 wan mu (1 wan mu is around

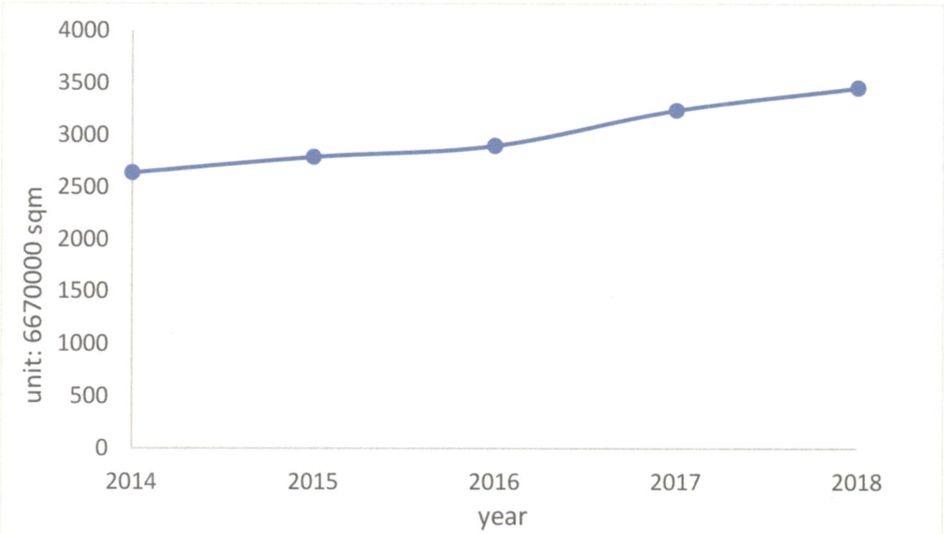

Figure 1.
Annual changes in planting area of Chinese herbal medicines (2014–2018).

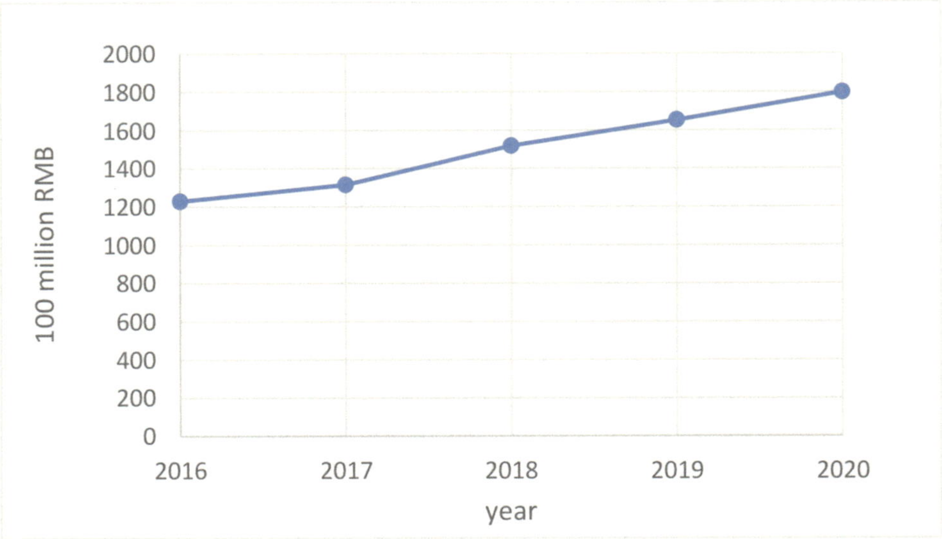

Figure 2.
Annual sales of Chinese crude herbal (2016–2020).

6,670,000 sqm). This figure increased to 3462 wan mu in 2018, with 31% growth within 5 years.

Given the increased area of planting, the annual sales of crude herbal have also increased continuously since 2016. As shown by **Figure 2**, in 2020, when a global pandemic occurred, the annual sales of crude herbal reached the highest of RMB 179 billion. According to WHO, 70–80% of CHM exported by China is crude herbal, indicting China is key player in the downstream of global value chain.

Notably, crude herbal is featured by its geographical origin, which indicates where the plant was cultivated and harvested. According to TCM theories, herbal plants grown in different geological conditions (such as soil, water, weather, and sunshine conditions) may vary dramatically in terms of their clinical effect. By distinguishing its geographical origin, one can tell the quality and authenticity of the material. However, with increased market demand, artificial cultivation of herbal plants is more adopted despite criticism of its impact on herbal quality. According to the Ministry of Agriculture and Rural Affairs (MARA)[6] of the P.R. China, by 2018, more than 600 kinds of crude herbal materials are commonly used in China, among which more than 300 kinds are cultivated artificially rather than in natural environment.

2.2 Herbal pieces

Herbal pieces refer to those processed or refined medicinal materials that are ready to be directly used for treatment or to be mixed with other materials for treatment. At present, herbal pieces are developed into several types including: (1) ordinary herbal pieces; (2) herbal pieces without the need of stir-frying; (3) granule herbal pieces; (4) broken herbal pieces, and (5) refined herbal pieces. Nowadays, the processing or refining methods for making herbal pieces follow a combined method that

[6] TCM development plan (2018–2025) can be found from MARA's official website at http://www.moa.gov.cn/gk/tzgg_1/tz/201812/t20181219_6165190.htm [Accessed: February 14, 2023].

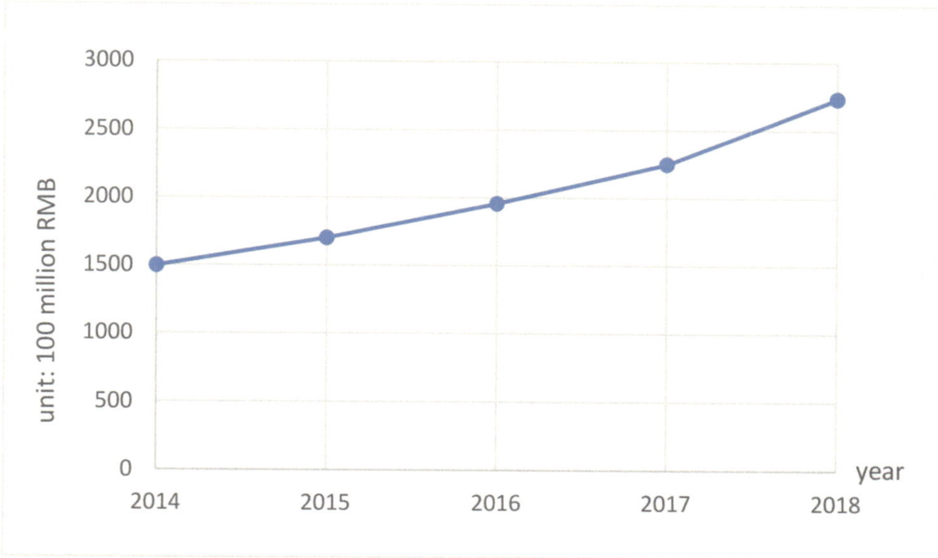

Figure 3.
Annual sales of herbal pieces (2014–2018).

incorporates traditional processing principles into modern processing technologies, such as cleaning, cutting, stir-frying, crafting, steaming, crushing, calcining, etc.

Talking about traditional processing principles, the TCM theories suggest that different parts of a plant and different ways of processing them could affect the clinical effect of herbal pieces. After plants are collected, they will undergo raw processing, including selecting, grading, washing, bleaching, slicing, hulling, steaming, boiling, scalding, sulfing, sweating, and drying of fresh medicinal materials. A plant can be processed by separating its fruit, tuber, grass, head, rhizomes, etc. Further processing include picking, washing, bleaching, slicing, desiccating, and so on. These processing methods have been formed over more than a thousand years of practices and are still believed important to ensure the CHM effect.

Like crude herbal, annual sales of herbal pieces also witnessed a continuous increase over the past years. As shown in **Figure 3**, the annual sales of herbal pieces reached RMB 273 billion in 2018. This figure almost doubled the annual sales of RMB 149 billion in 2014.

2.3 Herbal drugs

Herbal drugs refer to a class of CHM that can be used directly for disease prevention and treatment in the forms of pills, powder, injections, etc. With the development of modern pharmaceutical technologies, the Chinese herbal drug market has been increasing. In addition, the herbal drug market is also becoming increasingly integrated into the global market, especially in developing compounds, synthesizing natural drugs, or combining the usage of drugs.

Refining is crucial to ensure drug safety and a better curative effect. CHM refining addresses the removal of impurities and nonmedicinal parts to make the material clean and pure. Herbal properties are also refined by reducing or eliminating toxicity and eliminating unwanted side effects. Refining will inevitably trigger various physical and chemical reactions, so the composition of drugs can be created. In this process, both qualitative and quantitative changes are made to achieve pharmacological reactions so that clinical effect can be achieved. Around 30% of CHM exported by China are herbal drugs.

3. The traditional knowledge-based advantages of TCM

3.1 The unique philosophical foundation of TCM

Part of TCM philosophy concerns the relationship between humans and the universe. The Chinese believe a person fells unwell and gets a disease because of the fluctuations of *yin yang* and the resonances of *wu xing*. To keep a healthy status, people should model their behaviors on the four seasons (si shi) to maintain in balance with the *qi* of the universe. TCM regards human body and mind as "a dynamic self-regulating interconnected whole" ([8], p. 64). Unlike the Western approach, such as Greek traditional medicine, which is more interested in material constituents, the essential concern of TCM is the constant change and transformation (bian hua) about the human-universe relationship.

We here only mention a few ancient texts here. The *Yellow Emperor's Inner Canon* (Huan Di Nei Jing) compiled during the Qin and Han times (221 BC–220 AD) "defined the framework of TCM ... symbolizing the transformation from the accumulation of clinical experience to the systematic summation of theories".[7] The *Treatise on Cold Damage and Miscellaneous Disorders* (Shang Han Za Bing Lun) or the Treaties, from the Eastern Han Dynasty (206 BC–220 AD) collated by Zhang Zhongjing advanced the principles and methods to treat miscellaneous illnesses caused by internal ailments. The Ben Cao Gang Mu or Materia Medica in the Ming Dynasty (1368–1644) by Li Shizhen (1518–1593) was the first book in the world that scientifically categorized medicinal herbs in terms of their main and alternative names, property, growth environment, function, and limitation in the usage.

3.2 The diagnosis principles and practices

Four diagnostic methods came from the *Nan Jing—Sixty-one* by Bian Que., a famous physician during the Warring States Period (770–221 BC). The four methods are inspection, auscultation and olfaction, inquiry, and palpation. Inspection refers to the method by which a doctor needs to observe the whole body, parts, and excretions of the body purposefully through vision, to understand the health status and detect the disease condition. Auscultation and olfaction mean that through distinguishing the changes of sound and smell, a doctor can judge the physiological and pathological changes of viscera, which provide a basis for the diagnosis and syndrome differentiation. Then the most important part is inquiry, by which a doctor can understand the health status and diagnose the disease through purposeful inquiry of patients or companions. The last one is palpation, by which a doctor uses touch, press, and press certain parts of patients with fingers or palms, to understand the condition and diagnose diseases.

---

[7] The historical development of TCM can be referred to a white paper published on Dec. 6, 2016 by China's State Council Information Office, at http://english.scio.gov.cn/2017-01/17/content_40621689.htm [Accessed: February 14, 2023].

Notably, TCM classical literature was created in ancient times, and few physicians could understand or know how to apply it. Xu Shuwei (1080–1154), a physician and scholarly official, addressed that physicians need to understand the underlying causes of disease when applying the doctrines of the Treaties. Xu compiled nighty cases drawing from his clinical experience into the 90 *Discussions on Cold Damage Disorders* to deal with issues concerning both theories and various facets of clinical practices. Goldschmidt [9] noted Xu's book provided details of his diagnosis processes, including records of the most important diagnostic method, the palpated pulse, the dialog with patient's family members, and discussions with other physicians at the scene.

3.3 The treatment principles and therapies

One of the oldest Chinese treatises is *Shennong's Classic of Materia Medica* (Shen Nong Ben Cao Jing), believed written between 206 BC and 220 AD. This three-volume treatise contains almost 400 entries on medicaments and their descriptions. Shennong (a celestial farmer) was a respected national figure who risked his life tasting a hundred herbs to identify their medical properties. More pharmaceutical theories about CHM were documented, emphasizing principles such as distinguishing the main and subordinate functions of a herb, the Yin and Yang nature co-exist and must coordinate each other, to differentiate four properties and five tastes, to accommodate seven types of human emotions that they must exist in harmony. Leung, Fong ([10], p. 1) commented that TCM is based on "the complex recipes and formula derived from historical and anecdotal evidence of Chinese medicine practitioners," which differs from Western herbal medicine.

A typical TCM recipe is a combination of several drug ingredients. We can see it as a "cabinet" according to Leung, Fong [10]. To use a metaphor,[8] it must have "monarch" drugs, which directly deal with the disease; the "minister" drugs, which supplement the main function; the "assistant" drugs, which balance the need of other parts of the body; the "messenger" or the "servant" drugs, which induce the best function of the formula. These drugs must work together to achieve harmonized effect rather than just the targeted main effect alone. No single active constituent is responsible for the overall efficacy of the whole formula. Apparently, this principle reflects the ancient TCM philosophy mentioned earlier. Experienced physicians know how to adjust these drug components according to the specific case of the patient and the stage of that patient dynamically. This differs from the Western approach, which often applies the same treatment to patients labeled with the same disease.

4. The institutional disadvantages of TCM

4.1 The systematic challenges in protecting traditional knowledge

According to World Intellectual Property Organization (WIPO),[9] traditional knowledge (TK) "is knowledge, know-how, skills, and practices that are developed,

[8] A similar metaphor explanation can be referred to "Traditional Chinese Medicine in China" in a white paper on the development of traditional Chinese medicine (TCM) in China on Dec. 6, 2016, available at http://english.scio.gov.cn/2017-01/17/content_40621689.htm [Accessed: February, 14, 2023].

[9] More can be found from "Traditional Knowledge" at https://www.wipo.int/tk/en/tk/ [Accessed: February 7, 2023].

sustained and passed on from generation to generation within a community, often forming part of its cultural or spiritual identity." Although as important part of TK, TCM is highly appreciated, its IP value cannot find proper protection from current IP systems. Below we recall a few key milestones in the development of the international IP system to indicate systematic challenges faced by TCM.

A more direct agenda to protect TK is seen in the Berne Convention[10] [11], which for the first time, raised the issue of protecting traditional creation stories and artistic works in 1886. Although this did not trigger much action on protecting IP rights of traditional medicine, it started drawing people's attention to protect traditional culture. Since then, international institutions such as WIPO and the United Nations Educational, Scientific and Cultural Organization (UNESCO) have launched a series of agendas regarding TK protection.

One important footprint of protecting TK can be found in the Agreement on Trade-Related Aspects of Intellectual Property Rights (TRIPS) or the TRIPS Agreement, signed in 1994. The TRIPS Agreement, for the first time, declared that its member states can have enforcement rules in IP protection and incorporate the rules in the multilateral trading system. For example, Article 27.3 (b) of the TRIPS Agreement "deals with whether plant and animal inventions should be covered by patents, and how to protect new plant varieties." A related debate regards how disclosure of the source of TK should be practised. Especially, some developing countries "want to amend the TRIPS Agreement so that patent applicants are required to disclose the country of origin of genetic resources and traditional knowledge used in the inventions...".[11]

In 2000, the "WIPO Intergovernmental Committee on Intellectual Property and Genetic Resources, Traditional Knowledge and Folklore" or the IGC[12] was established which marked a big step to promote TK protection more systematically. IGC is a forum where WIPO member states could discuss issues regarding the protection of IP based on TK. In 2000, IGC published *Matters Concerning Intellectual Property and Genetic Resources, Traditional Knowledge and Folklore* [12] which further detailed how TK should be protected.

The protection of TCM in China started in the 1980s. In China, Article 43 of the *Law of TCM of P. R. China* (2007) stipulates that the state shall establish a database, protection directory, and protection system to protect the TCM knowledge. The owner of TCM knowledge has the right to inherit and use the knowledge. Also, the owner has the right to know, to permit, and to share the benefits when other people want to obtain and use the TK. Owners of some classic prescriptions which contain secret composition and production techniques can apply for IP protection. Also, what is perhaps unique in China, is that the classic TCM know-how is regarded as the state treasured secrets and are exercised with special protections.

Specific to the IP protection of CHM, the Chinese IP protection system and the international system are not compatible. Also, many well-known medicinal materials have been neglected within the Chinese IP system without IP protection. For example, traditional knowledge about some famous CHM such as honeysuckle, cangshu,

[10] More can be found from "Berne Convention for the Protection of Literary and Artistic Works" at https://www.wipo.int/treaties/en/ip/berne/ [Accessed: February 7, 2023].

[11] More can be refer to "TRIPS: Reviews, article 27.3(b) and related issues" at https://www.wto.org/english/tratop_e/trips_e/art27_3b_background_e.htm [Accessed: February 7, 2023].

[12] More about IGC can be found at "Intergovernmental Committee (IGC)" at https://www.wipo.int/tk/en/igc/ [Accessed: February 10, 2023].

angelica, contains unique processing techniques but has been neither protected by the National List of Intangible Cultural Heritage nor covered by the List of World Intangible Cultural Heritage. Below we explain further why CHM is exposed with limited IP protection options.

4.2 The limited options for protecting TCM both at home and abroad

Patent: From WIPO IP Statistics Data Centre, TCM patent applications account for only 0.3% in the herbal and botanical medicines applications. This is because formulas of CHM, especially those derived from ancient recipes, are not patentable internationally. The patentable scope of CHM covers CHM extraction, extraction methods, compounds, or compositions of compounds. To obtain patent within this scope immediately exposes the competitive disadvantages of CHM due to less developed R&D or processing techniques compared with those in developed economies.

Taking Japan as an example, its domestic patenting system has been designed following international patenting system. Japan has applied for 210 patents internationally based on ancient recipes recorded by classical Chinese treaties. In comparison, it is hard for a CHM to meet the international IP application standard, mainly because the novelty cannot be fully evidenced with poor information on its chemical properties. Consequently, CHM suffers a substantial loss due to knowledge leaking to its competitors without patent protection.

Copyright: The fundamental knowledge of TCM, as manifested by classical works, texts, and treatises, could not get protection through copyright. Like TK in other fields, the innovative development of TCM has gone beyond the input of any individual person rather, it has been created by collective wisdom and then passed from generation to generation over a long history. Therefore, it is impossible to recognize and inappropriate to assign one person as the right subject of TCM knowledge.

Trademark: For decades, the naming of TCM products in China has followed its unique norm: using the herbal name to label the trademark. In compassion, the corporate trademark is less addressed. Consequently, we can see the same or similar product names available in the market but made by different CHM companies. Such a trademark system also nurtures nonfamous corporates to secretly use famous corporate brand names to promote poor quality or even fake medicines. Consequently, people trust and prioritize CHM over old and famous corporate brands such as Tong Ren Tang or Jiu Zhi Tang. When CHM makers want to compete internationally, they suddenly realize they need to register and build their corporate trademarks, and often famous corporate brand names have been preregistered by local counterparties.

Geographical indication: The geographical indication is crucial information that suggests quality differences subject to where and how the herbal material is cultivated and harvested. However, in the China context, geographical indication almost equals the authenticity nature of CHM. The two concepts are interchangeably used and heavily supported by domestic laws such as China's Trademark Law and Chinese Medicine Law. For CHM going global, geographical indication and authenticity indication should be separated. For example, in 2020, the "EU-China Agreement on Protection of Geographical Indications"[13] was signed, which includes a total of 275

[13] More about "EU-China Agreement on Protection of Geographical Indications" can be found at https://eur-lex.europa.eu/EN/legal-content/summary/eu-china-agreement-on-protection-of-geographical-indications.html [Accessed: February 10, 2023].

mutually recognized geographical indication products. Still, many CHM is facing the problem of having no proper trademark, or the existing trademark is not protected.

Trade secret: Trade secrets in the field of TCM mainly include unpatented ancestral secret recipes, new drug formulas, processing methods, preparation techniques, compound matching ratios, Chinese herbal cultivation techniques, identification techniques, etc. The protection of trade secrets is the traditional and dominant protection method in China. In the survey conducted by the State Administration of Traditional Chinese Medicine on 120 key TCM enterprises and their 401 important TCM products, 61.8% of the enterprises adopted trade secret protection measures. However, for CHM going global market, trade secret protection has its limitations. In applying international IP protection or international collaborations, it is virtually very difficult to keep the secret.

5. The case study of Lianhua Qingwen

5.1 Background of Yiling Pharmaceutical Co. Ltd

Yiling Pharmaceutical Co. Ltd. (hereinafter called YL), was established in 1992 headquartered in Shijiazhuang, the capital city of Hebei province in China. YL originated as a small clinic from the Shijiazhuang Development Zone Medical Research Institute. The company was named after its founder, Professor Wu Yiling. As a pharmaceuticals and biotech company YL's main area is TCM varieties "focusing on the core treatment fields such as cardio-cerebrovascular diseases, respiratory diseases, digestive diseases, endocrine diseases, immunological diseases, and urologic diseases."[14] In 2011, YL was publicly listed in the Shenzhen Stock Exchange. By 2023, YL will have more than 16,000 employees. It is also a multinational corporate with offices and agents located in 30 countries and regions around the world. By carrying out clinical trials in a standardized and scientific manner, it is one of the few Chinese pharmaceutical companies certified by the Global Manufacturing Practices (GMP).

YL won many national prizes with titles such as "National Key Hi-tech Enterprise," "Top 20 Listed Pharmaceutical Company," and "China Famous Brand," and recently the "2020 Corporate Social Responsibility Pioneer Award".[15] But what makes YL attract international spotlight is its famous herbal drug, Lianhua Qingwen (hereinafter called LHQW). Western media [13] commented that because of LHUQ, YL's stock price jumped more than 60% since the end of December 2022. According to Zhong Nanshan, a famous epidemiologist and head of expert group at the National Health Commission (NHC), LHQW "is effective in treating mild and moderate [Covid] symptoms. Not only domestically, we can also promote it overseas" [14]. As shown by **Figure 4**, the annual sales of LHQW have increased dramatically from 2016 to 2021, especially in the outbreak year of the global pandemic in 2020. The sales jumped from RMB 1.7 billion in 2019 to RMB 4.23 billion in 2020, reaching RMB 4.49 billion in 2021.

LHQW represents a typical TCM case in China, which seems extraordinarily successful in the domestic market and is now targeting to tap more into the global

---

[14] More information can be referred to "New Fields Exploration" at https://en.yiling.com/science/ [Accessed: February 9, 2023].

[15] More background can be referred to "Company History" at https://en.yiling.com/company-history/ [Accessed: February 9, 2023].

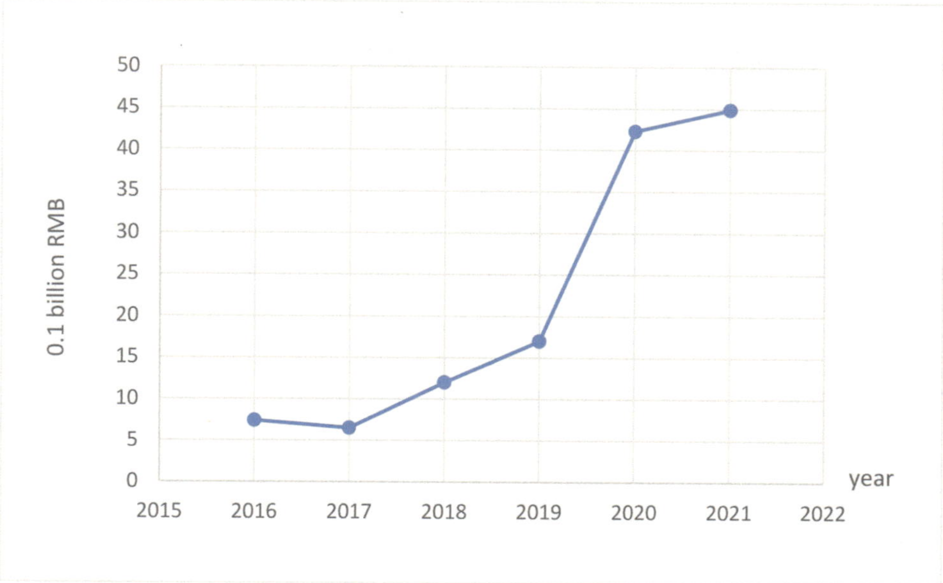

Figure 4.
Sales growth of LHQW (2016–2021).

market. Below we look at its TK base and IP status to explain why companies like YL may face a dilemma, as this chapter addresses.

5.2 The traditional knowledge-based advantages of LHQW

The development of LHQW was based on Chinese TK—three classic Chinese medicine remedies for infectious diseases (pestilence): "Maxing Shigan Tang" (Ma Ren Shi Gan Tang), "Yinqiao San"(Yin Qiao San) and "Shengjiang San" (Sheng Jiang San). Its ingredients include honey suckle, liquorice root, apricot seed, and forsythia, as a treatment for coronavirus. According to TCM theories, the main function of LHQW is to collect and distribute external evils, cleanse internal fires, and drive away plague and evil acts on our body. LHQW demonstrates strong TK-based advantages due to its broad spectrum of antiviral effects during several serious events [15].

The first event (SARS: 2002–2004): LHQW was developed in 2003 as a treatment for severe acute respiratory syndrome (SARS) following the outbreak of the epidemic in Guangdong, China in November 2002. Professor Wu Yiling, the founder, and an academician of the Chinese Academy of Engineering, led his team to carry out research on the SARS. After analyzing the SARS situation in Guangzhou and other places, the research team successfully launched LHQW based on the essence of ancient prescriptions of the Han, Ming, and Qing dynasties, combined with modern pharmacological research. It was the only medicine approved by the China State Food and Drug Administration (SFDA) in the treatment of SARS in 2004.

The second event (H1N1: 2009–2010): In December 2009, the H1N1 influenza or the Swaine flu was first identified in Mexico and then spread rapidly around the world, causing serious social disruption. LHQW capsule was proven to have a good therapeutic effect [16]. Not only does it have better effect than another famous drug, such as Tamiflu, but the cost of treatment is only 1/8 of Tamiflu. Therefore, LHQW was selected as the "Type A" drug to deal with H1N1 by China's health authority in 2009.

The third event (MERS: 2012–2015): In 2012, the Middle East respiratory syndrome (MERS) a respiratory disease, was first detected in Saudi Arabia. On May 23, 2013, the WHO named the novel coronavirus infection "Middle East respiratory syndrome." In May 2015, MERS had a large-scale outbreak in South Korea. In response to this new coronavirus, YL quickly carried out relevant research. Again, LHQW was recognized as an effective treatment for MERS. During this period, China was experienced very serious air pollution in most big cities, and LHQW was also recognized as an effective drug for dealing with diseases caused by air quality. In the first half of 2015, LHQW has sales reached to 169 million yuan.[16]

The fourth event (Covid-19: 2020–2023): Since the outbreak of the Covid-19 epidemic in 2020, LHQW has demonstrated its attacking power against the virus. Based on its effect, it was recognized as one of the most important front-line drugs. In 2020, LHQW was selected officially as the top "Three TCM drugs and Three Herbal Formulas"[17] to deal with Covid-19. It was also listed in the 3rd and 9th edition of the *New Coronavirus Diagnosis and Treatment Guide*. The government endorsement of LHQW added further official affirmation of the medicinal effect of LHQW. The revenue of YL jumped since 2019. In 2021, it achieved sales revenue of 4, 060 billion yuan.[18]

5.3 The aggressive IP performance at home vs. zero IP protection abroad

YL presents a successful example in TCM industry. First, YL has always been proactive in following the market status and reacting responsibly, as shown from our review of its quick reaction to SARS, H1N1, MERS, PM2.5, to Covid-19. Second, YL appreciates TK and treats TK as its core knowledge based in building R&D capabilities. Long before SARS, the company started the development related TCM. Thirdly, YL has a clear IP strategy. From 2003 to 2023, YL applied for as many as 49 invention patents around LHQW products. Among the 49 patents, 2% related to the formulation of TCM, 8% related to the improvement of production methods, 11% related to the detection of active ingredients of TCM, and 79% related to medicinal uses [17].

As the core product, the LHQW series generate great market value for YL. According to the company's annual report, LHQW's B2B (to hospitals) market share has increased from 10.10% in 2017 to 43.50% in 2021. Its retail market share has increased from 2.44% in 2017 to 6.63 in 2021. Apar from the mainland China, Hong Kong, Macau, and other regions, it has been approved for entering into nearly other 30 countries and regions including Brazil, Canada, Thailand, and Russia, etc., and start building its global brand.

It is not totally surprising to us that LHQW has not obtained any patent internationally. Compared to its success in the domestic market, LHQW has not been promoted globally or even accepted as an effective medicine. The role of CHM in treatment is still controversial. For example, "The US Food and Drug Administration, as well as Singaporean and Australian authorities, have warned that there was no evidence that Lianhua Qingwen had any effect on the virus, and cautioned against its

[16] The financial performance can be found from the annual report at https://www.yiling.cn/%E5%B9%B4%E5%BA%A6%E6%8A%A5%E5%91%8A/ [Accessed: February 14, 2023].

[17] More about "The three therapies and three drugs" can be found at http://health.china.com.cn/2022-12/09/content_42199603.htm [Accessed: February 10, 2023].

[18] The financial performance can be found from the annual report at https://www.yiling.cn/%E5%B9%B4%E5%BA%A6%E6%8A%A5%E5%91%8A/ [Accessed: February 14, 2023].

use" [13]. Also, some raised the concern that the counterfeit version of the remedy could be spread in the market without a clear verification of LHQW.

Acknowledged the fundamental theoretical differences between traditional and modern medicines, the therapeutic effects of TCM usually come from the synergistic action of certain ingredients that are more difficult to be evaluated for their efficacy and safety [16]. In this regard, Japan provides a different example. Its domestic patenting system has been designed following the international patenting system. In Japan, a new herbal medicine invention must meet the three core principles of any invention: to be novel, useful, and not obvious. In comparison, it is hard for companies like YL to meet the international IP application standard, mainly because the novelty cannot be fully evidenced.

6. Conclusion

This chapter uses CHM as the context and the case of LHQW to explain a dilemma faced by TCM. We argue TCM is not just China's national treasure it is also the treasure of world civilization. With its rich TK base, TCM is creating unique medical value that are not available by normal herbal medicine. However, we find that the globalization of TCM is suffering because of incomplete IP protection systems both at home and at the global level. In 2016, China's State Council Information Office issued a white paper on the development of TCM.[19] In viewing this white paper, we provide the following dimensions to highlight our advice and directions for future research.

Advancing the national R&D capacity of TCM: One technical barrier for TCM to go global is how to enhance the accuracy of its medical ingredients. Chen, Pang [18] noted that the number and variety of medical plants could reach to more than 70,000 different species that need to be distinguished; otherwise, patients' safety and herbal efficacy can be severely affected. Yet the traditional methods to authenticate herbal materials such as morphological, microscopic, and chemical identification are insufficient to get accurate and reliable authentication from enormous species, especially from those closed related species and plant parts that share similar morphological or chemical structures. Recently, the DNA barcoding technique has been adopted to resolve the problem. DNA barcoding information is publicly accessible through online databases, which include almost all crude herbal drugs listed in Chinese Pharmacopeia, Japanese Pharmacopeia, Korean Pharmacopeia, Indian Pharmacopeia, United States Pharmacopeia, and European Pharmacopeia. TCM should go further to advance such technologies to catch up with R&D development.

Promote international standard of TCM*:* China became a member of the WHO in 1978, and there is still a long way to go to make TCM globally accepted and competitive. In 2022, WHO launched a five-year project (2016–2021) to create standard terminologies on TCM in English. One important principle followed in developing the terminology book was keeping the integrity of the theoretical framework of TCM. The project aims to promote safe and effective use of TCM, TCM knowledge transfer, and TCM research at the global level. The terminologies include fundamental terminologies, terminologies on diagnosis, patterns, constitution, and treatment principles/methods and therapies. China should seize opportunities as such to promote

[19] The detail of the white paper on "Traditional Chinese Medicine in China" can be found at http://english.scio.gov.cn/2017-01/17/content_40621689.htm [Accessed: February 14, 2023].

international integration. Zou [19] reported during the 13th Five-Year Plan Period (2016–2020), the country formulated 37 international standards on TCM.

Upgrade domestic IP protection system into a "China TCM protection model": The case LHQW shows a typical example of CHM that enjoys domestic success but could not get into global market despite of potentially great market demand. Having strong IP protection at home does not mean CHM could obtain IP protection internationally. To this point, the Japanese development model can be referred by the Chinese policymakers in terms of getting China's domestic IP protection system integrated into the global IP protection system. However, we suggest the Chinese government should not simply replicate the Japanese model. Currently, the most widely adopted IP protection in China is trade secret method. However, trade secret protection is not ideal because in practice it does not prevent knowledge leaking to international collaborators. In our view, the Chinese government really needs to form the "China TCM protection model," which allows TCM to go global in exchange for technology advancement, but not at the cost of IP assets, especially IP assets derived from China's TK.

Author details

Yue Xu[1*] and Yumao Wang[2]

1 International Business and Management, Cardiff Business School, Cardiff, UK

2 Pharmaceutical Intellectual Property, Intellectual Property Publishing House Co., Ltd., Beijing, P.R. China

*Address all correspondence to: xuy63@cardiff.ac.uk

References

[1] WHO. WHO Expert Meeting on Evaluation of Traditional Chinese Medicine in the Treatment of COVID-19. Geneva: World Health Organization; 2022

[2] WHO. WHO International Standard Terminologies on Traditional Chinese Medicine. Geneva: World Health Organization; 2022

[3] Maegawa H, Nakamura T, Saito K. Regulation of traditional herbal medicinal products in Japan. Journal of Ethnopharmacology. 2014;**158**:511-515

[4] Benjamin AE. Antiquarianism, Language, and Medical Philology: From Early Modern to Modern Sino-Japanese Medical Discourses. Leiden: Brill; 2015

[5] Saito H. Regulation of herbal medicines in Japan. Pharmacological Research. 2000;**41**(5):515-519

[6] Zhou M. Historical figures promoting the communication of Ben Cao Gang Mu (《本草纲目》Compendium of Materia Medica) in Japan. Chinese Medicine and Culture. 2018;**1**(3):112-115

[7] Chen L, Fu Y, Zhang L, Zhao S, Feng Q, Cheng Y, et al. Clinical application of traditional herbal medicine in five countries and regions: Japan; South Korea; Mainland China; Hong Kong, China; Taiwan, China. Journal of Traditional Chinese Medical Sciences. 2015;**2**(3):140-149

[8] Hill S. The importance of the classics in the transmission of Chinese medicine to the west. Chinese Medicine and Culture. 2019;**2**(2):62-65

[9] Goldschmidt A. Three case histories on cold damage disorders from ninety discussions on cold damage disorders by Xu Shuwei (1080-1154). Asian Medicine (Leiden, Netherlands). 2013;**8**(2):459-471

[10] Leung P-C, Fong HHS, Xue CC. Current Review of Chinese Medicine Quality Control of Herbs and Herbal Materials. Hackensack, NJ: World Scientific; 2006

[11] WIPO. Intellectual Property and Genetic Resources, Traditional Knowledge and Traditional Cultural Expressions. Geneva: World Intellectual Property Organization; 2020

[12] WIPO. Matters Concerning Intellectual Property and Genetic Resources, Traditional Knowledge and Folklore. Geneva: World Intellectual Property Organization; 2000

[13] Riordan P, Ho-him C, Lockett H, Li G. Chinese traditional medicine company's shares surge on Covid outbreak. Financial Times. 6 Apr 2022. Available from: https://www.ft.com/content/4330f5d0-6d3f-430c-bd3f-63c951e60916

[14] Riordan P, Li G, Ho-him C, Lockett H. China Covid-19 tsar pushed treatments without revealing business ties. Financial Times. 25 Apr 2022. Available from: https://www.ft.com/content/fcac2cbc-4bff-44f5-81bf-66db32b99fca

[15] Li R, Hou Y, Huang J, Pan W, Ma Q, Shi Y, et al. Lianhuaqingwen exerts anti-viral and anti-inflammatory activity against novel coronavirus (SARS-CoV-2). Pharmacological Research. 2020;**156**:104761

[16] Duan Z-P, Jia Z-H, Zhang J, Liu S, Chen Y, Liang L-C, et al. Natural herbal medicine lianhuaqingwen capsule

anti-influenza a (H1N1) trial: A randomized, double blind, positive controlled clinical trial. Chinese Medical Journal. 2011;**124**(18):2925-2933

[17] Bai G, Yu L, Ma Q. Cultivation Practices of High-value Pharmaceutical Patents (in Chinese only). Beijing, China: Intellectual Property Publishing House; 2017

[18] Chen S, Pang X, Song J, Shi L, Yao H, Han J, et al. A renaissance in herbal medicine identification: From morphology to DNA. Biotechnology Advances. 2014;**32**(7):1237-1244

[19] Zou S. Significant TCM cooperation seen in last decade. China Daily. 24 Sept 2022. Available from: https://www.chinadaily.com.cn/a/202209/24/WS632e408ba310fd2b29e79814.html

Chapter 6

The Utilization of the Economic Value of Geographic Indications as a Communal Right in Increasing Community Welfare (In the Perspective of Indonesian Trademark Law and Geographical Indications)

Sentosa Sembiring

Abstract

This paper attempts to analyze the benefits gained by the community by including Geographical Indications as one of the scopes of Intellectual Property Rights. Observing the nature contained in Geographical Indications as a material right, it is appropriate for the community that produces Geographical Indications to benefit economically. This is an opportunity and at the same time a challenge for stakeholders in disseminating Geographical Indications whose existence has its own characteristics, when compared to other types of Intellectual Property Rights. To implement what is described in the TRIPs Agreement, the Government of the Republic of Indonesia issued Law Number 20 of 2016 concerning Marks and Geographical Indications. With the issuance of this law, the existence of Geographical Indications as a part of getting legal certainty as a communal right. To obtain communal rights as exclusive rights to Geographical Indications, communities are required to register with the Directorate General of Intellectual Property, Ministry of Law and Human Rights of the Republic of Indonesia. For community groups that have registered Geographical Indications, a Geographical Indication certificate will be issued. By having a legal certificate, Geographical Indications get legal protection.

Keywords: geographical indications, communal rights, registration and well-being, community welfare, intellectual property rights

1. Introduction

For some people, the term Geographical Indication is not something new in their lives, why? Because the results of the production of Geographical Indications are not only used to meet the needs of daily life but have also been used as objects of trade. When it is intended to be used as a trading object, the Geographical Indications that are produced require a sign that is associated with the uniqueness of that area. In short, manufactured goods known as Geographical Indications only exist in that area. To distinguish it from similar goods, it is necessary to give a trade name by the manufacturer.

However, for some people it may be that discussing Geographical Indications is something foreign to them. However, along with the development of science and technology, relations between countries are increasingly open, especially with the establishment of the World Trade Organization in 1994, in one of the attachments to the agreement establishing the World Trade Organization, it is regulated Trade Related Aspects of Intellectual Property Rights (TRIPs). The terminology of Geographical Indications as part of Intellectual Property Rights is increasingly recognized by various groups of people. Therefore, it is reasonable for the opinion put forward *Trias Palupi Kurnianingrum*:

> *"TRIPs are considered an important milestone in efforts to liberalize international trade, therefore the protection of geographical indications is one of the central topics to be accommodated in the provisions of TRIPs." [1].*

Observing the existence of Geographical Indications which have increasingly existed since the signing of the TRIPs, from a business perspective, Geographical Indications have quite high economic value and need to be regulated in laws and regulations. The purpose of this arrangement is to provide protection to the area of origin that produces goods which have their own characteristics according to the geographical conditions of the goods produced or produced. As stated *Ranitya Ganindha and Sukarmi*:

> *"It is necessary to realize that talking about Geographical Indications is not merely looking at the context IPR, but more than that Geographical Indications are very closely related to the cultural roots of society. Respect for historical value needs to be maintained. The character that shows the element of ownership is of collective or communal value. Geographical indications have the potential to guarantee that economic benefits can be felt from a product by producers from various regions of origin of the product." [2].*

It is possible that when the delegation leaders present at the formation of the World Trade Organization realized the importance of regulating Geographical Indications as one of the scopes of Intellectual Property Rights (IPR), they agreed to regulate Geographical Indications in separate laws and regulations. This can be seen from the formulation contained in Article 22 paragraph (2) point (a) Agreement TRIPs:

> *"In respect of geographical indications, Members shall provide the legal means for interested parties to prevent the use of any means in the designation or presentation of a good that indicates or suggests that the good in question originates in a geographical area other than the true place of origin in a manner which misleads the public as to the geographical origin of the good".*

Indonesia as one of the countries that signed the agreement to establish the World Trade Organization (WTO), ratified the agreement with the Law of the Republic of

Indonesia Number 7 of 1994 concerning Ratification of the Agreement Establishing the World Trade Organization (UU No.7/1994). As a follow-up to the issuance of law No.7/1994, the Government of Indonesia issued a series of laws and regulations in the field of Intellectual Property Rights. As is well known, the scope of the IPR study field is quite broad. Precisely in part II of TRIPs it is explained that the scope of IPR includes:

1. Copyright and related rights;

2. Trademarks;

3. Geographical indications;

4. Industrial designs;

5. Patents (patents);

6. Layout-designs of Integrated Circuits; and.

7. Protection of trade secrets (protection of undisclosed information).

In connection with the regulation of Marks and Geographical Indications, the Government of Indonesia initially issued the Law of the Republic of Indonesia Number 15 of 2001 concerning Marks. In this law the regulation regarding Geographical Indications (GI) is quite short. Meanwhile, the development of Geographical Indications at the global level is growing quite rapidly. Considering the economic value contained in Geographical Indications is quite important not only for national interests, but also can cross between countries as objects of trade, the Government of Indonesia renewed the regulation regarding Geographical Indications by issuing Law Number 20 of 2016 Concerning Trademarks and Geographical Indications (hereinafter referred to as Law No. 20/2016). Regulations regarding GI are regulated in Articles 53-71. More detailed arrangements regarding Geographical Indications are described in Government Regulations and Regulations of the Minister of Law and Human Rights of the Republic of Indonesia.

With the issuance of Law No. 20/2016, the existence of Geographical Indications is increasingly getting legal certainty. This is felt to be important, because judging from the existing potential, Indonesia as an archipelagic country, is rich in natural and biological resources. The large amount of potential that is owned by the area that produces Geographical Indications also comes from the fact that the community as a community that produces Geographical Indications benefits from the production of the Geographical Indications produced. The problem is whether the automatically generated Geographical Indications will receive legal protection, so that the public can automatically enjoy the results of using Geographical Indications as objects of trade transactions both nationally and across national borders? Or are there requirements that must be met to obtain the protection of Geographical Indications so that the public can enjoy the results of the Geographical Indications produced or produced in their area? It seems that this is where the problem lies, not all people are necessarily aware that goods produced from regions that have a unique geography can produce a product that has economic values that can prosper if it is managed properly by the community and/or government agencies that have public authority granted by state legislation.

2. Geographical indications as part of intellectual property rights

2.1 Background

The question may arise what is meant by Geographical Indications? Providing a definition or definition of Geographical Indications is not an easy job, why? Because discussing Geographical Indications there are relations that cannot be simply separated, namely those related to culture and traditional knowledge. On the other hand, Geographical Indications are also very close to Marks. For this reason, if one pays attention to the various intellectual property rights literature, even experts seem to have difficulty making an understanding that can be accepted by all parties. As stated by *Miranda Risang Ayu*:

> *"the definition of Geographical Indications is still quite varied, both in terms of definition and scope of protection. There is difficulty in making a definition, because Geographical Indications are influenced by the values of society and/or the nation of a country." [3].*

Referring to the opinion expressed by the Intellectual Property Rights expert above, it is better to first understand the nature contained in the Geographical Indication itself. Looking at the legal literature that discusses this matter, experts explain that the concept of Geographical Indication cannot be separated from what is called an Indication of Origin. The concept of an indication of origin is essentially the right of the public to use a mark on a product which is generally made in the agricultural sector due to special features or special characteristics of the geographical environment where the said product material is produced. Therefore, when viewed from a cultural perspective, it is necessary to build a bridge first. The need for this bridge according to *Basuki Antariksa*:

> *"to maintain a balance between the interests of community groups based on the concept of collectivism and the legal protection of Intellectual Property Rights based on the understanding of individualism. As is known, the legal regime of Geographical Indications can provide protection for a product produced by a community in a certain geographical area, such as Champagne wine, which was made by a community in the region with the same name in France since the 17th century." (Basuki [4]).*

It is worth contemplating what the experts above have said, because with an increasingly open market for trading products based on regions that have specificity in producing production, it is quite reasonable for Geographical Indications to be given legal protection, bearing in mind that Geographical Indications are property rights that have value economy. Indonesia as an archipelagic country certainly has a variety of cultures and products based on regions that have unique products that are known and have a place in the international market. In business has a high economic value. In an atmosphere like this, bad intentions from people who want to get instant profits can happen. For this reason, legal protection of Geographical Indications is one thing that must be done, as stated *Muh. Ali Masnun*:

> *"to protect and avoid misuse of Geographical Indications from people who want to benefit without regard to product quality, it is felt that it necessary to follow legal protection to be able to protect these commodities from unfair competitive practices in*

trade in the era of today the boundaries between countries are increasingly borderless." [5].

2.2 Legal basis for regulating geographic indications

How is the implementation of communal rights in Indonesia? In this context it is interesting to pay attention to what is described in the 1945 Constitution of the Republic of Indonesia (1945 Constitution) which states as follows:

"The state recognizes and respects customary law community units along with their traditional rights as long as they are still alive and in accordance with the development of society and the principles of the Unitary State of the Republic of Indonesia, which are regulated in law."[1]

It can be seen that in accordance with the constitution, the State recognizes traditional rights with a broader understanding such as cultural rights, customs, tangible and intangible movable objects. It's just that, in Indonesia, the arrangements regarding community communal rights are still not specific. Arrangements are still scattered in various laws and regulations related to Intellectual Property Rights, including in the Law on Trademarks and Geographical Indications [6]. The notion of Geographical Indications is normatively explained in Law No. 20/2016 as follows:

"Geographical indication is a sign indicating the area of origin of goods and/or products which due to geographical environmental factors including natural factors, human factors or a combination of the two factors give reputation, quality and certain characteristics to the goods and/or products produced."[2]

From the definition of Geographical Indications as described above, there is one thing that needs to be stated here, namely a Geographical Indication is a sign attached to the goods being traded. This sign is used as a trademark. As explained by expert and practitioner of Intellectual Property Rights *Suyud Margono:*

"Sometimes a business person wants to introduce a brand or use a place or geographical name to explain where the goods/services come from. Trademark Law regulates Geographical Indications that use the name of the geographical location of the goods." [7].

Goods traded have distinctive characteristics. The peculiarities or characteristics of the goods are due to geographical factors. In an environment like this, so that goods produced and of course used as objects of business transactions are not imitated or falsified by other people, it is necessary to provide legal protection for these Geographical Indications. The purpose of providing protection is to protect an item as a sign of the area of origin of an item due to several unique factors that are only owned by certain areas. This factor can be caused by natural conditions, humans, or a combination of the two with certain quality characteristics of the goods produced. Meanwhile, what is meant by internal geographical protection is Mark protection based on Geographical Indications.

---

[1] See Article 18B of the 1945 Constitution of the Republic of Indonesia.

[2] See Article 1 point 6 of Law Number 20 of 2016 Marks and Geographical Indications.

It is necessary to state here that what is meant by a Mark according to Law No. 20/2016 is a sign that can be displayed graphically in the form of an image, logo, name, word, letter, number, color arrangement, in the form of 2 (two) dimensions and/or 3 (three) dimensions, sound, hologram, or a combination of 2 (two) or more of these elements to distinguish goods and/or services produced by persons or legal entities in the activities of trading in goods and/or services.[3] What is described in these provisions, it can be seen that the Mark is a sign to distinguish it from similar goods that are produced or traded by the brand holder.

2.3 Legal protection

Further provisions regarding how to provide similar goods in differentiating goods like Geographical Indication products, are further elaborated in the Regulation of the Minister of Law and Human Rights of the Republic of Indonesia Number 10 of 2022 concerning Amendments to the Regulation of the Minister of Law and Human Rights Number 12 of 2019 concerning Indications Geographical. This Ministerial Regulation explains the logo and code of origin. The meaning of the Indonesian Geographical Indication Logo is a symbol or symbol consisting of images and writing which is the official identity of a geographical indication product that has been registered and has received a certificate of geographical indication from the Directorate General of Intellectual Property, Ministry of Law and Human Rights.[4] Whereas what is meant by the Code of Origin for Indonesian Geographical Indication Products is a sign in the form of letters or numbers that identify the origin of a geographical indication product that has been registered and obtained a certificate of geographical indication from the Directorate General of Intellectual Property, Ministry of Law and Human Rights.[5]

If this is related to Geographical Indications, the holder of the Geographical Indication is granted exclusive rights to the marks used in producing or trading the Geographical Indications. This is confirmed in Law No. 20/2016: The right to Geographical Indications is an exclusive right granted by the state to the right holders of registered Geographical Indications, as long as the reputation, quality, and characteristics that serve as the basis for providing protection for such Geographical Indications still exist.[6] There is one thing that needs to be considered in order to obtain exclusive rights to Geographical Indications, namely the obligation to register Geographical Indications with the Minister. As for what is meant by the Minister in this case is the minister who organizes government affairs in the field of law. In the government system in Indonesia it is organized by the Ministry of Law and Human Rights of the Republic of Indonesia.[7]

Paying attention to the existence of Geographical Indications in this decade has become one of the objects of business transactions not only on a national scale but has crossed countries, for this reason, business actors and consumers feel it is very

---

[3] See Article 1 point 1 of Law Number 20 of 2016 Marks and Geographical Indications.

[4] See Article 1 point 14 Regulation of the Minister of Law and Human Rights of the Republic of Indonesia Number 10 of 2022.

[5] See Article 1 point 14 Regulation of the Minister of Law and Human Rights of the Republic of Indonesia Number 10 of 2022.

[6] See article 1 point see Article 1 point 7 Regulation of the Minister of Law and Human Rights of the Republic of Indonesia Number 10 of 2022.

[7] See Article 1 point 20 of Law Number 20 of 2016 Marks and Geographical Indications.

important to be given legal protection. Manufacturers certainly do not want goods originating from their blood to be counterfeited by other people. Illegal use like this can damage the image of the producer. Geographical Indication For consumers, as the end user of a product, it is enough to feel doubtful about the low quality of the goods purchased because they are not produced according to actual quality.

Starting from this idea in the Intellectual Property Rights literature, experts explain why Geographical Indications need to get legal protection, namely: first, Geographical Indications refer to the identification of the origin of the product. Second, Geographical Indications can inform consumers that the goods being traded originate from areas that provide quality, reputation, and/or characteristics of the area concerned, both geographically and in natural resources. Third, Geographical Indications can represent business interests because they guarantee the authenticity of an item with characteristics from a certain area [8].

Therefore, it is not an exaggeration if there are those who are of the view that the existence of Geographical Indications which have their own characteristics, in terms of the aspect of international trade, the use of a geographical name as a guide or indication of where an item originates has a comparative advantage capable of increasing competitiveness of the commodity in question [9].

3. Geographical indications as communal rights

3.1 Existence of geographical indications

The struggle carried out by various countries to include Geographical Indications as one of the objects of study in the field of Intellectual Property Rights is not in vain. This can be seen in the provisions of TRIPs that have included Geographical Indications as one of the scopes of Intellectual Property Rights. This struggle is certainly understandable, because seen from the context of trade, Geographical Indications are trade objects that have the potential to increase transaction objects. If viewed in the context of a state, it is possible that Geographical Indications can be used as a commodity in the import-export trade which of course can generate foreign exchange. On the other hand, when viewed from the location where it is produced or the production of Geographical Indications, Geographical Indications are referred to as communal rights. This means that the public as holders of exclusive rights will benefit from the legal protection given to Geographical Indications.

As can be seen from the various opinions expressed by experts, the exclusive rights of Geographical Indications granted by the state to applicants who have been registered with the Director General of Intellectual Property Rights of the Ministry of Law and Human Rights of the Republic of Indonesia, are not individual rights but community rights.

Figure 1 describes the steps and process for registration application.[8]

The emergence of the concept of community rights cannot be separated from the party having the authority to apply for the registration of Geographical Indications is a community organization. The appointment of a representative agency to apply for registration is a combination of all the elements involved in a geographical indication protection. This is certainly in line with the principle of protecting Intellectual

[8] Taken from the official website of the Indonesian Directorate General of Intellectual Property Right, https://dgip.go.id/menu-utama/indikasi-geografis/syarat-prosedur

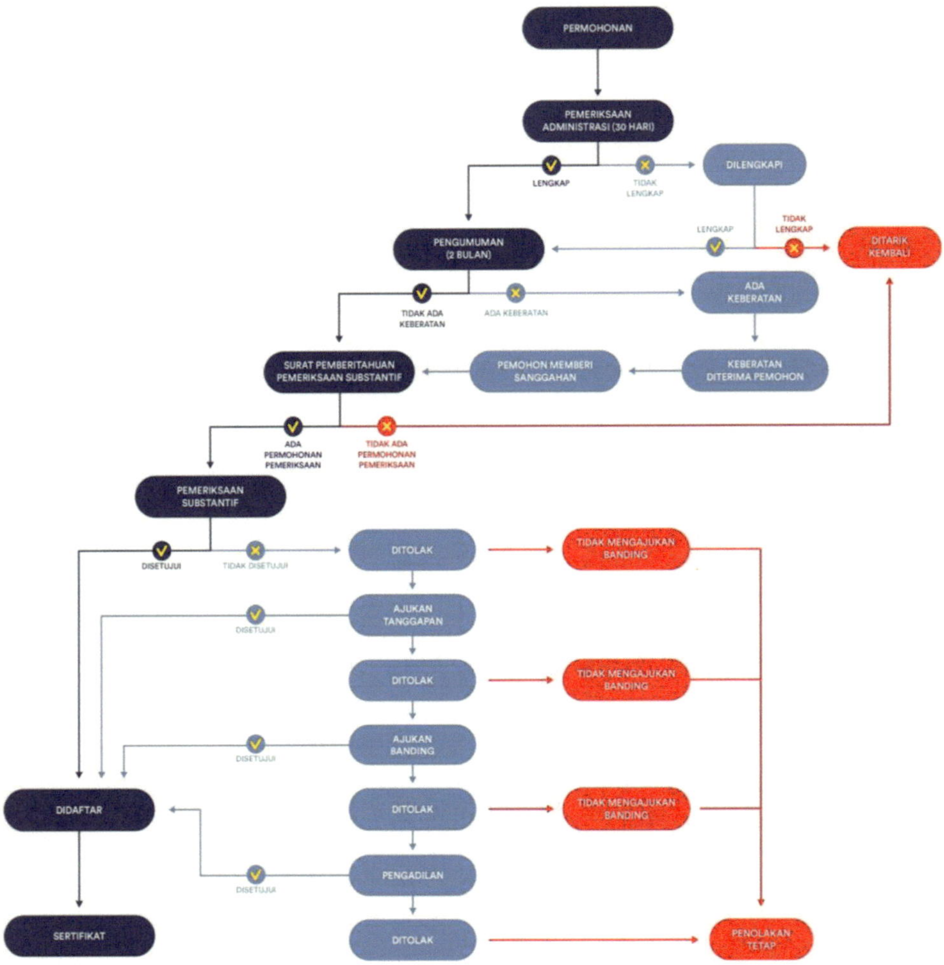

Figure 1.
Procedure for Registration of Geographical Indications at the Directorate General of Intellectual Property Rights, Ministry of Law and Human Rights of the Republic of Indonesia.

Property Rights, namely the principle of social justice, that the granting of rights by law should not be solely to fulfill individual interests but for the benefit of society. As stated by *Yeti Sumiyati; Tatty Aryani Ramli and Rusli Iskanda*r:

> *"when the utilization of economic rights from geographic indications is used both by the community and outside the community, it will become the right of all elements of the community. The benefits of economic rights can be enjoyed equally by all components of society. This is certainly understandable, because to produce a Geographical Indication product, it is not done by one person but is a collective work, so that producers can strengthen relations between other producers and can also increase the dynamics of rural areas which in turn can increase income. The community in the area where the Geographical Indication is produced" [10].*

What was stated by the Intellectual Property Rights research team above is understandable. The existence of Geographical Indication products does automatically gives a reputation to an area, and this will have an impact on the development of agro-tourism areas, with Geographical Indications it will also stimulate the emergence of other related activities such as further processing of a product. All economic activities because of the Geographical Indications, automatically contribute to the economic growth of the Protected Geographical Indications area itself. As stated *Desty Anggie Mustika*:

> *"Legal protection of Geographical Indications can increase the value of the product to a high level. Granting recognition to Geographical Indications, either indirectly or indirectly, can stimulate the economy of the area of origin of the Geographical Indication products and more importantly, Geographical Indications are addressed to the producer, not to the creator. In this context the concept of Geographical Indications is referred to as communal protection." [11].*

The above, supports the idea that Geographical Indications as Intellectual Property Rights are communal in nature. When compared to other types of Intellectual Property Rights, Geographical Indications have their own characteristics. According to *Idris,* an expert and official at the Director General of Intellectual Property Rights of the Ministry of Law and Human Rights:

> *"As for the characteristics of a communal Geographical Indication, it can be seen that the rights attached to GI are basically: first, the rights of the local community or customary community; secondly, shared or communal property so that it can be shared with community members and third, compiled, guarded and maintained by tradition in a sustainable manner." [12].*

In relation to communal rights, it is interesting to examine the requirements for registering Geographical Indications with the Director General of Intellectual Property Rights. Unlike the case with other types of Intellectual Property Rights, registration is carried out individually by the owner or holder of Intellectual Property Rights. What about the registration of Geographical Indications? In Law No. 20/2016 it is implicitly stated that to apply for registration of Geographical Indications must be submitted by a community group. This shows that legislators have realized that Geographical Indications have their own characteristics. For this reason, it is quite reasonable why community groups should apply for geographic indication rights, because if it is possible for individuals to do so, you can imagine the legal consequences that may arise, individuals are given exclusive rights, in the end the community gets nothing and it could even be that the community is prohibited from producing, trading Geographical Indications without permission from the exclusive rights holder of Geographical Indications.

Meanwhile, community groups that are authorized to apply for registration of Geographical Indications to the Director General of Intellectual Property Rights are explained in Government Regulation No. 51 of 2007 concerning Geographical Indications (GR No. 51/2007). Applicants for Geographical Indications consist of:

a. an institution that represents the community in the area that produces the goods in question, consisting of:

1. parties who cultivate natural products or natural resources;

2. producers of agricultural products;

3. manufacturers of handicraft products or industrial products; or.

4. traders who sell the goods;

b. institution that is authorized to do so; or.

c. group of consumers of the goods.[9]

From the criteria described in the provisions above, it further strengthens the idea of Geographical Indications as communal rights. What the public needs to realize is that to obtain legal recognition for products based on Geographical Indications, a legal action is required, namely the obligation to register Geographical Indications at the Office of the Director General of Intellectual Property Rights. The requirements and procedures for registering Geographical Indications are further elaborated in the Regulation of the Minister of Law and Human Rights of the Republic of Indonesia Number 12 of 2019 concerning Geographical Indications which has been updated with the Regulation of the Minister of Law and Human Rights of the Republic of Indonesia Number 10 of 2022 concerning Amendments. On Regulation of the Minister of Law and Human Rights Number 12 of 2019 Concerning Geographical Indications (hereinafter referred to as Permenhukham RI No. 10/2022). In Article 3 of RI Minister of Law and Human Rights No. 10/2022 stated:

(1) In order to obtain the protection referred to in Article 2, the applicant must apply to the Minister.

(1a) The applicant as referred to in paragraph (1) is:

a. an institution that represents the community in a certain geographical area that operates goods and/or products in the form of:

1. natural resources;

2. handicrafts; or.

3. industrial products; and.

b. provincial or district/city regional government.

One thing that is interesting from the provisions above is that the government, either the provincial government or the district/city government, may act as an applicant in registering Geographical Indications. This should be welcomed, as stated *Balqis Siagian; Saidin; Suhaidi and Sunarmi:*

> *"The role of the government can be the best solution to speed up the registration of Geographical Indices in the regions. With the intervention of the government, the people in locations where products based on Geographical Indications feel cared for develop the potential that exists in the area." [13].*

---

[9] See Article 5 paragraph 3 GR No 51/2007.

On the other hand, the public also needs to be given an understanding of what a Geographical Indices is. For this reason, through education and socialization programs regarding the meaning of Intellectual Property Rights in general and Geographical Indications in particular, it is hoped that the public can become actors and at the same time as guardians and maintainers, guardians of product quality, so that the continuity of Geographical Indication products that have been and will be registered by the government will remain can be well maintained. If this is fulfilled, then the characteristics of Geographical Indications which are the main requirements for providing legal protection for Geographical Indications can always be fulfilled in accordance with what is required in the laws and regulations on Geographical Indications.

The characteristics of Geographical Indications are also explained in the Government Regulation of the Republic of Indonesia Number 51 of 2007 concerning Geographical Indications (GR No. 51/200). In this PP it is stated: Geographical Indications are protected if the distinctive characteristics and qualities which form the basis for the protection of said Geographical Indications still exist.[10]

From this provision, the right to Geographical Indications can basically be used continuously by the holder of Geographical Indications if the quality of the Geographical Indications can be maintained as a basis for considering the protection of Geographical Indications. Therefore, it is quite reasonable, the registrant of Geographical Indications is given exclusive rights. This is confirmed in the Regulation of the Minister of Law and Human Rights of the Republic of Indonesia Number 12 of 2019 concerning Geographical Indications, the Right to Geographical Indications is an exclusive right granted by the state to registered Geographical Indication rights holders, if reputation, quality, and characteristics form the basis the granting of protection for the Geographical Indication still exists.[11]

If so, what are the benefits of registering Geographical Indications? By registering, Geographical Indications receive legal protection. The purpose of providing legal protection is inseparable from the existence of Geographical Indications as part of collective Intellectual Property Rights. Hence, legal protection of Geographical Indications requires the cooperation of all parties. Legal protection and potential development of Geographical Indication products are a means for local governments and other stakeholders to create local economic strength. The protection of Geographical Indications is not only beneficial for environmental sustainability, but also for the development of natural and human resources in the locality.

Efforts to obtain legal protection require the cooperation and proactivity of all parties, as stated by Ranitya *Ganindha and Sukarmi*:

> *"Protection of Geographical Indications requires proactive efforts from interested parties, starting from registration to maintaining the quality of Geographical Indications. Another important thing from Geographical Indications is the consistency of a product with the name of a region."*[12]

Therefore, it is also reasonable why Geographical Indication products being marketed must include a logo. More on this matter is described in the Regulation of the Minister of Law and Human Rights of the Republic of Indonesia Number 10 of 2022.

---

[10] See Article 4 GR No 51/200

[11] See Article 1 point 2 of the RI Minister of Law and Human Rights No 12/2019

[12] Ranitya Ganindha and Sukarmi. supra.

It was further stated, every Geographical Indication product packaging must include the certificate number and the Code of Origin of Indonesian Geographical Indication Products.[13] Referring to the provisions above, the registration of Geographical Indications is very important for trading Geographical Indications. According to *Idris*, the benefits that can be obtained from the protection of Geographical Indications are:

> *"firstly, to protect well-known product names from misuse and counterfeiting; secondly, to encourage rural-regional development and thirdly to assist consumers by providing them with information about the specific characteristics of the products produced or marketed."*[14]

If this is related to economic development, both on a local and national scale with the protection of Geographical Indications, at the implementation level it is not merely the result of economic value that is the goal. But also, the process must be in accordance with Regional Government policies in realizing regional original income and of course also in the context of improving people's welfare. Therefore, all parties must maintain the consistency and quality of Geographical Indications, as stated by *Teng Berlianty and Yosia Hetharie*:

> *"Stakeholders related to the management of Geographical Indications need to play an active role based on the principles of modern management but still use local sources because it is carried out by regions that produce Geographical Indications." [14].*

3.2 Geographical indications as objects of trade transactions

What has been stated by the authors above, regarding the importance of the active role of all parties involved in maintaining and maintaining the quality of Geographical Indications, is very reasonable, because Geographical Indications are a national economic potential that can become superior commodities, both in national and international trade. Therefore, the various steps that have been taken in providing legal protection both normatively and empirically are time to be carried out. This step is important to follow up, because other parties, both foreign and national, have very open opportunities to take advantage of its Geographical Indications for business purposes, the impact of which can be detrimental to the community producing the Geographical Indications themselves.

Seeing the vast potential of natural resources, it is very possible for those who want to take advantage of the opportunity for their own benefit. It is in this case that various loopholes that may be exploited by other people need to be prevented by providing legal protection to the producer of the Geographical Indications. Experts and parties concerned with the existence of Geographical Indications have provided various recommendations, among others, *Candra Irawan* said:

> *"In this decade, the trade that is being developed relies on science. As a result, geographical indications that have not been registered will become the target of economic actors and have the potential to be used individually, and this will harm the interests of the people who have been making and trading these products. For this reason, the*

[13] See Article 37A the Regulation of the Minister of Law and Human Rights of the Republic of Indonesia No 10/2022.

[14] Idris. Op.cit.

> *government, both the central government and regional governments, must immediately seek registration of geographical indications that have the economic potential to be commercialized, provide legal protection, and utilize them for the benefit of society."* [15].

What was stated by the experts above shows that to provide protection to Geographical Indications, it is important to register Geographical Indications. For this, it is necessary to pay special attention to local governments. As described elsewhere in this paper, each region in Indonesia has its own unique types of food and agricultural products. Unlike the other areas. If this is managed properly, economically it can generate a source of income for the area concerned. As stated by *Devica Rully Masrur*:

> *"The sharing of regional superior products has an important meaning for the progress of the regional economy, especially for the sake of increasing the welfare of the local community. Therefore, the existence of superior products that have specific unique values such as location needs to be preserved. Maintaining the existence of regional superior products that have a unique taste, distinctive shape, of course, requires strong efforts to protect them. This is where the importance of protecting Geographical Indications for a regional superior product, which according to law can be protected by registering it."* [16].

By registering, legally the registrant will get exclusive rights. If you already have exclusive rights, this means that Geographical Indications can be produced, traded and licensed to other parties. From the sale of production and or royalties, the people in the location where the Geographical Indications are produced benefit, so that ideally, they can prosper.

4. Conclusion

Geographical indications as one of the scopes of Intellectual Property Rights have their own characteristics when compared to other types of Intellectual Property Rights. There are distinct characteristics of the Geographical Indications, which may be due to geographical factors or the local environment and culture. Therefore, it is reasonable that what is produced from the area concerned is also different from other regions. What is produced in this case, can be in the form of agricultural products, handicrafts that have their own uniqueness.

For the product or production of geographical indications for the area concerned to receive legal protection, in accordance with the provisions stipulated in Law Number 20 of 2016 concerning Marks and Geographical Indications, Geographical Indications must be registered. The parties authorized to apply for registration according to this law are community groups and local governments. If all the requirements for registering Geographical Indications have been met, the applicant for registration of Geographical Indications will be given a registration certificate. With a registration certificate, the certificate holder whose name is included in the certificate has exclusive rights. This means that the registrant has the right to produce, reproduce, trade and license Geographical Indications.

By producing and selling, it means that the holder of exclusive rights, in this case the community, ideally can also enjoy the results or economic value of Geographical

Indications. By obtaining economic value from Geographical Indications, conceptually the community will become prosperous, because basically the exclusive rights of Geographical Indications belong to the community.

Author details

Sentosa Sembiring
Faculty of Law, Parahyangan Catholic University, Bandung, West Java, Indonesia

*Address all correspondence to: sentosa@unpar.ac.id

References

[1] Trias Palupi Kurnianingrum. Pelindungan Hak Ekonomi Atas Indikasi Geografis (protection of economic right to geographical indications). Jurnal Negara Hukum. 2016;7(1). DOI: 10.22212/jnh.v7i1.947

[2] Ranitya Ganindha dan Sukarmi. Peran pemerintah daerah dalam mendukung potensi indikiasi geografis produk pertanian. (the role of local government in supporting the potential of agricultural product geographic indications). Jurnal Cakrawala Hukum. 2020;**11**(2):211-221. DOI: 10.26905/idjch.v11i2.3970

[3] Miranda Risang Ayu. Memperbincangkan Hak Kekayaan Intelektual Indikasi Geografis. (Discuss Intellectual Property Rights of Geographical Indications). Bandung: Alumni; 2006

[4] Basuki Antariksa. Landasan Filosofis Dan Sejarah Perkembangan Perlindungan Hak Kekayaan Intelektual: Relevansinya Bagi Kepentingan Pembangunan Di Indonesia (Philosophical Basis and History of the Development of Intellectual Property Rights Protection: Its Relevance for the Interests of Development in Indonesia). Available from: https://jdih.kemenparekraf.go.id/asset/data_puu/Art_19-Landasan%20Filosofis%20HKI.pdf

[5] Muh. Ali Masnun. Menakar Peluang Pelindungan Indikasi Geografis Pada Bidang Jasa Dalam Kerangka Hukum Indonesia: Sebuah Diagnosa Awal. (assessing the opportunity to protect geographical indications in the service sector with in the Indonesian legal framework: An initial diagnosis). Dialogia Iuridica: Jurnal Hukum Bisnis dan Investasi. Nov 2021;**13**(1):47-58. DOI: 10.28932/di.v13i1.3198 [Last accessed: 1 July 2022]

[6] Adawiyah R, Rumawi R. Pengaturan Hak Kekayaan Intelektual Dalam Masyarakat Komunal Di Indonesia. (regulation of intellectual property rights in communal society in Indonesia). Repertorium: Jurnal Ilmiah Hukum Kenotariatan. 2021;**10**(1):1-16. DOI: 10.28946/rpt.v10i1.672

[7] Margono S. Komersialisasi Aset Intelektual Aspek Hukum Bisnis. (Commercialization of Intellectual Assets Aspects of Business Law). Jakarta: Grasindo; 2002

[8] Kementerian Hukum Dan Hak Asasi Manusia Republik Indonesia Badan Pembinaan Hukum Nasional. Hasil Penyelarasan Naskah Akademik RUU Tentang Merek. (Results of Alignment of Academic Papers on the Draft Law on Brands). Jakarta: Kementerian Hukum Dan Hak Asasi Manusia Republik Indonesia Badan Pembinaan Hukum Nasional; 2015

[9] Sasongko W. Indikasi Geografis: Rezim HKI Yang Bersifat sui generis. (intellectual property rights regime which is sui generis). Jurnal Media Hukum. 2012;**19**(1)

[10] Yeti Sumiyati; Tatty Aryani Ramli Dan Rusli Iskandar. Kajian Yuridis Sosiologis Mengenai Indikasi Geografis Sebagai Sumber Pendapatan Asli Daerah (PAD). (sociological juridical study regarding geographical indications as a source of regional original income). Mimbar Jurnal Sosial dan Pembangunan. 2008;**24**(1). DOI: 10.29313/mimbar.v24i1.256

[11] Desty Anggie Mustika. Batik Tradisional Megamendung Ditinjau Dari Sistem Perlindungan Indikasi Geografis. (Megamendung traditional batik in terms

of geographical indication protection system). Yustisi. Jurnal Hukum dan Hukum Islam. 2018;**5**(2):70-91

[12] Idris. Perlindungan Indikasi Geografis Untuk Pembangunan Ekonomi Masyarakat Lokal Berbasis Potensi Sumber Daya Daerah. (Protection of Geographical Indications for Local Community Economic Development Based on Regional Resource Potential). Makalah Yogyakarta; 2019. Available from: https://penelitian.ugm.ac.id/wp-content/uploads/sites/295/2019/03/Pak-Idris_Sosialisasi-IG.pdf

[13] Siagian B, Saidin, Sunarmi SD. Pelindungan Hukum Atas Potensi Indikasi Geografis Di Kabupaten Tapanuli Utara. (legal protection for potential geographical indications in north Tapanuli regency). Iuris Studia: Jurnal Kajian Hukum. 2021;**2**(3):653-663

[14] Teng Berlianty dan Yosia Hetharie. Urgensi Pendaftaran Dan Perlindungan Hukum Terhadap Embal Sebagai Indikasi Geografis Maluku Tenggara (registration urgency and legal protection of enbals as a geographic indication southeast maluku). Jurnal IUS Kajian Hukum dan Keadilan. Aug 2020;**8**(2):246-255. DOI: 10.29303/ius.v8i2.793 [Last accessed: 25 July 2022]

[15] Candra Irawan. Pendaftaran Indikasi Geografis Sebagai Instrumen Perlindungan Hukum Dan Peningkatan Daya Saing Produk Daerah Di Indonesia. Proceeding Seminar Nasional Multi Displin Ilmu and Call for Papers Unisbank Ke 3 (Sendi U 3) 2017. (Registration of Geographical Indications as an Instrument for Legal Protection and Increasing the Competitiveness of Regional Products in Indonesia. Proceeding of the 3rd Unisbank Multi-Discipline National Seminar and Call for Papers). Available from: https://media.neliti.com/media/publications/174023-ID-pendaftaran-indikasi-geografis-sebagai-i.pdf

[16] Devica Rully Masrur. Perlindungan Hukum Indikasi Geografis Yang Telah Didaftarkan Sebagai Merek Berdasarkan Instrumen Hukum Nasional Dan Hukum Internasional. (legal protection of geographical indications that have been registered as trademarks based on national legal instruments and international law). Jurnal Lex Jurnalica. 2018;**15**(2):1-13

Section 4

Impact of IPR in World Economy

Chapter 7

Intellectual Property in the Innovative Development of the World Economy

Vladlena Lisenco

Abstract

Interest in intellectual property has increased in the XXI century as the basis of the global innovation economy. The subject of the presented analysis is intellectual property as a factor influencing the innovative development of the economies of different states. The article notes the dependence of the level and quality of economic growth on the pace and scale of innovation activity, the degree of involvement in the process of scientific and technological development. The results achieved by the countries in the field of intellectual property and innovative development presented. The introduction notes the dependence the level and quality of economic growth on the pace and scale of innovation, the degree involvement in the process of scientific and technological development. The main part contains exogenous and endogenous factors of innovative development, the role of the institute of intellectual property as one of the key factors for the successful functioning of the innovation macro- and micro-level systems. Global recognition of intellectual property as the main instrument of innovative transformation is confirmed by the inclusion of indicators use of intellectual property in the main world indices of innovative development. The article concludes that most innovations are based on intellectual property.

Keywords: innovation, modernization, commercialization of intellectual property, transformation of law, digital market

1. Introduction

World experience proves that the sustainable long-term development of the economy of a single country depends not so much on its resource capabilities as on the ability to develop and implement innovations. Thanks to innovations, science becomes a direct productive force, and innovations in the form of intangible assets become the main capital of the economic development of the state. In this regard, it becomes important to study the institute of intellectual property, which is understood as a set of norms, relations, mechanisms and processes of formation and circulation of intellectual labor products. Within the framework of this institute, innovation is reproduced by turning the results of intellectual activity into objects of intellectual property.

Its analysis involves the study of the sphere of intellectual activity and the creation of an intellectual product, which comes to the fore in the "new" innovative economy.

As you know, in the modern world, the "survival" of the state depends, in the broad sense of the word, mainly on ensuring its competitiveness [1]. In turn, competitiveness is impossible without maintaining the world level of scientific and technological progress. This means the need to maintain a constant and increasing flow of innovations (mainly technical), today this is called the term "innovation". To a large extent, such innovations are nothing more than the results of intellectual activity.

In a general sense, innovation activity affects all scientific, technological, organizational, financial and commercial activities. This include investments in new knowledge, which, in turn, lead to the emergence of innovations or innovative processes. It follows that innovations can be present in every area of human activity. They represent ideas implemented as a real product of intellectual activity and present in economic turnover. In modern conditions, the economic development of any country increasingly depends on the creation and effective use of high technologies, the introduction of fundamentally new technology and the widespread use of information resources. All this can be expressed in such a category as "innovation". Innovation is a new phenomenon in various fields of human activity. Innovation means carrying out a number of measures leading to fundamental improvements in the field of production, management, education, social sphere and much more. The achievements of scientific and technological progress are an example of the greatest innovations of our time. Therefore, when forming national strategies for the innovative development of states, we are primarily talking about innovations in the field of production, i.e. technological innovations. Innovative achievements in the field of research and development are transferred to the business sphere. Thus, it can be argued that in all cases when intellectual property objects are created and used, we are dealing with innovations. In other words, most often innovations are objects of intellectual property applied in practice [2, 3].

The concept of "intellectual property" was first used in 1967 by the Stockholm Convention in Sweden, which established WIPO (World Intellectual Property Organization). According to article 2 of the Convention, intellectual property includes: literary, artistic and scientific works; inventions in all spheres of human activity; trademarks, service marks, trade names and commercial designations; industrial designs; scientific discoveries; other objects of intellectual activity in the industrial, scientific, literary and artistic fields [4]. Intellectual property may include objects of copyright, related rights and industrial property protected by law. All types of intellectual property are united by the fact that they all relate to the results of creative activity (**Figure 1**).

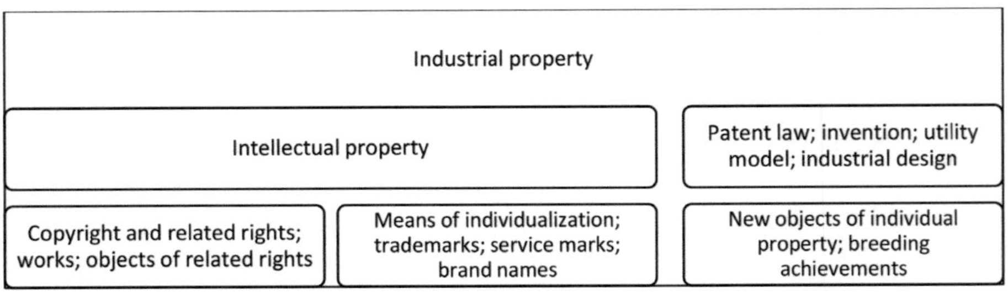

Figure 1.
The relationship between intellectual and industrial property.

Industrial property was first used in the text of article 1 of the Paris Convention on the Protection of Industrial Property. Objects of industrial property protection: patents for inventions; utility models; industrial designs; trademarks; service marks; trade names; indication of origin or the name of the place of passage [5].

Intellectual property is not only a system of legal norms, but also a separate economic institution that has a very strong impact on the innovation process. The effectiveness of innovation creation depends on the degree of legal protection of the results of intellectual activity. Increasingly, intellectual property objects – products of intellectual labor – are initially created precisely for successful functioning on the market.

2. Economics of intellectual property

The history of innovative development of leading countries in the middle of the XX - beginning of the XXI century gives many examples when the creation, modernization and accelerated development of national economies took place due to the large-scale use of the latest national and foreign results of intellectual activity that have legal protection. Thus, the restoration of the national economies of Japan, Germany, and other European countries destroyed as a result of World War II and the formation of new knowledge-intensive industries (electronics, nuclear and space industries, computer technology, information technology, and much more) took place not on the basis of existing technologies. It went primarily through the acquisition and development of advanced foreign technologies, as well as domestic developments. In the absence or acute shortage of material, technical and financial resources, scientific base and fierce competition in the markets of high-tech products, previously applied classical methods of gradual development of national innovative economies have become unacceptable for many countries. They faced the challenge of losing their former leading positions in the world economy.

The beginning of the existence of intellectual property (XVIII—XIX centuries) as an independent sector of the world economy is legitimately associated with the adoption during this period of national laws on privileges, patenting, copyright and related rights in leading countries and the conclusion of international agreements in this area.

Focusing on national goals in economic development, an increasing number of countries consider the sphere of intellectual property as an independent object of strategic planning. For the purposes of the study, the experience of implementing strategies in the field of intellectual research development of the leading countries of the WIPO rating, demonstrating stable growth in patent activity: the USA, China, Japan, Austria, India, was summarized. China's practice deserves special attention [6 , p.27]. From 2012 to 2021, China rose from 34th place to 11th in the ranking of the Global Innovation Index, China became one of the innovative countries. The construction of high-speed railways, 5G networks and much more occupies a leading position in the world, and major breakthroughs have been achieved in the field of manned space flights and Mars exploration. According to the International Monetary Fund, China's economy ranks second in the world in terms of GDP ($13.407 trillion) [7].

The United States has adopted a strategic plan for the development of intellectual property for the period 2018–2022. Being the undisputed leader of patenting, the United States aims the following strategy to strengthen its position by improving legislation and the quality of service of the work of national patent offices. In addition, the need to improve the quality and timing of consideration of applications for inventions and trademarks was noted.

Singapore's ambitious strategic goals to create an IP Hub as the basis for the country's innovative development and ensuring the economy of the future are explained by the achievement of a sufficiently high level of innovation of the economy. In 2013, the Singapore government announced a 10-year plan to help the country become a global IP hub in Asia. The IP Hub Master Plan aims to use the opportunities presented by the expansion of activities at the international level to stimulate business and economic growth in Singapore [8].

Over the past decades, India has transformed from a backward third world country into a global locomotive of the digital economy. Today, many international companies see great opportunities in the local market. The Indian economy as a whole is free and highly competitive, especially against the background of other developing countries. Back in 2013, it was on the 142nd place in the ranking of ease of doing business, and by 2021 it moved to 63rd place, overtaking countries such as Greece and South Africa. The IT sector, which today is the main driving force of the national economy. The total market size is $191 billion and creates about 10% of GDP. India accounts for 55% of the global IT services outsourcing market. Many international companies began moving their offices here in the 1990s to save on labor [7, 9].

3. Global innovation index and innovation clusters

Currently, a large number of international studies are conducted, according to the results of which various ratings are formed. These ratings evaluate the achievements of the countries of the world in certain areas of life. In the context of the generation and dissemination of protected knowledge, we can name such ratings as: KET (Knowledge Economy Index); GCI (Global Competitiveness Index): BCI (Business Competitiveness Index); GII (Global Innovation Index); HDI (Human Development Index); ISI (Information Society Index).

Within the framework of this work, it seems appropriate to include the Global Innovation Index, calculated according to the INSEAD International Business School [7], in the composition of indicators of innovation activity. The Global Innovation Index 2022 analyzes the latest global trends in innovation in the context of the ongoing COVID-19 pandemic, slowing labor productivity growth and other urgent challenges. Assessing the effectiveness of innovation activities of about 132 economies and noting their strengths and weaknesses in the relevant area, the authors identify the most advanced countries in the world in terms of innovation.

In 2022, for the twelfth time, Switzerland ranks first in the ranking of the most innovative countries and territories in the world, followed by the United States of America, Sweden, the United Kingdom and the Netherlands. China is getting closer to the top ten, and Turkey and India are among the top 40 leaders in terms of innovation development for the first time.

The secrets of the success of the economies of the world leaders of innovative development include the following components: the state strategy of innovative development through the intellectual property market; a centralized horizontal and vertical system of state administration of processes in the field of intellectual property in order to reduce administrative barriers to market development; uniform rules – standards for the formation, turnover (commercialization) and protection of intellectual property; trained staff of professional intermediaries in the field of law, economics and intellectual property management.

The Global Innovation Index 2022 lists the world's leading scientific and technological innovation clusters with the largest concentration of inventors and authors of scientific articles. Such clusters are often called centers of scientific and technical activity (**Table 1**).

In 2022, the Tokyo-Yokohama cluster became the world's leading scientific and technological cluster, followed by Shenzhen – Hong Kong –Guangzhou (China and Hong Kong, China), Beijing (China), Seoul (South Korea) and San Jose –San Francisco (United States of America).

The engine of the global movement is the innovation clusters of the USA. Since the 1980s, the government has been actively working on creating programs designed for their education and development, one of them is the "Regional Cluster Initiative". For this purpose, significant sums of money are allocated annually from the country's budget.

In 2006, the European Union issued the "Manifesto of Clustering in the EU countries", which makes it possible to increase the competitiveness of individual EU members and improve the position in the world markets of the Union as a whole. In high-tech Germany, federal cluster programs such as Bioregio are working, which stimulate cooperation between local enterprises and organizations in order to accelerate innovation processes. India is also known for its innovation clusters. There are 2000 units operating on the territory of the country. The biggest one's work in IT, foundry and pharmaceutical industries [7, 9, 10].

Innovation clusters or innovation clusters are global economic "hot spots" where new technologies are developing at an amazing rate and where the pooling of capital, experience and talent contributes to the development of new industries and new ways of doing business. These are vibrant, bubbling ecosystems consisting of startups, businesses supporting the startup process, and mature businesses, many of which have developed rapidly. In these ecosystems, human resources, capital and know-how are smoothly mobile, and the speed of transactions is determined by the relentless pursuit of the possibility of phased financing and short business model cycles.

Innovation clusters, according to X. Ferras-Hernandez and P. Nylund, can be defined as "engines" of innovative development ([11], p. 55). An innovation cluster is similar to the generally accepted understanding of a business cluster, but somewhat different from it. In 1990, Michael Porter described business clusters as a geographical

1	Switzerland	(1-st) place in 2021	11	China	(12)
2	USA	(3)	12	France	(11)
3	Sweden	(2)	13	Japan	(13)
4	United Kingdom	(4)	14	Hong Kong, China	(14)
5	Netherlands	(6)	15	Canada	(16)
6	Republic of Korea	(5)	16	Israel	(15)
7	Singapore	(8)	17	Austria	(18)
8	Germany	(10)	18	Estonia	(21)
9	Finland	(7)	19	Luxembourg	(23)
10	Denmark	(9)	20	Iceland	(17)

Table 1.
Ranking of the countries of the world according to the innovation index 2022 [7].

concentration of a critical mass of interconnected companies and institutions in a certain area. This clustering concept explains how areas specializing in a particular industry gain competitive advantages through economies of scale and reduced transaction costs. But he does not explain how highly innovative clusters can support the continuous emergence of fast-growing firms, some of which diverge from the initial concentration of business.

Innovation-oriented business clusters began to attract more and more attention in the 1990s. The term "innovation cluster" began to be used more widely, but it still lacked a separate definition.

Issues of formation and increasing attention is paid to the development of clusters in the world economy. The experience of foreign countries in this area shows a high effect from their creation, which is to increase the competitiveness of organizations and improving the well-being of the population based on the strengthening of innovative enterprise activity. The specifics of the functioning of innovative clusters that allow creating new technologies, carrying out deep technological modernization and innovative development of industry based on their own or borrowed technologies, as well as training personnel for work in a new industrial and technological formation are characterized by the presence of three components: the presence of fundamental practice-oriented science, innovative industry, developing education.

4. Research and development (R&D) and protection of intellectual property rights

In the conditions of an innovative economy, achievements in the field of science, technology and innovation have become the determining factors of economic growth. Therefore, today the place of any country in the world economic system is determined by the knowledge-intensive economy of this country. Accordingly, countries with economies in transition will be able to successfully integrate into the system of world economic relations only if the knowledge intensity of their national economies increases. To fulfill this requirement, special attention within the framework of innovation policy should be paid to scientific and research developments, especially in the field of priority areas. In world practice, there is a steady increase in the volume of R&D financing. This trend is primarily determined by the leading countries of the world, where over the past 20 years absolute R&D expenditures have increased 2–3 times. The relative expenditures of the leading countries on R&D in the gross domestic product also show a positive trend.

The level of national spending on R&D is a relative value, which is calculated as the total amount of public and private spending on all types of research and development work during the calendar year, including government budgets at all levels, budgets of commercial organizations, grants and donations from private foundations and non-governmental organizations. The level of R&D spending is expressed as a percentage of gross domestic product (GDP). R&D is a set of activities aimed at obtaining new knowledge and its practical application to solve specific problems. It includes three main groups of activities: fundamental research; applied research; experimental design and technological developments. National spending on R&D is considered one of the key indicators of a country's scientific and technological development.

The indicator is calculated on the basis of data from national statistics and international organizations. The source of information is the database of the Institute of

Statistics of the United Nations Educational, Scientific and Cultural Organization (UNESCO), which is updated annually, but is delayed by an average of two years and does not cover all states, since many countries cannot provide annual statistics for this indicator [7, 9].

More than 30 countries raised their research spending between 2014 and 2022. Although research expenditure rose in most regions between 2014 and 2020, 80% of countries still invest less than 1% of GDP in R&D. The G20 countries still account for nine-tenths of research expenditure, researchers, publications and patents. Following the Covid-19 pandemic, research spending as a share of GDP may see a mechanical rise as the GDP of many countries declines. It remains to be seen whether countries will maintain stable investment in research in monetary terms (**Table 2**) [7, 9, 10].

In the context of widespread globalization, one of the most difficult problems of the modern market is the protection of intellectual property rights.

The concept of intellectual property rights protection includes a whole range of issues, such as the fight against intellectual piracy, ensuring the interests of free competition, problems of parallel import and much more.

Securing intellectual property rights is one of the main requirements of the Agreement on Trade-Related Aspects of Intellectual Property Rights (abbreviated TRIPS Agreement). The issues of intellectual property rights protection are also a priority for countries with economies in transition. In most of these countries, there are industries related to innovation and creativity that benefit from effective protection of intellectual property rights [12].

Experts note a significant increase in the number of copyright violations on the Internet. It should be noted here that in the conditions of the information society, the issues of protection of intellectual property rights and, first of all, copyright in the digital environment have grown into a huge problem. This problem urgently requires independent research and, based on them, the adoption of separate documents at the international level.

Country	**Expenditure on R&D (in % of GDP) by years**		
	2013	**2016**	**2020**
Austria	2.95	3.13	3.2
Great Britain	1.64	1.68	1.72
Germany	2.82	2.92	3.1
Israel	4.09	4.51	5,4
India	0.71	0.67	0.65
China	2.0	2.12	2.19
Luxemburg	1.30	1.30	1.1
Norway	1.65	2.03	2.3
USA	2.71	2.76	3.5
France	2.24	2.22	2.4
Sweden	3.30	3.27	3.5
South Korea	4.15	4.23	4.81

Table 2.
Level of expenditure on R&D in some countries of the world.

As is known in world practice, there are different approaches to solving this problem. In some countries, special courts for intellectual property rights have been established, in other countries, issues are considered in courts of general jurisdiction. Specialized courts, for example, in the field of intellectual property operate in the following states: Belarus, Hungary, Greece, Russia, Slovakia, Turkey, Czech Republic, Romania. In a number of other countries, special judicial boards have been established as part of the courts, for example, in Ukraine, in the system of economic courts there are specialized courts on intellectual property issues and a specialized Panel of judges in the Supreme Economic Court.

Customs authorities are an important link in the general system of intellectual property rights protection. The Customs Register of Intellectual Property Objects, which has been created in many countries, is a modern tool for combating intellectual piracy.

5. Intellectual property objects and artificial intelligence technologies

The rapid development and widespread use of artificial intelligence technology raises a number of questions, including whether artificial intelligence can create intellectual property objects. There are still numerous discussions about the legal consequences of using such technologies in the world [13].

The World Intellectual Property Organization, as an international organization, emphasizes the relevance of the question of where the line should be drawn between human and machine creativity, that is, what should be the amount of contribution or the degree of human participation so that the result of labor belongs to the first or second category mentioned above.

The experience of Great Britain seems to be an interesting experience in regulating relations in the field of intellectual property implemented using artificial intelligence.

In accordance with the existing patent legislation of the United Kingdom, only an individual (that is, a person) can and should be indicated as an "inventor" in a patent application (Article 7 of the UK Patent Law 1977 3). This rule has recently been reflected in various decisions concerning patent applications for inventions created using an artificial intelligence system called DABUS [14].

In the USA, there is a separate approach to copyright objects created by artificial intelligence technology. As a rule, two main conditions are required to grant copyright. Firstly, the work must be in a tangible form, and secondly, it must be original. Since one of the modern fields of application of artificial intelligence is the creation of literary and artistic works, the study of copyright in the context of artificial intelligence is an urgent area of legal science and practice in the United States. Understanding the main problems in this context is possible by analyzing the oldest fundamental precedents: Burrow Gilles Lithographic Co. v. Saroni ([15], p. 76), Bleistein v. Donaldson's lithograph ([16], p. 23), Alfred Bell & Co. against Catalda's fine Arts [17].

As for the actual American approach to copyright objects, in the creation of which a person did not directly participate, the approach still prevails in the law enforcement practice of the competent authorities of the United States [18].

In the context of the analysis of regulatory approaches to the regulation of relations using artificial intelligence technology, the experience of the European Union as an example of the unification of norms at the regional level is noteworthy. Currently, the EU is increasing investments in the development of artificial intelligence technologies, expanding the scope of its application everywhere.

Considering the question of whether exclusive rights to copyright objects created by artificial intelligence are recognized, we turn to Article 2 of Directive 2009/24/ EC of April 23, 2009 "On the legal protection of computer programs" [19], as well as Article 4 of Directive 96/9/EC of the European Parliament and of the Council of March 11, 1996. "On the legal protection of databases" [20], in which an individual or a group of individuals who created the object is indicated as the author, implying the human factor.

In October 2020, the European Parliament adopted three important documents regulating various spheres of relations within the framework of the functioning of artificial intelligence technology: Resolution of October 20, 2020 "Ethical principles in the field of artificial intelligence, robotics and related technologies", dedicated to ethical approaches in the field of regulating relations related to the implementation of artificial intelligence technologies; Resolution from October 20, 2020 "The regime of civil liability arising from the use of artificial intelligence technology", dedicated to civil liability for damage caused by artificial intelligence technology, as well as considering the issue of intellectual rights to works created directly by artificial intelligence or with the help of it; Resolution of October 20, 2020 "On Intellectual Rights in the development of artificial Intelligence technologies", which contains approaches to regulating attitudes in the context of the relationship between artificial intelligence and intellectual rights.

The European Parliament also enshrined in the above resolutions the concept of an artificial intelligence system (paragraph "a" of Article 4 of the Regulations, the text of which is contained in the Resolution of October 20, 2020 "Ethical principles in the field of artificial intelligence, robotics and related technologies", as well as paragraph "a" of Article 3 of the Regulations, the text of which is contained in the Resolution dated October 20, 2020, "The regime of civil liability arising from the use of artificial intelligence technology") [21–23].

6. Conclusions

In modern conditions, the practical application and wide dissemination of the results of scientific, technical and research activities, formalized in the form of objects of intellectual property, is a necessary factor in the economic development of any country. The relevance of innovative activity has now increased significantly and determines the position of the countries on the economic and political map of the world.

In modern society, achievements in the field of science and technology have begun to determine the dynamics of economic growth of states, the level of competitiveness of products and services, the degree of integration into the world economy. World experience shows that there is no other way of development for a knowledge-based economy other than innovation. The main factors in the growth of production, employment, investment, and foreign trade turnover are the creation, introduction and widespread dissemination of new products, services, and technological processes.

Science and high technology are international in nature, although the contribution of each country to the global scientific potential is unique in its own way. Today, big science from the state positions of the leading countries of the world is considered in the system "science - innovations - real economy". In civilized market conditions, the main engine in moving along this chain is intellectual property, its protection, regulation of the transfer of rights and commercialization.

Author details

Vladlena Lisenco
Researcher of European University, Moldova

*Address all correspondence to: vlada.lisenco@gmail.com

References

[1] Helpman E. Innovation, Imitation and Intellectual Property Rights. Cambridge: The National Bureau of Economic Research; 1992. DOI: 10.3386/w4081

[2] Terroir P. Rebalancing the patent economy. In: Intellectual Asset Management. Vol. 71. 2014, 2014

[3] Useche D. Are patents signals for the IPO market? An EU–US comparison for the software industry. Research Policy. 2014;**43**(8):1299-1311

[4] Convention of WIPO 1967 г. Electronic resource (date of the application 02.01.2023): Available from: https://www.wipo.int/treaties/ru/convention/summary_wipo_convention.html

[5] Paris Convention for the Protection of Industrial Property, 1883. Electronic resource (date of the application 02.01.2023): Available from: https://www.wipo.int/export/sites/www/treaties/en/docs/pdf/paris.pdf

[6] Abrami RM, Kirby WC, McFarlan FW. Why China can't innovate: And what it's doing about it. Harvard Business Review. 2014;**92**(3):107-111

[7] Global Innovation Index 2022. Electronic resource (date of the application 28.12.2022): Available from: https://www.wipo.int/publications/ru/details.jsp?id=4622

[8] Williamson PJ, Yin E. Accelerated innovation: The new challenge from China. MIT Sloan Management Review. 2014;**55**(4):27-34

[9] UNESCO Science Report 2022 Electronic resource (date of the application 02.01.2023): Available from: https://www.unesco.org/reports/science/2021/en

[10] UN Department of Economic and Social Affairs Statistics. SDG Indicators Database. Electronic resource (date of the application 02.01.2023): Available from: https://unstats.un.org/sdgs/dataportal

[11] Ferras-Hernandezи X, Nylund P. Clusters as Innovation Engines: The Accelerating Strengths of Proximity. Electronic resource (date of the application 02.01.2023): 2018. Available from: https://www.researchgate.net/publication/328973025_Clusters_as_Innovation_Engines_The_Accelerating_Strengths_of_Proximity

[12] Deere C. The Implementation Game: The TRIPS Agreement and the Global Politics of Intellectual Property Reform in Developing Countries. New York, NY: Oxford University Press; 2008

[13] Hochberg YV, Serrano CJ, Ziedonis RH. Patent Collateral, Investor Commitment, and the Market for Venture Lending. NBER Working Paper No. 20587; 2014

[14] Dinapoulos Elias SP. Intellectual property rights, multinational firms and economic growth. Journal of Developmental Economics. 2010;**92**(1):13-17. DOI: 10.1016/j.jdeveco.2009.01.007

[15] Burrow Gilles Lithographic Co. v. Sarony, 111 U.S. 53 (1884)

[16] Bleistein V. Donaldson Lithographing, 188 U.S. 239 (1903)

[17] Alfred Bell & Co. v. Catalda Fine Arts, 191 F.2d 99 (2d Cir. 1951)

[18] Chang H. Intellectual property rights and economic development: Historical lessons and emerging issues. Journal of Human Development. 2001;**2**(2):287-309. DOI: 10.1080/14649880120067293

[19] Directive 2009/24/EC of the European Parliament and of the Council of 23 April 2009 on the legal protection of computer programs. Electronic resource (date of the application 28.12.2022): Available from: https://eur-lex.europa.eu/LexUriServ/LexUriServ.do?uri=OJ:L:2009:111:0016:0022:EN:PDF

[20] Directive 96/9/EC of the European Parliament and of the Council of 11 March 1996 on the legal protection of databases. Electronic resource (date of the application 25.12.2022): Available from: https://eur-lex.europa.eu/legal-content/EN/ALL/?uri=celex%3A31996L0009

[21] European Parliament resolution of 20 October 2020 with recommendations to the Commission on a framework of ethical aspects of artificial intelligence, robotics and related technologies (2020/2012(INL)). Electronic resource (date of the application 05.01.2023): Available from: https://www.europarl.europa.eu/doceo/document/TA-9-2020-0275_EN.pdf

[22] European Parliament resolution of 20 October 2020 with recommendations to the Commission on a civil liability regime for artificial intelligence (2020/2014(INL)). Electronic resource (date of the application 05.01.2023): Available from: https://www.europarl.europa.eu/doceo/document/TA-9-2020-0276_EN.pdf

[23] European Parliament resolution of 20 October 2020 on intellectual property rights for the development of artificial intelligence technologies (2020/2015(INI)). Electronic resource (date of the application 05.01.2023): Available from: https://www.europarl.europa.eu/doceo/document/TA-9-2020-0277_EN.pdf

Chapter 8

Remuneration of Employee Inventions: Building a Typology of Existing Approaches

Pavel Svačina

Abstract

The remuneration of employee inventions in corporations is a relatively controversial topic in the field of intellectual property. In many countries, there are ongoing lawsuits over the amount of remuneration between the inventor and the employer. The available scholarly literature and professional sources suggest that there are many ways in which countries approach remuneration legislation and practice. However, the evidence is fragmented, and there needs to be more knowledge of whether there are recognizable typical approaches. To fill this gap, this chapter aims to find and define several recognizable types of compensation that exist in the world and their underlying principles and theories. We use Eisenhardt's comparative template for qualitative theory-building research (multiple case study) and formulate four recognizable types of approaches to the remuneration of employee inventions. The results of this chapter can serve, for example, innovative corporations in the correct setting of the reward mechanism for employee inventions when entering various foreign markets.

Keywords: employee invention, patent, remuneration, reward, case study

1. Introduction

Intangible assets have become a source of significant competitive advantages in today's market economies [1–3], and many authors and studies suggest a strong relationship between intangible assets' value and companies' market value [4–7]. The creators of these intangible assets are people (often employees), so one of the popular research areas is the remuneration of creative employed individuals, especially creators of technical innovations like inventions [8–10]. In many countries, there are disputes and even official court litigation over the amount of these rewards [11–15].

These disputes stem from the fact that many countries remunerate employed inventors by law [16], so the remuneration is then reviewable by an independent court. When and how are these rewards paid out? What are the critical conditions, and how do these conditions differ across countries? These are questions answered to some extent by analyses of the remuneration systems of different countries [17–21]. To some extent, there is also a more in-depth comparison of a particular sample of European countries [16, 22].

However, the literature lacks a deeper theoretical-empirical synthesis of the extent to which these approaches are similar or what are the deeper conceptual differences between them. This study aims to fill this space in the literature and offer, based on an empirical analysis of available approaches, a condensed typology of existing systems for rewarding employee inventions.

The text of the study is divided into the following sections: the second section outlines the issue of employee inventions and the current state of knowledge in relation to the aim of the study, the third section describes the research approach used, the data used and the selection of cases, the fourth section presents the results of the analysis of the investigated cases, followed by a discussion and conclusions.

2. Employee inventions: overview of literature

2.1 Remuneration and controversies around employee inventions

According to the latest statistics from the World Intellectual Property Organization (WIPO), in developed countries more than 90% of patent applicants are filed by organizations [23]. And, as shown in **Figure 1**, the (growing) majority of these patent applications are filed by the business sector. This number shows that most inventions are very often the result of the creative activity of individual persons employed in various (private or public) organizations.

Thus, new knowledge is mainly created as a direct or indirect result of employee tasks and are thus "employee inventions." However, modern intellectual property law allows for ownership rights to these intangible results to be exercised by employers for several understandable reasons [24].

The topic of employee inventions is considered quite controversial. The main reason is that it is situated at the intersection of patent, labor, and contract law [25, 26]. The labor law allows the employer to generally use the results of his employee's work. However, the ownership and use of intangible results in the form of inventions are governed by the patent law, because only a specific person may be designated as the creator (originator) of the invention. In addition, the contractual arrangement

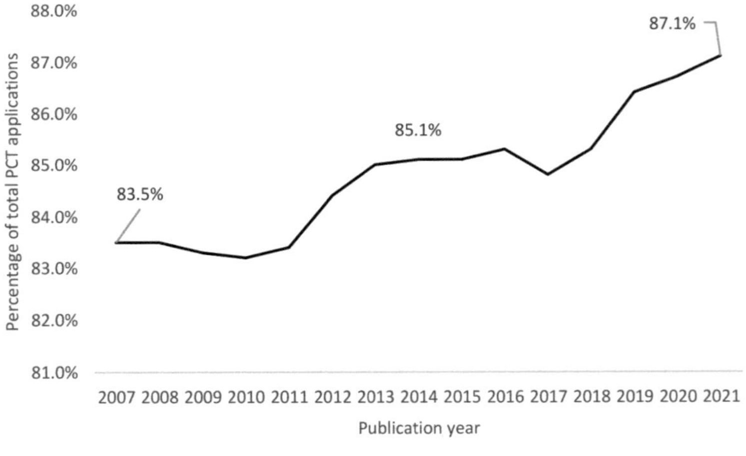

Figure 1.
Business sector share of all PCT applications. Source: Compiled from WIPO PCT Yearly Review ([23], p. 24).

between the employee and the employer can further specify the relationship in this area. The law of employee inventions therefore constitutes a certain "bridging" between the principles of labor and patent law in particular [27]. This "bridging" is made possible by defining the rights and obligations of the employee and the employer, whereby the employer's main property right is to exercise the rights to the given invention and to deal with it (within the patent law) without restrictions, and his main obligation is to pay the employee a certain reasonable remuneration.

The statutory regulation of employee inventions is purposefully not harmonized internationally, so each country regulates this area on its own [16]. In this regard, Germany is a relatively often cited country in the literature; it was one of the first countries to adopt a special law on employee inventions in 1957 [17, 28]. Like Germany, some other countries have taken the path of detailed legal regulation of employee inventions in special laws (Sweden, Denmark, Norway, Finland). Other countries, including Italy, Spain, Austria, Japan, France or Czechia, leave a relatively broad regulation within their patent laws [16, 18, 19, 29, 30]. Anglo-Saxon countries have a disproportionately different approach to employee inventions. There is often no legal regulation at all; these matters are usually regulated in the employment contract between the employee and the employer [24, 31–33].

Different surveys and case analyses also offer an insight into the level of the remuneration is in different countries, such as France [19, 34, 35], Japan [36], Germany [17], Sweden [21], USA [37–39], or European countries as a whole [40, 41].

2.2 Available theoretical frameworks in employee inventions literature

The theoretical framework of the theory of motivation prevails in the scientific literature regarding the remuneration of employee inventions. Within this framework, many authors examine the relationship between the amount of remuneration (as an incentive) and the number and quality of inventions produced by employees, in the private [36, 42–45] or public [46, 47] sector. The same framework also includes the examination of the relationship between the amount of remuneration and the number of inventions disclosed by employees to employers [48, 49].

An interesting but not very explained theoretical view is offered by Trimborn [17]. He distinguishes between rewarding employee inventions on the so-called monopoly principle and on the so-called extra-service principle. The monopoly principle is described as a system in which each employee must receive a reward, regardless of his/her job position, because the employed inventor is considered a quasi-license provider to his/her employer. However, this approach does not prevent the differentiation of remuneration due to the type of his/her work position. The second, the principle of extra-service, is based on the idea that an employee should receive extra compensation beyond his/her salary when he/she creates a benefit for his/her employer that is beyond what is expected.

Another way of looking at the issue of ownership of employee inventions (including related remuneration) is offered by Wolk [50]. She distinguishes the approach of countries with a civil law tradition from the approach of countries with a case-law tradition. Civil tradition countries generally attribute the rights to the created invention to the employee and only then are they transferred to the employer. Conversely, case-law countries grant property rights to the created invention directly to the employer. The concept of different legal traditions is followed in a certain sense by the concept of dividing countries into liberal market economies (LME—mainly case-law countries) and coordinated market economies (CME—mainly civil-law countries) [51]. The typology of LME and CME economies is put by the authors of this concept in connection with the creation of a different type of innovation—while the CME countries are mainly adapted to the creation of small/incremental innovations, the LME countries are much better adapted to the creation of radical innovations.

The last, well-generalizable concept in the field of rewarding employee inventions is the concept of economic benefit (or value) of the invention. As some authors summarize through various country comparisons [16, 22], in countries that apply the legal right to this remuneration, the unifying concept for determining the amount of the remuneration is precisely the economic benefit (or value) of the invention created by the employee. In this context, rewarding employee inventions can therefore be considered meritocratic, as explicitly mentioned by Harhoff and Hoisl [28].

3. Methodology, data, and research design

The aim of this study is to give a certain answer to the research question "How and why countries organize their remuneration systems for employee inventors?" by creating a typology of well-recognizable approaches. Since this study needs a deeper investigation of individual countries, we apply a qualitative, mostly inductive approach—multiple case study [52–54]. Although the study is primarily based on the inductive approach formulated by K. Eisenhardt [52], we use selected theoretical constructs for the organization of evidence, described at the end of Section 2.2. The overall research procedure is illustrated in **Figure 2**.

For the purposes of this study, we used primary and secondary data—specific laws of individual countries, their legal interpretations, but also other descriptions of these systems and their comparison in various individual aspects [16, 22, 31, 55, 56]. The selection of countries for the analysis was made purposefully [57], using certain differences already indicated by earlier literature. At the same time, the selection is made in such a way that it is varied in terms of the size of the countries (we used GDP data from World bank), in terms of different legal systems, etc., so that several recognizable types can subsequently be identified in such a sample (cf. a similar strategy in [58]. We excluded from the study countries with strong authoritarian political leadership as they may have various specifics not comparable across analyzed market-economy countries.

The analysis is focused only on the remuneration rules for employee inventions in the private sector. The collected evidence is presented in Appendix 1.

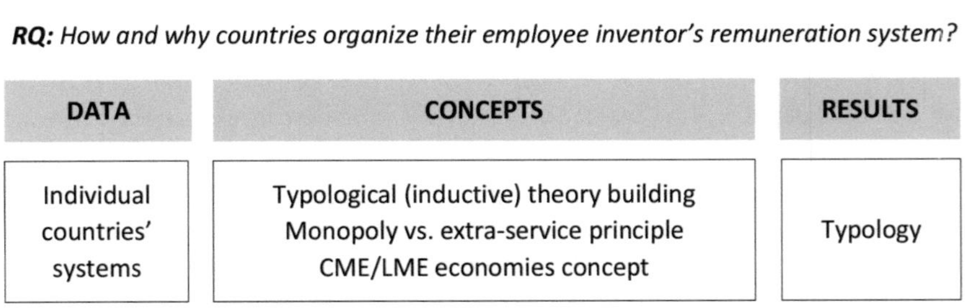

Figure 2.
Overview of the research process.

4. Results

In accordance with the defined literature [52], we performed within-case and cross-case analysis. The coded dataset is presented in Appendix 2. Four relatively well distinguishable types of remuneration systems for employee inventions emerged by systematic iterative comparison of the attributes of analyzed countries. An overview of the identified types is shown in **Figure 3**. A description of the four identified types is given in the following text.

4.1 Type 1

It is a remuneration system dominated by the principle of monopoly. In this type each employed inventor is entitled to a certain remuneration in addition to his salary, regardless of his job position, although the type of job position affects the amount of this remuneration. This type is dominated by the principle of civil law—the inventor is considered the originator (original owner) and the employer claims and subsequently acquires ownership rights for a certain quasi-license fee (remuneration).

4.2 Type 2

This is a system similar to the first type, however, with one significant difference—inventors, whose job tasks include inventing, are usually not entitled to special remuneration beyond their salary. The monopoly principle is therefore to a certain extent replaced by the principle of extra service, that is, for a specific reward, the employee's performance needs to be beyond the performance expected in his job position.

4.3 Type 3

In this type (in contrast to type two) there is a fairly noticeable application of the principle of extra service. Countries in this type have a system that covers most

	TYPE 1	TYPE 2	TYPE 3	TYPE 4
Key idea	**rewards each employee inventor**	**employee inventor "hired to invent" excluded**	**rewards only in exceptional cases**	**pure internal rules-based remuneration**
Underlying principle	monopoly	extra-service (weak)	extra-service (strong)	extra-service (strong)
Countries included	DE, JP, SWE, CZ, FR	AT, SP, IT	UK, NL	USA
Law perspective	patent-law based	→	→	labour / contract-law based
Economy perspective	CME logic	→	→	LME logic

Figure 3.
Typology of employee inventors' remuneration systems.

invented innovations with a negotiated wage. The discussion about a specific remuneration over and above the wage occurs only rarely and in very exceptional cases. For example, the United Kingdom defines these cases as inventions that bring an extraordinary benefit to the employer.

4.4 Type 4

The last type identified is the type that prevails in Anglo-Saxon countries, such as the United States. It is a system in which the payment of various rewards is entirely voluntary and contractual. These rewards, often defined by internal company regulations, are tied to a certain extra performance of the employee, so they are also philosophically constructed on the principle of extra service.

Created types can also be viewed from additional perspective views. For example, from the perspective of the dominant type of rights (patent (civil)-labor-contractual), one can see from the first type toward the fourth type a certain degree of erosion of the principles of patent law (i.e., the rights of the inventor/citizen) toward the principles of labor law, in which the fruits of the employee's work are primarily by the ownership of the employer, or contractual law, in which what the employee and the employer agreed upon in the contract primarily applies.

The identified types also well reflect the overall way the economy is organized (CME-LME). In the CME system of economies in which emphasis is placed on specific education at the expense of limited employee flexibility, it makes sense to grant inventors a certain specific remuneration through patent law, which is more difficult for them to negotiate on a relatively inflexible labor market. And conversely, in a situation where in the LME system the innovative employee is relatively flexibly educated, it seems reasonable to leave the reward system in the flexible labour market and perceive the whole process through motivation theories.

5. Discussion

Previous literature indicated the existence of a relatively large number of different remuneration systems for employed inventors, with the German approach being mainly discussed. The typology developed in this text suggests that, at a certain level of abstraction, several distinguishable types can be observed across countries. The main underlying principle for differentiating the created types is the principle of monopoly and extra services [17], while additional interpretation of the differences is helped by legal and market concepts applied to some extent differently in countries with different legal and economic traditions [50, 51].

However, it should be mentioned that the German approach, although it is often criticized for its uniformity [28, 42], may be used in disputes in other countries as well, as shows the evidence from, for example, Austria [29] or Italy [59]. This use of the German model in other countries is useful since uniform rules may be too rigid to grasp employee motivation at the firm level, however, in a situation where there is a legal dispute between an employee and an employer, some robust estimation model must be available which would verify that the reward was reasonable. Thus, countries that do not have detailed rules can be inspired by the German approach when solving court disputes. In this context, the German approach also remains a sui generis type.

Although four types can be well distinguished at a given level of abstraction, some variability remains even within the defined four types. From the empirical evidence (listed in Appendix 1), we can see, for example, relatively substantial differences between Germany and Japan. Japan, unlike Germany, does not have a uniform methodology for calculating the remuneration, has no arbitration board for dispute resolution, and has recently emphasized the binding nature of clearly described internal company remuneration rules [18]. However, the inclusion of Japan in the group with Germany is done because the amount of remuneration remains reviewable by the court and also because Japan does not deny the right to remuneration even to employees with R&D contracts. Similarly, we can see differences within the third type between the UK and the Dutch systems. While the terms of an "extraordinary situation" are defined within the UK [55], the Netherlands seems to be awaiting this definition [20].

The long-term existence of these different types indicates the fact that there is no one best system applicable across the globe. Rather, it appears to be the case that the systems applied in individual countries are the result of many different legal and market principles and their interactions, and one cannot simply transfer a particular system to another country. The given results can also be explained by the concept of equifinality, often observed in typologies [53], meaning that an equivalent result (adequate remuneration system) can be reached in several ways. Research carried out at the level of individual organizations of one country [58] also suggests the same—the variability of ways how to comply with one given statutory rules.

The results must also be seen within the accepted limitations. The first such limitation is the fact that only a limited number of countries were analyzed, and additional research may identify another well-differentiated type of reward system. Such other types may (but may not) be current systems used in countries with strong control over political and market events, which were not the subject of this analysis. The system used in socialist countries without private property [31] can also be recognized as another separate type.

6. Conclusions

This chapter dealt with the topic of rewarding employee inventions in private sector. Unlike the principles of patent law, this is a topic that is not harmonized across countries (not even in the EU) and represents a potential risk for innovative organizations entering foreign markets. This risk lies in potential conflicts between organizations and their local innovative employees. Although each country takes a somewhat different approach in this area, this chapter identifies four distinguishable types of remuneration systems for employed inventors. The analysis works with empirical evidence based on knowledge of the remuneration systems in many countries. The main key to differentiating the four defined types of remuneration systems seems to be the degree to which individual countries apply either the so-called monopoly principle or the so-called extra service principle.

Acknowledgements

The preparation of this chapter was funded by the Prague University of Economics and Business research project—VSE IP 100040.

Appendix 1. Collected evidence

	Germany	France	Japan	Sweden
GDP (2021, constant 2015 mil. USD)	3,554,676	2,577,596	4,435,431	565,187
Specific law	Yes	No	No	Yes
General rules on remuneration (private sector)	Yes	Partly	No	Partly
Specific arbitration board for remuneration issues	Yes	Yes	No	Yes
Types of employee inventions	1) **Mission/ service invention**—devolves into employer	1) **Mission invention**—research contract; rights devolve to employer	1) **Mission invention**—created within employer's activities/employee duties; employer may claim	1) **Research-based invention**—belongs to employee
	2) **Free invention**—patent belongs to the employee	2) **Non-mission invention**—relates to employer's field; belongs to employee; employer may claim the rights	2) **Free invention**—patent belongs to the employee	2) **Mixed inventions**—other than research duties of employee; employer has right to non-exclusive license and option to buy or for excl license
		3) **Free invention**—patent belongs to the employee		3) **Other inventions**—not service-related but within employer's field—option for employer
Remuneration of employee inventions	Reasonable compensation for 1)	Additional remuneration for 1). Fair price for 2 (or for 3).	Reasonable remuneration for 1). Fair price for 2)	Reward for disclosure; additional remuneration after patent grant.

	Czechia	Austria	Italy	Spain
GDP (2021, constant 2015 mil. USD)	210,996	405,146	1,862,306	1,238,778
Specific law	No	No	No	No
General rules on remuneration (private sector)	No	No	No	No
Specific arbitration board for remuneration issues	No	No	Yes	Yes

	Czechia	Austria	Italy	Spain
Types of employee inventions	1) **Employee invention**—one type, passes automatically to the employer	1) **Employee invention**—created within employer's akctivities/employee duties; employer may claim	1) **Paid for inventive step**—patent belongs to the employee	1) **Research-based inventions**—belongs to employer.
	2) **"free" invention**—not expressly regulated; if its criteria are not met, the right belongs to the employee	2) **"free" invention**—not expressly regulated	2) **not paid for inventive step**—belongs to the employer	2) **Mixed inventions**—created using means of employer (not directly service inventions) belong to employee; employer may claim non-exclusive license
			3) **free invention**—patent belongs to the employee	3) **Other**
Remuneration of employee inventions	Reasonable reward, additional remuneration for employee inventions	No specific reward for 1)—only wage for research contracts; when situation changes, then additional compensation	No specific reward for 1)—only wage	Wage sufficinet; supplementary remuneration only beyond reasonable situations for 1). Additional remunerations for 2).

	UK	Netherland	USA
GDP (2021, constant 2015 mil. USD)	3,036,532	846,873	20,529,460
Specific law	No	No	No
General rules on remuneration (private sector)	No	No	No
Specific arbitration board for remuneration issues	Partly	No	No
Types of employee inventions	1) **Service invention**—created within employee work duties belongs to employer	1) **Hired to perform R&D**—employer is entitled to file the patent	1) **Employee invention**—hire to invent—belong to employer
	2) **Other inventions**—belong to employee	2) **Not hired to perform R&D**—employee is entitled to file the patent	2) **Employee invention**—not hired to invent—belongs to employee, shop-right for employer
			3) **Other—free invention**—belongs to employee
Remuneration of employee inventions	Remuneration only in case of outstanding benefit to employer	Yes, but very restrictive interpretation of courts. Remuneration only in exceptional circumstances	Only wage, usual pre-emptive agreements. Internal remuneration rules

Appendix 2. Coded evidence

	Austria	Italy	Spain	UK	Netherland	USA
Specific law	No	No	No	No	No	No
General rules/ details on remuneration	No	No	No	No	No	No
Specific arbitration board	No	Yes	Yes	Partly	No	No
Law tradition	Civil law	Civil law	Civil law	Case law	Civil law	Case law
Typ of economy	CME	CME	CME	LME	CME	LME
Overall arrangement	Institutional	Institutional	Institutional	Institutional/ motivation	Institutional/ motivation	Motivation
Overall principle	Extra service (weak)	Extra service (weak)	Extra service (weak)	Extra service (strong)	Extra service (strong)	Extra service (strong)
Type evaluation	2	2	2	3	3	4

	Germany	France	Japan	Sweden	Czechia
Specific law	Yes	No	No	Yes	No
General rules/details on remuneration	Yes	Partly	No	Partly	No
Specific arbitration board	Yes	Yes	No	Yes	No
Law tradition	Civil law	Civil law	Civil law	Civil law	Civil law
Typ of economy	CME	CME	CME	CME	CME
Overall arrangement	Institutional	Institutional	Institutional	Institutional	Institutional
Overall principle	Monopoly	Monopoly	Monopoly	Monopoly	Monopoly
Type evaluation	1	1	1	1	1

Author details

Pavel Svačina
Prague University of Economics and Business, Prague, Czechia

*Address all correspondence to: svacina@vse.cz

References

[1] Sullivan PH. Value-Driven Intellectual Capital: How to Convert Intangible Corporate Assets into Market Value. New York: Wiley; 2000. p. 276

[2] Teece DJ. Capturing value from knowledge assets: The new economy, markets for know-how, and intangible assets. California Management Review. 1998;**40**(3):55

[3] Lev B. Intangibles: Management, Measurement, and Reporting. Washington, D.C: Brookings Institution Press; 2001. p. 216

[4] Hall BH, Jaffe A, Trajtenberg M. Market value and patent citations. The RAND Journal of Economics. 2005;**36**(1):16-38

[5] Sandner PG, Block J. The market value of R&D, patents, and trademarks. Research Policy. 2011;**40**(7):969-985

[6] Belo F, Gala VD, Salomao J, Vitorino MA. Decomposing firm value. Journal of Financial Economics. 2022;**143**(2):619-639

[7] Chen YS, Shih CY, Chang CH. Patents and market value in the US pharmaceutical industry: New evidence from panel threshold regression. Scientometrics. 2013;**97**(2):161-176

[8] Claire B. The incentives for innovation in the private sector. Recherches Economiques de Louvain. 2013;**79**(2):45

[9] d'Andria D. Why are researchers paid bonuses? On technology spillovers and market rivalry. Research Policy. 2016;**45**(10):2105-2112

[10] Giarratana MS, Mariani M, Weller I. Rewards for patents and inventor behaviors in industrial research and development. Academy of Management Journal. 2018;**61**(1):264-292

[11] Craft L. Yen for patents. ASEE Prism. 2005;**14**(5):17

[12] Atherton H. Inventors awarded fair share of employer's outstanding patent profits [Internet]. Bird & Bird. 2009. Available from: http://www.twobirds.com/en/news/articles/2012/inventors-awarded-fair-share-of-employers-outstanding-patent-profits

[13] Kim, Lee CH, Bang ST. Supreme Court recognizes compensation to employee for work-for-hire invention as co-inventor | Lexology [Internet]. 2016. Available from: http://www.lexology.com/library/detail.aspx?g=aecf0128-feba-47e6-8e42-7501bbe3a17c

[14] Normile D. Blue LED inventor sues former company. Science. 2001;**293**(5535):1575

[15] O'Driscoll C. UK pharma employees win (sic)1.5m for invention. Chemistry & Industry. 2009;**4**:7

[16] Wolk S. Remuneration of employee inventors - Is there a common European ground? A comparison of national laws on compensation of inventors in Germany, France, Spain, Sweden and the United Kingdom. IIC International Review of Intellectual Property and Competition Law. 2011;**42**(3):272-298

[17] Trimborn M. Employees' Inventions in Germany: A Handbook for International Businesses. Frederick, MD: Kluwer Law International; 2009. p. 186

[18] Okuyama S. New employee invention scheme in Japan. les Nouvelles.

Journal of the Licensing Executives Society. 2017;**LII**(3):111-113. Available from: https://papers.ssrn.com/abstract=2961886

[19] Declercq F, Intes D. Employee inventions in France. les Nouvelles. Journal of the Licensing Executives Society. 2017;**LII**(3):91-94. Available from: https://papers.ssrn.com/abstract=2961831

[20] Pors W. Employee Inventions in the Netherlands [Internet]. Rochester, NY: Social Science Research Network; 2017 Report No.: ID 2961889. Available from: https://papers.ssrn.com/abstract=2961889

[21] Wolk S. Compensation of Employed Inventors in Sweden [Internet]. Rochester, NY: Social Science Research Network; 2008 Report No.: ID 1557560. Available from: http://papers.ssrn.com/abstract=1557560

[22] Peberdy M, Strowel A. Employee's rights to compensation for inventions - A European Perspective [Internet]. Inside EU Life Sciences. 2010. Available from: https://www.insideeulifesciences.com/2010/03/05/employees-rights-to-compensation-for-inventions-a-european-perspective/

[23] WIPO, editor. Patent Cooperation Treaty Yearly Review 2022. Geneva, Switzerland: World Intellectual Property Organization; 2022. p. 1 (PCT Yearly Review)

[24] Merges RP. The law and economics of employee inventions. Harvard Journal of Law and Technology. 1999;**13**:1

[25] Langley M, Lee Y. Employees' inventions: Statutory compensation schemes in Japan and the UK. European Intellectual Property Review. 2005;**27**(7):250

[26] Oehlrich M. Induced innovation of the German employees' invention act. Pharmaceuticals Policy and Law. 2013;**15**(3-4):127-135

[27] Mark J. 'But It Was My Idea!' A Statutory Compensation Scheme for Employee Inventors? [Internet] [A dissertation submitted in partial fulfillment of the degree of Bachelor of Laws (Honours)]. Dunedin, New Zealand: University of Otago; 2007. Available from: https://www.otago.ac.nz/law/research/journals/otago036269.pdf

[28] Harhoff D, Hoisl K. Institutionalized incentives for ingenuity—Patent value and the German Employees' Inventions Act. Research Policy. 2007;**36**(8):1143-1162

[29] Wolzt C. Employee‘s inventions - The austrian concept. In: Presented at the Conference of LES Austria - Czech Republic & Slovakia – Hungary. Wien; 2019

[30] Svačina P, Rýdlová B, Bohácek M. Remuneration of employee inventions at Czech universities. Scientific Papers of the University of Pardubice, Series D: Faculty of Economics and Administration. 2018;**26**(43):232-245

[31] Svačina P, Boháček M, Bačárová R, Rýdlová B. Odměňování zaměstnaneckých (podnikových) vynálezů a jeho přiměřenost: právní a ekonomické aspekty. Praha: Wolters Kluwer; 2020. p. 357

[32] Gloor A. Levelling the global field: A case for mandatory employee compensation in Canadian Patent Law. Intellectual Property Journal. 2010;**23**(1):37-62

[33] Orkin N, Burger S. Employee invention rights in the twenty-first century. Labor Law Journal. 2005;**56**(1):82-88

[34] Loum NF. Current judicial practice concerning additional remuneration for employee inventors and inventions by trainees under French Patent Law. International Review of Intellectual Property and Competition Law. 2007;**38**(3):328-342

[35] Doyen D, Fortune E. La Rémunération des Inventions de Salariés: Pratiques en vigueur en France, Analyses. INPI. 2016. Available from: https://www.inpi.fr/fr/la-remuneration-des-inventions-de-salaries

[36] Onishi K. The effects of compensation plans for employee inventions on R&D productivity: New evidence from Japanese panel data. Research Policy. 2013;**42**(2):367-378

[37] Cockburn IM, Henderson R. Survey results from the 2003 Intellectual Property Owners Association Survey on Strategic Management of Intellectual Property. Intellectual Property Owners Association. 2003. Available from: http://www.ipo.org/index.php/2003/10/survey-results-from-the-2003-intellectual-property-owners-association-survey-on-strategic-management-of-intellectual-property/

[38] Malanowski S. Innovation Incentives: How Companies Foster Innovation [Internet]. Wilson Group; 2007. Available from: https://www.wilsongroup.com/wp-content/uploads/2011/03/InnovationIncentives.pdf

[39] Fradkin H, Vaughn A. A survey of aerospace industry inventor incentive awards. les Nouvelles - Journal of the Licensing Executives Society. 2009;**XLIV**(4):261-264

[40] Briner RG, Eck M. Employee inventor rewards survey. CMS. 2014. Available from: https://cms.law/en/CHE/Publication/CMS-Employee-inventor-rewards-survey

[41] Giuri P, Mariani M, Brusoni S, Crespi G, Francoz D, Gambardella A, et al. Inventors and invention processes in Europe: Results from the PatVal-EU survey. Research Policy. 2007;**36**(8):1107-1127

[42] Leptien C. Incentives for employed inventors: An empirical analysis with special emphasis on the German Law for Employee's Inventions. R&D Management. 1995;**25**(2):213-225

[43] Lerner J, Wulf J. Innovation and incentives: Evidence from corporate R&D. The Review of Economics and Statistics. 2007;**89**(4):634-644

[44] Honig-Haftel S, Martin LR. The effectiveness of reward systems on innovative output: An empirical analysis. Small Business Economics. 1993;**5**(4):261-269

[45] Burhop C, Lübbers T. Incentives and innovation? R&D management in Germany's chemical and electrical engineering industries around 1900. Explorations in Economic History. 2010;**47**(1):100-111

[46] Arqué-Castells P, Cartaxo RM, García-Quevedo J, Godinho MM. Royalty sharing, effort and invention in universities: Evidence from Portugal and Spain. Research Policy. 2016;**45**(9):1858-1872

[47] Lach S, Schankerman M. Incentives and invention in universities. The RAND Journal of Economics. 2008;**39**(2):403-433

[48] Baumann O, Stieglitz N. Rewarding value-creating ideas in organizations: The power of low-powered incentives. Strategic Management Journal. 2014;**35**(3):358-375

[49] Svačina P, Rýdlová B. Identifying specifics affecting the remuneration of employee inventions. In: Proceedings of the European Conference on Knowledge

Management, ECKM, Barcelona. 2017. pp. 964-972

[50] Wolk S. Intellectual Property Law and Ownership in Employment Relationships [Internet]. Rochester, NY: Social Science Research Network; 2008 Report No.: ID 1557603. Available from: http://papers.ssrn.com/abstract=1557603

[51] Hall PA, Soskice DW, editors. Varieties of Capitalism: The Institutional Foundations of Comparative Advantage. Oxford, UK; New York: Oxford University Press; 2001. p. 540

[52] Eisenhardt KM. Building theories from case study research. Academy of Management Review. 1989;**14**(4):532-550

[53] George AL, Bennett A. Case Studies and Theory Development in the Social Sciences. Cambridge, MA: MIT Press; 2005. p. 331

[54] Kluge S. Empirically grounded construction of types and typologies in qualitative social research. Forum Qualitative Sozialforschung/Forum: Qualitative Social Research [Internet]. 2000;1(1). Available from: http://www.qualitative-research.net/index.php/fqs/article/view/1124

[55] Rýdlová B, Svacina P. Employee inventor's remuneration: An evidence from Great Britain. In: Proceedings of the 11th International Scientific Conference INPROFORUM 2017: "Innovations, Enterprises, Regions and Management" [Internet]. České Budějovice; 2017. pp. 276-283. Available from: http://omp.ef.jcu.cz/index.php/EF/catalog/book/51

[56] Schörghuber B, Schultes R, Lunze A, Epping M, England P. Compensating employee inventors in Austria, Germany and UK [Internet]. Taylor Wessing. 2014. Available from: https://united-kingdom.taylorwessing.com/synapse/ti_compensation_employee_inventors.html#austria

[57] Suri H. Purposeful sampling in qualitative research synthesis. Qualitative Research Journal. 2011;**11**(2):63-75. DOI: 10.3316/QRJ1102063

[58] Svačina P. Rewarding employee inventions in corporations: Designing a framework to evaluate adequacy of remuneration and offering an optimal remuneration system. European Journal of Innovation Management. 2021;**24**(2):258-289

[59] Zanettin G. Taking the German approach to Italian employees' inventions [Internet]. IAM. 2013. Available from: https://www.iam-media.com/article/taking-the-german-approach-italian-employees-inventions

Chapter 9

The Role of Intellectual Property in Assuring Cultural and Gender Diversity in Labor Force in an Internationalized World

Tatiana Ertner, Diericon Cordeiro, Ramon Miranda and Lucas Aguiar

Abstract

When we think of a globalized world, whose development is based on internationalized actions, the ease of communication, access to information, cultural and commercial exchanges, and the technological development that they ignite immediately come to mind. Clearly, much is earned from internationalization; however, what is lost is rarely considered. A rigorous assessment of the changes that internationalization represents for a nation is needed in order to understand its effective costs and handle it properly. It is common sense that the main impact of internationalization is on the culture of a people. Internationalization, as a mechanism to facilitate sharing of information, products, and knowledge, certainly has an impact on cultural diversity; however, it is not always clear if it is positive or negative. Regarding intellectual property, it often influences authorship recognition and, therefore, ownership of innovative creations. Often, cultural issues affect the way in which authorship recognition occurs, especially when it comes to different ethnicities and genders. In this chapter, we will explore the aspects of intellectual property related to traditional knowledge that influence cultural and gender diversity, worldwide, evidencing their pros and cons, aiming to collaborate with public policies to bridge the gender gap and truly protect diversity.

Keywords: gender gap in intellectual property rights, ownership, cultural diversity, globalized regulations, traditional knowledge

1. Introduction

Diversity ensembles a complexity of participants that are used to designate similar characteristics that identify a group. Although it aims to distinguish the interesting and unique aspects of tangible contributions, ambiguously, it also denotes the expected products that can be obtained from a selected group of people, practices, or actions.

IntechOpen

Cultural diversity, therefore, resembles the distinct contributions of distinct communities to humanity. It encompasses everything that is produced by a specific community by means of the learnings passed on to its members from generation to generation. This is an internationalized behavior, recognizable in any part of the world.

It is generally referred to as traditional knowledge, and it is comprehended worldwide as related to a community as its own way of being productive and distinguishable. Due to this characteristic, traditional knowledge is an intellectual property and, as such, must be protected. It is a cumulative body of knowledge due to the mechanism by which it is passed on through generations, conserving its first traces and being modified only by the next generation.

Traditional knowledge refers to know-how, innovations, and practices of a specific community, formed by people from a location, sharing the same backgrounds, as provided by their ancestors. There are several products, knowledge and practices that are understood as traditional because of their long-standing interactions with their natural surroundings.

These constant interactions result in these unique practices and products that are, then, transmitted through language and oral traditions inherited from ancestors. Moreover, this knowledge also contributes to the well-being of the communities, and their insertion in the environment, therefore, they also refer to medicinal knowledge, products and practices. Diversity is then an intangible heritage of humanity that must be protected to ensure the sustainable development of every corner of the world [1–4].

Gender diversity is a reflex of cultural diversity, since it assumes distinct aspects depending on the community and the production that are in focus. For instance, if products are related to crafts and clothes or tools for agriculture, there is a predominance of female work and knowledge in the prior example and male knowledge in the late one.

In traditional knowledge, there is a significant aspect of the social organization of communities that results in a workload share that considers the differences between male and female abilities, giving rise to knowledge provided by them, differently, and originating gender diversity into traditional knowledge.

Since the needs of a community are influenced by their environments and available resources, and these needs are supplied by the efforts of every member of the community, gender diversity assumes significantly distinct aspects that can be neither anticipated nor controlled by broad parameters [5]. It is evident that there is a disparity of opportunities and access to education, positions and payment offers, socialization mechanisms, and personal development between men and women all over the world, which have profound impacts not only on behavioral development but on cultural-social, scientific-technological and economic developments [6]. Nevertheless, it is crucial to know the essential causes of this diversity and its local and global impacts to establish legislations that foster equity.

With this regard, it is noteworthy that what is common in gender diversity worldwide is the fact that it differs in the quality of intellectual property produced by men and women, and the impact of this, generally, is negative for the overall development of all nations.

Although the reasons for the gender gap, especially in intellectual property rights, have distinct origins, it is clear that it has a negative impact on a country's technological and economic development, at least because there is an evident waste of creativity and intellectual abilities and, therefore, must be broadly bridged [7–9].

To bridge the gender gap can be a powerful tool to strengthen the intellectual property of a community and to achieve the desired economic development. Also, attention must be paid to the traditional knowledge in all kinds of communities, searching for mechanisms to adequately protect them. It is because traditional knowledge is often underrespected by other communities and nations. It means that very often they are subject to misappropriation especially because of their commercial value to several kinds of industries [4, 10].

Specifically biopiracy, as a result of the misappropriation of knowledge of indigenous people on medicinal products and plants, has been ascendant and, especially in Brazil, as a nation with a enormous biodiversity, regulations are not efficient in preventing it.

The country had approved in 2015 its biodiversity law [11] to specify the rules for access to traditional knowledge and genetic heritage, which is essential for the sustainable conservation and use of biodiversity. However, it must be efficient and aligned to the context of the Convention on Biological Diversity (CBD) and, in fact, it has been proven to provoke violations of international agreements and has been denounced for excluding indigenous and traditional people's rights, having inadequate legal provisions on access and benefit-sharing (ABS) [12].

Brazil is not the only example of biopiracy and disrespect to traditional knowledge. Worldwide, misappropriation of traditional knowledge has occurred due to inadequacies of the existing intellectual property regulations that can greatly differ in distinct nations. In an effort to equalize the protection mechanisms, several organizations with diverse visions of traditional knowledge have been discussing the aspects of protection of the broad forms of knowledge. World Intellectual Property Organization (WIPO), United Nations Educational, Scientific and Cultural Organization (UNESCO), World Trade Organization (WTO) International Labour Organization (ILO), the World Health Organization (WHO), United Nations (UN) through its United Nations Environment Program (UNEP) and the Convention on Biological Diversity (CBD) have been, in 2005 starred in a discussion that culminated with the initiative of a Sui Generis protection for traditional knowledge, among others [13, 14].

The rules for the protection are, since then, been established and adopted, giving rise to several national regulations to provide *Sui Generis* protection for traditional knowledge [14–16], most of them taking into account the definitions and perceptions of the characteristics of the traditional knowledge presented by those organizations in several meetings and conferences.

Particularly relevant are the discussions in COP 8, where the participants agreed that *"urge the Governance to develop, adopt national and local sui generis models for the protection of knowledge, innovations and traditional practices, with the full and effective participation of indigenous and local communities"*. It is equally relevant to consider the UNESCO – Convention on the Protection and Promotion of the Diversity of Cultural Expressions perception that *"Cultural diversity is an essential characteristic of humanity, constituting, in itself, a heritage that must be valued and preserved."*

They also agreed that culture should be incorporated as a strategic element of national and international development policies, which provides the view of heritage promotion to ensure maintenance for future generations, with a humanistic focus.

Allied to that are the visions of WTO and WIPO that this knowledge must provide economic support and financial return to the communities in order to foster their preservation and development by means of defining authorship and ways to compensate the communities′ members for the inappropriate use of cultural creativity, having a focus on commercial exploitation. Also relevant is the vision of CBD, which values respect for traditional communities, and the right to a fair division of benefits from the use of traditional culture, in a community focus.

In this work, we provide an overview of the intellectual property rights application worldwide, taking into account how the protection of traditional knowledge is supported, the female participation in the labor force in distinct countries, and how cultural and educational differences may support or devast gender equity.

Also, we evaluated the relevance of national regulations and how they are attached to international approaches, and the impacts they have in distinct communities worldwide. We examined the characteristics of the gender gap in the global economy, considering its growth especially related to technology and innovation promotion, by analyzing the participation of women in patent application and in startup creation and management, also considering it as a tool to provide equity among genders, despite cultural differences.

With this effort, we aim to evidence the pros and cons of the intellectual property related to traditional knowledge, which directly influences cultural and gender diversity, and, therefore, contribute to public policies to bridge the gender gap and foster diversity.

2. Methodology

To acquire the data that are explored in this work, searches in patent databases and in scientific publications were conducted, in a bibliometric mean. To perform the analysis presented in this work, some developing and developed countries were selected to have their tendencies of women in the labor market and as inventors and entrepreneurs evaluated in the time flow.

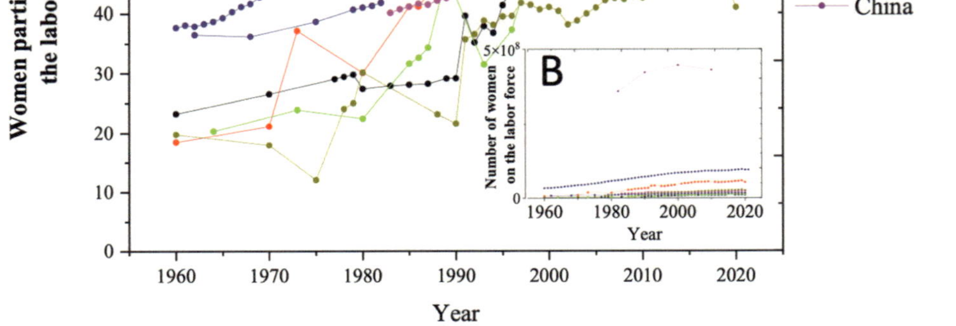

Figure 1.
A) Female participation in the working market, per country, per year from 1958 to 2020 and B) absolute number of women in the working market, per country, from 1958 to 2020.

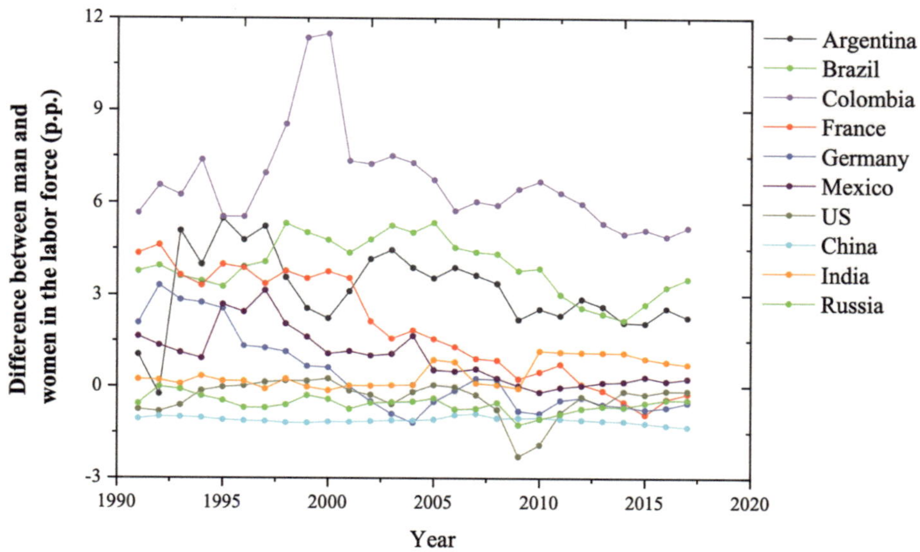

Figure 2.
Percentage difference of employment between men and women, from 1990 to 2020, in selected countries.

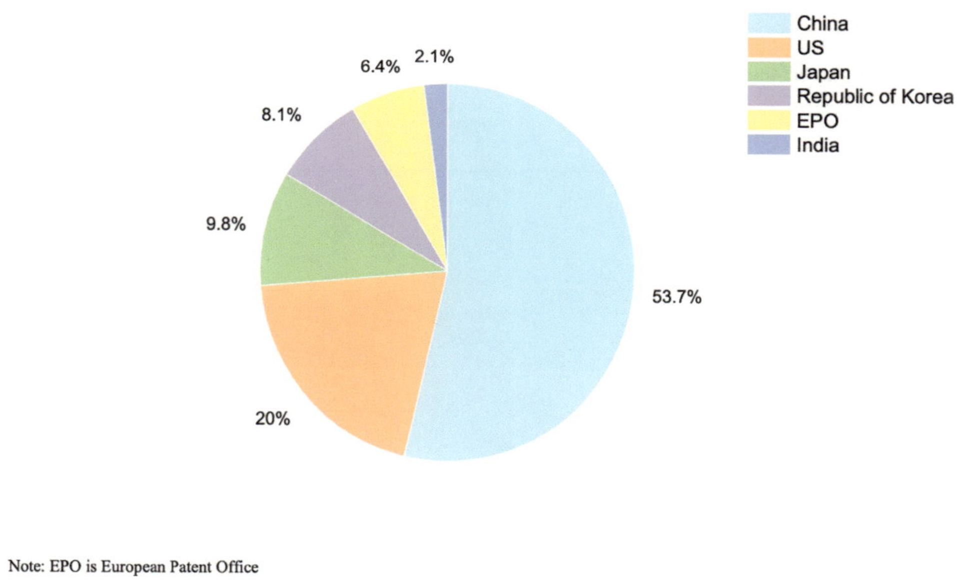

Figure 3.
Patent application in 2021 via PCT, per country. Source: WIPO statistics database, November 2022.

2.1 Countries selection

To illustrate women's participation in the economy, countries with similar socio-economic development indices were selected, such as those referring to education, health, and income. The chosen countries are economically and culturally significant, so that it is possible to analyze the barriers that women in developing countries have to overcome in the path to a better future.

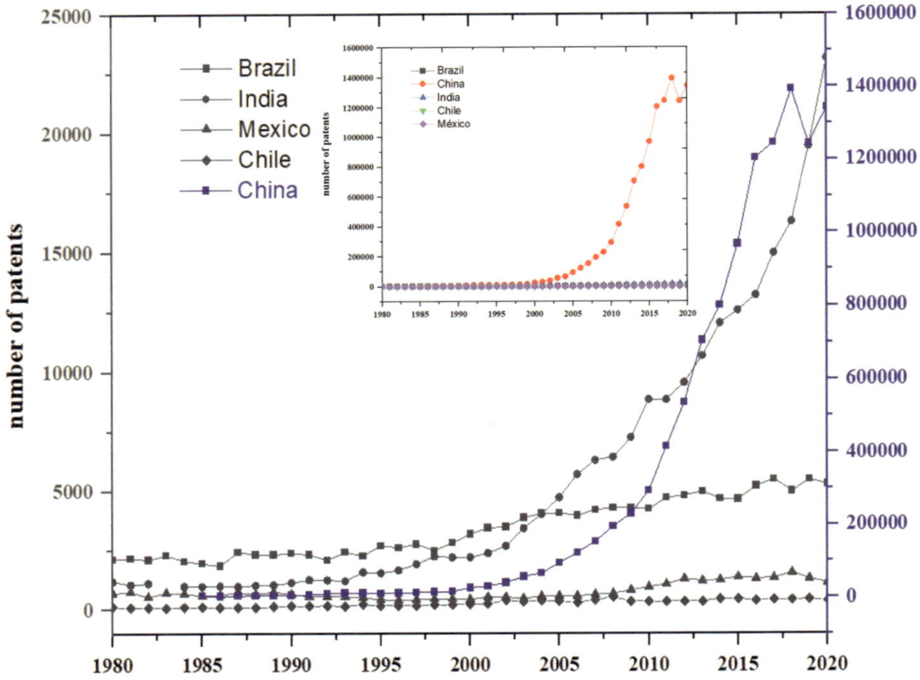

Figure 4.
Patent-filling growth from 1980 to 2020, in selected countries.

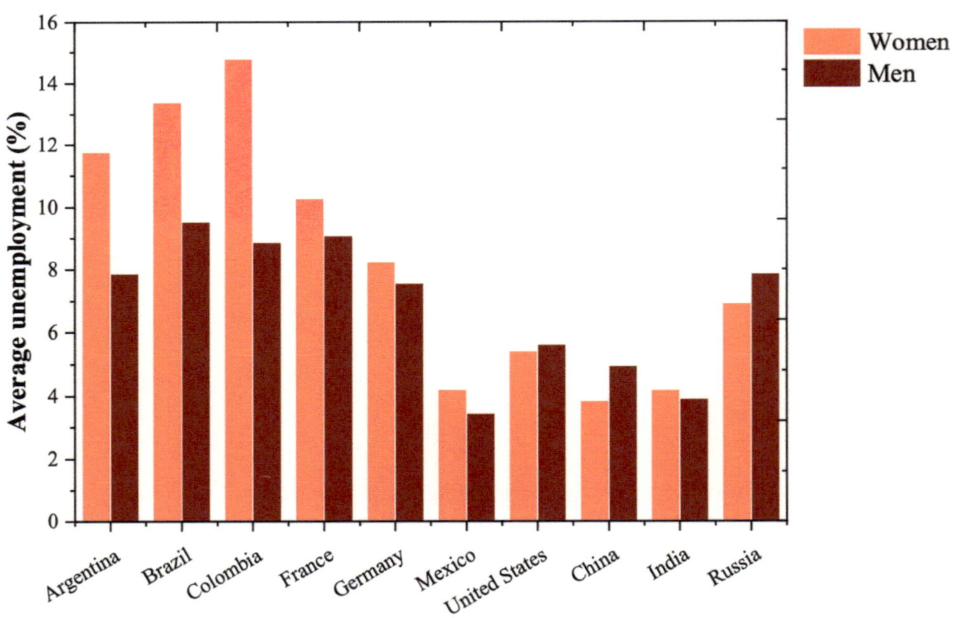

Figure 5.
Unemployment rate of men and women in selected countries.

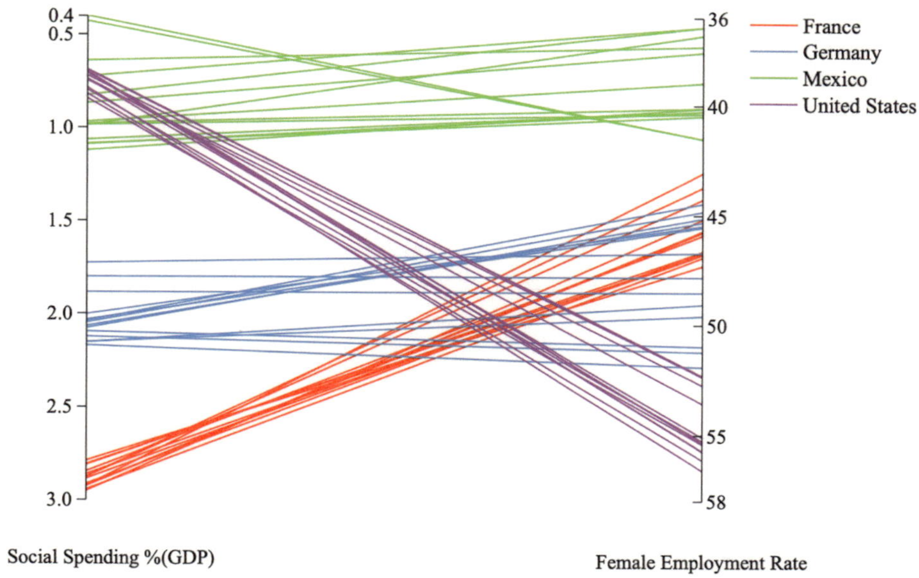

Figure 6.
Governmental investments in family aid policies and the employment rate of women in selected countries.

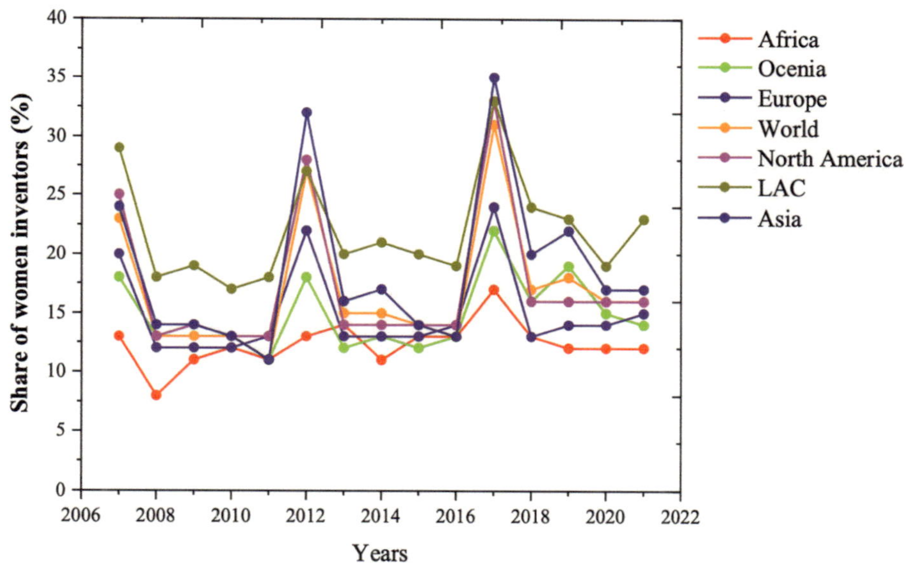

Note: LAC is Latin America and the Caribbean.

Figure 7.
Percentage of women listed as inventors in PCT patent applications per year, per geographical region.

2.2 Data gathering

Part of the data used for analysis was made openly available at the Our World in Data website, at the Status of Women in the States website (which seeks to monitor

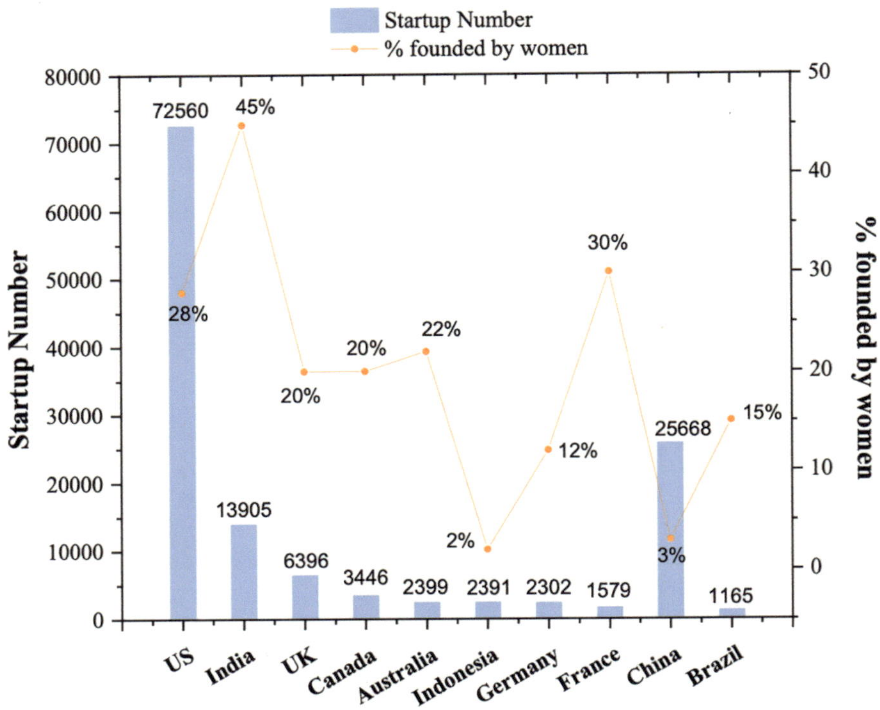

Figure 8.
Number of startups that were founded by at least one woman, in the ten countries with more startups launched worldwide.

socioeconomic data related to the labor market and the performance of women) and in WIPO reports and statistics, made available through WIPO intellectual property data center (free online service that provide access to WIPO statistical data on intellectual property activity), which can be accessed also in their website, all under the Creative Commons BY license. Part of the data used was acquired from studies carried out by third parties and duly referenced.

Data were collected to produce graphics presented in **Figures 1–8**.

3. Findings

As showed by Montanari and Bergh [17], women's traditional knowledge is usually related to the manufacturing and creation of several products that uses natural raw materials. Their practices are often taught by them to their children, by traditional means, learned from their mothers. Information natural resources uses and compositions are also taught this way; all of these are considered traditional knowledge of people. Therefore, women have a vital role in the preservation of a culture, but also in the preservation of the environment and biodiversity conservation.

Although it is evident that women greatly contribute to the preservation and dissemination of traditional knowledge of their communities, the lack of data in this matter that can register their efforts is a threat to their perseverance. With low information, adequately and methodologically acquired, statistics on how important women play in preserving biodiversity and cultural knowledge cannot be reliable.

Therefore, it results in the lack of dedicated funding or interest in funding preservation activities conducted by women. It also damages their participation in policies formulation to address their own needs and their views in decision-making processes are often not taken into account [18, 19].

All organizations that are focused on biodiversity conservation, knowledge dissemination, and even climate change fight recognize that it is essential that women participate in equal levels to men in decision-making. Their abilities must provide them enrollment also in the design of programs on biodiversity and environmental management, to promote a reliable adaptation and mitigation of climate change consequences, and improving local development, having the premises of the 2030 Agenda for sustainable development in target [20].

Although the participation of women in directly protecting traditional knowledge and promoting biodiversity is not discernible, it is easily comprehensible once their participation in the economy and labor market, especially those related to innovation and traditional knowledge is correctly analyzed. Therefore, in the following sections, we will present available data related to women's participation in the economy worldwide, how they are involved with intellectual property protection, and how they economically benefit from their efforts toward innovation and development.

3.1 Women's participation in economy

Women's participation in the economy worldwide has been followed since 1980s and has been at an increased rate since then [21–23].

However, there is a sensible difference between the rates and the mechanisms to bridge the gender gap among the nations. The main reason for the distinct rates of participation of women in the economy of distinct countries is the changes in legislation and/or actions to promote gender equality, as well as education and gender equality awareness in each country.

Changes in legislation are often related to labor laws aimed at promoting gender equality in the workplace. The 1990s was marked by the main changes in labor laws that allowed the increase of women's participation in the labor market. The adoption of these laws contributes to women's economic emancipation and is also a significant reason for the economic growth observed in developing countries. These changes that have been contributing to the benefit changes are: 1. prohibition of discrimination of gender and/or sexual orientation in the hiring process; 2. guarantee of equal wages for women and men in similar jobs; 3. guarantee of paid maternity leave; 4. ensuring shorter working hours for pregnant women; 5. prohibition of the dismissal of pregnant women; 6. guarantee of licenses to care for sick family members; 7. guarantee of equal labor rights for women and men and 8. guarantee of rights to education for women [24].

Although all these measures are understood in terms of human rights and guarantee of health specifically related to the UN 2023 agenda, they are often characteristic of women responsibilities in a family and are often the reason for their professional drawback.

Figure 1 shows the evolution of women participation in the labor force in the selected countries, in the period of 1980 to 2020. Evidently, there was an increase in female participation over the years, with a constant growth rate until near 2008, when most of the countries presented stable participation from that year on, which can be related to the economic crash of the USA that had significant effects worldwide due to the bankruptcy announced by Lehman Brothers Bank [25–28].

Notably, in Germany, the growth of women's participation in the labor force has continued to increase at a constant rate due to a higher level of qualification among women that has increased considerably, approaching that of men, enabling them to participate in several sectors [29]. However, it is expected that the next data will not be as favorable as these due to the negative impact the COVID-19 emergency had on employment in all sectors worldwide [30].

Also, countries, such as Brazil and Colombia, presented relatively high growth rates in female participation in a workforce that was growing after a brief recovery between 2012 and 2018 but that is expected to decrease again due to COVID-19 pandemic effects. Especially in Brazil, 11% of the women immediately lost their jobs related to domestic work and tourism due to the lockdown needs [31, 32].

Figure 1B shows the absolute number of women participating in the labor force. In absolute terms, China is the market with the highest participation of women in the labor force. Historically, it also had shown low levels of women unemployment; however, the available data is insufficient to infer the behavior of the current situation, but it evidences a decrease in women participation after the years 2000 that occurred at least until 2010. Yet, China is a country in which women have been over 60% of the labor force.

The United States also presents a high population of women actively participating in the labor market. Currently, they are around 57% of the labor force, and this participation has been kept since 2000, after a strong growth that occurred since 1940, pulling the female participation from nearly 40% to over 60%, and changing drastically the situation of the American labor force. However, according to the OECD, the levels practiced today are similar to those of 1993 [33].

This observed growth between 1940 and 1970 is due to two main reasons: 1) the massive high school education, graduation rates that rose substantially and included women and 2) the advent of new technologies that urged for new skilled employees and leaving old positions in the open, ready to be taken mainly by married women, such as clerical workers, that were understood as suitable for the new female labor force [34].

Figure 1 also shows that there is a general tendency to increase the participation of women in the labor market in both developed and developing countries. It also evidences that a crisis of any kind immediately causes a decrease of women in labor force and the reasons for that vary from culture to culture, but always proving a distinction that drawback women from the productive sectors, even if they are skilled and with education levels similar to those of men.

In a general manner, data show that there is an increase in women's participation in the labor market since the 1960s. However, this behavior is changed according to the social and economic moment experienced by each country's society.

In American society, the end of the 1990s can be pointed out as the apex of women participation in labor market. On the other hand, in China, the share of women active in the labor market by 2010 is higher than those of any other countries, with its apex occurring in the mid-1990s. In Brazil, the apex occurred before other Latin American countries that are part of this analysis, such as Colombia, Argentina and Mexico. In Latin American countries it occurs in the following decades, but at a relatively lower rate when compared to the American society. The causes for these distinct apexes may have independent reasons, possibly related to lower birth rates and population aging, commonly characterized by higher longevity rates among women. In the United States, for instance, this dynamic is related to the development of the so called Baby Boomer generation and its retirement. In 2010, the oldest Baby Boomers were about

64 years old and by 2019 they were 73. This phenomenon has led to a decrease of women's participation in labor market participation rates, even when participation rates by age group have increased [35].

Unemployment is also higher among women, worldwide. In **Figure 2** the unemployment rate is presented, considering men and women of distinct countries.

Figure 2 shows that female unemployment rates are higher in developing countries than in developed ones. Countries that experience a dynamic of economic growth, such as China and India, present much lower unemployment rates, evidencing their actual scenario of full employment, contrasting with the chronic unemployment scenarios experienced by other developing countries. Although the employment is higher in such countries, especially due to their economic growth promoted by the fast technological development implemented in these countries, it is not the main reason for the difference in economic growth experienced by other developing countries.

In China and India, they invested in technological development as a way to move forward their economy and lifestyle, which has positively impacted their industrial diversity, therefore, promoting gender diversity to fill the job vacancies created by the new fields of productions originated by the technological development. But countries such Brazil, Chile, and Mexico also had invested in technological development in this period; however, their achievements in promoting industrialization and diversification are far lower.

To promote a better understanding and use of the intellectual property system, WIPO has provided special services for developing countries, by producing information, guidelines and providing training on the Patentscope database [36].

As shown in **Figure 3**, China has been the greatest patent-filling country in the world, which evidences its strategy of investing in the technological development of quality to ensure new markets for their new industries.

Data collected by The World Bank (available under Creative Commons license (CC.BY.4.0)) and from the WIPO Patent Report: Statistics on Worldwide Patent Activity [37] were used to plot the graph in **Figure 4**, which shows the progression of patent filling in selected developing countries. Comparing these data shows that since 2000 China has been producing innovations in an exponential rising behavior, and in 2020 its patent portfolio is over 64 times larger than other developing countries in the analysis. India has also increased its patent application numbers, as a strategy of specializing its industry and to enter in the market of high value products. Other developing countries also had invested in patent applications to specialize their industries, but in a very modest fashion, compared to China and India, mainly due to distinct strategies of incentive to science and education and technological development in these countries. This also has an impact on the participation of women in their labor market, confining them to sectors that are usually more affected, such as services and agriculture.

Even so, developing countries like those have also been experiencing the growth in women's employment. Specially India, South Africa, and Brazil have faced a significant increase in female participation in the workforce, which shows that women have made efforts to make progress economically and socially. In these countries, they had found positions mainly in agriculture, services, trade, manufacturing, and construction. Agriculture is the main source of employment for women, and it has been an important driver force to the economic and social development of developing countries.

While female participation in labor markets is increasing, there is still a long way to go to improve the position of women in developing countries. Discrimination is still a reality for many women, and therefore developing countries need to take policies to promote gender equality. In addition, women need access to education and training to acquire professional skills that allow them to compete with men in the labor market. Overall, the increased participation of women in productive sectors in developing countries has been a positive step toward improving women's living conditions. This trend has generated more opportunities for women to obtain economic independence and improve their contribution to society [38, 39].

However, this is distinct from what is observed in developed countries. In those countries, women have played an increasingly important role in the economy due to female participation increase in a broad productive field. For instance, in the United States, about 55% of the female labor force is concentrated in health and social services, and education and public administration sectors welcome nearly 40% of women. In addition, women have also increased their presence in the financial services industry, with about a third of the female labor force employed in financial services companies. Moreover, the manufacturing industry, have also employed more women, with 25% of women working in the area, and the construction industry, with a20% of women as labor force [38].

Yet in the United States, according to the most recent data, American women receive the highest salaries in government positions (whether at the federal, state, or local level). 40% of women occupy managerial functions, which require higher education, while 33% of men occupy such positions. Fields of science, technology and engineering have experienced an expressive growth in the number of positions occupied by women in the last decade, also being the sectors that are among those that provide better remuneration [38].

Therefore, the experience of the developed countries confirms that investing in science, technology and, thus, education can provide women with enough skills to enter any market as a reliable labor force. This assumption can be corroborated by unemployment rates, considering male and female, distinctly. **Figure 5** shows the unemployment rates by country, as it was determined in 2017. As shown in **Figure 5**, unemployment among women are generally higher than among men, but the discrepancy is more pronounced in developing countries such as Argentina, Brazil and Colombia. Notably, in India, which, likewise China, invests in technological development, unemployment rates among men and women are similar. In countries such as Russia and China, however, unemployment afflicted men and in the developed countries, unemployment rates tend to be close among men and women; despite it being slightly higher among women in the United States, unemployment is similar among men and women.

Since the unemployment rate is higher among women is a general feature, afflicting both developed and developing countries, it is to be assumed that it might have common origins. Evidently, women in the labor market have yet to deal with their usual tasks, for instance, taking care of family and being responsible for the children well-being and education. Therefore, often they leave their jobs in order to accomplish those tasks and this is even more pronounced in places where policies of family care and education are not efficient.

Figure 6 presents the correlation between the governmental investment in public policies as a percentage of the gross domestic product (%GDP) related to family aid and the employment rate among women in selected countries.

From **Figure 6**, it is observed that there is an overall direct relation between public policy expenses aiming for family aid and female employment rates. This is because, in general, governmental policies on social support for families include maternity assistance, family assistance, paid maternity leave, paternity leave and etc. However, countries do not uniformly adopt these social policies, but several Latin American and European countries adopt paid maternity leave to some degree, leading to higher employment levels as policies are fitted to the social needs of that country.

For instance, in France, the higher public investment in policies resulted in a level of female employment similar to that achieved by Germany, which invested less of its gross domestic product in those policies. It is noteworthy that, according to Martin [40, 41], France has been going through a relevant change in its labor force behavior. Between the years 1945 and 1975, women start to participate more effectively in the labor market, finding positions mainly in a simple part-time job, thus showing an expressive growth in the female employment rate. In these last decades, more qualified women have been working in full-time jobs, in similar regimens than men, resulting in less expressive employment growth but also indicating that the gender gap is closing. In fact, nowadays, nearly 49% of the French labor force is female.

On the other hand, the low investment of the United States in public policies for family aid resulted in a higher female employment rate. The United States is among the few developed countries that do not have specific legislation that guarantees paid maternity leave. Thus, only 23% of employees of US companies grant the benefit of paid maternity leave [42]. However, the United States has been investing in women's education as a way to provide equality in job opportunities [43, 44].

3.2 Women as inventors and patent owners

To understand the gender diversity in the labor market is essential to promote equity in a sustainable fashion. We were able to evidence that the national differences in female employment rates and characteristics can be related to public incentives, in the form of family aid and the promotion of female access to higher education. Also, we understood that countries focused on their technological and scientific development are more prepared to bridge the gender gap in the labor force. But, to be a sustainable process, meaning that gender equity must be achieved once and for all, women must be as well prepared as encouraged to value and realize their ideas; therefore, they must develop the same confidence in their abilities that are taught to men by all cultures.

To understand if the female qualification is rendering women that are confident and conscientious of their abilities to contribute to the technological development of a country, as well as to find a place in the challenging market of advanced technology industry, it is relevant to analyze the characteristics of the inventors of patent applications filed worldwide.

Data provided by the WIPO Intellectual property data center [45] and reported in WIPO Yearly PCT Review 2022, evidence that the female participation as inventors in patent applications, through the Patent Cooperation Treaty (PCT) is increasing at a faster rhythm, with women being responsible for near 30% of the patent filed worldwide. In 2021, the share of women as inventors in patent applications via PCT increased by 1%, compared to 2020, reaching the historical mark of 16.5% of the application having at least one female inventor. This increase is impressive, considering that it is similar to the increase noted between 2001 and 2011, suggesting that this is a recent endeavor for women.

However, even though this evidences a never experienced growth before and, therefore, a behavior change, it is still too slow, meaning that equity will only be achieved in 2050, if women participation evolute in the same rhythm it evolved in

2021 [46, 47]. **Figure 7** shows the women's participation as inventors in PCT applications worldwide, by year, in distinct regions of the world. **Figure 7** evidences that the growth acknowledged in WIPO Yearly PCT reviews [47] is, actually consisted of apexes that are related to a growth behavior if analyzed each 5 years, as in the report's methodology. However, they evidence a growth that hardly is higher than 30%.

From **Figure 7**, it is observed that participation of women inventors in PCT application is less than 30% in most geographical regions and that the mark of one-third of women as inventors was only achieved in 2017; however, it was not kept in 2021 by any region. Latin America and Caribbean countries counted with the highest participation in 2021, around 23%, and the most pronounced decrease was in Asian countries, followed by the decrease perceived in North America.

Due to the high PCT application number from both regions also affected the women participation counted in the world, resulting in a female share of 16.5% as inventors in PCT applications. These data, therefore, show that there is a tendency for an increase in women's participation as inventors in patents, as all geographical regions are perceiving their participation increase and, as for Latin America and the Caribbean, this can be more propounded from year to year. These observations sustain that this number may rise much faster from now on, since which may lead to equity earlier than expected.

Male participation as inventors in PCT application, in the same period, was never less than 95.5% and achieved 96% in 2021, one of the lowest participation in a long period [47]. It indicates that female participation may be increasing much faster in numbers, since most inventions have more than one inventor, as they result from collaborative work, where women have the most significant share in the labor force, have conquered positions that are now available to them due to their higher education access and that this increase is occurring worldwide. Therefore, it is a prognostic that countries are in the way of equity and, if they learn from each other experiences, it may occur faster than predicted.

3.3 Women as leaders in technological-based companies

The global startup economy is large and is rising. According to the Global Startup Ecosystem Report 2020 of the Global Entrepreneurship Network – Genome Startup [48], it creates nearly US$3 trillion in value with increasing economic participation. They reported that in 2019, 84 startup ecosystems, worldwide, had created a billion-dollar-value startups, known as unicorns, contrasting with the 4 unicorns created in 2013, when the term started to be used. It represents a growth of 26% considering the number of unicorns launched in the year before.

This is an innovation-domain environment and it can directly inform about the contribution of women to such promising businesses. To participate on that, a person must be enthusiastic about innovations, well trained, and develop skills in highly technological fields. Also, must be capable of generating new products, fundraising and understand about business launching. Therefore, it can promptly inform about any changes in the gender gap. (Unfortunately, bridge the gender gap is perceived as a challenge for such a specialized field. Only 14% of startup founders in the world are female, yet it is a business concentrated in specific cities in the world.) [48].

Figure 8 shows the number of startups that present at least a woman as founder, per country, among the ten countries with more startups in the eorld [49, 50].

Figure 8 shows that, on average, women founded around 20% of the startups in these countries. India is the country counting with more female participation in this market as founders of a startup company, being 45%, while Indonesia presents the lowest female participation as startups founders (2%), followed by China, where women founded 3% of the existing companies there. These number agree with the percentage of women listed as inventors in patent applications, as previously discussed (Section 3.2).

Considering that most startups are related to innovative business and products, in the technology field, it is expected that successful startups also present a vast intellectual property portfolio for two main reasons: it proves to investors that the business is serious and supported by a good idea and intellectual property portfolio also ensures a reliable asset that means value to the startup. Therefore, if women are similarly participating in intellectual property production and protection and in company launching, it may indicate that those women have access to more information and better training in technological fields, as well as having information about the business. Moreover, it also means that they understand their role in the technological development around the world, and they are seeking to have their adequate share of it.

Moreover, many well-funded startups failed in 2017; some examples are Jawbone, Juicero, Sprig, Beepi, Yik Yak, Quixey, and Luxe, which together had raised more than US$ 1 billion and yet, failed. It is interesting that also in 2017, female participation in patent applications via PCT had dropped. This may be related to a misinterpretation of the market needs for new technologies, which is also a reason for startup closures. However, startups are a risky business, and it is still unknown the effect that failure might have on female participation acceptance in such field. Most of the startups fail within a year, due to many factors, among them, lack of funding, lack of skills, and market misinterpretation. However, those that succeed and ultimately become unicorns are investing in their intellectual property portfolio and that is a strong reason for more and more women to seek information on intellectual property system worldwide.

4. Conclusion

Despite the lack of data enduring the efforts of women to preserve and disseminate the traditional knowledge of their people, it is perceived among all cultures that they play a crucial role to that. However, their significant contribution is not often recognized and, in most cultures and regions, women lack opportunities to create new products based on their knowledge, produce them, and profit from their efforts. It is not offered to them the same opportunities of training, knowledge, and working as men worldwide, as it is shown by the available data on women contribution to the work force in many countries.

Also, related to that is the lack of women's representation as inventors in patents. Its correlation to the innovation production points out that women are not innovating in the same degree as men. Or they do not know the intellectual property system as well as they do.

In addition, the same contribution women provide as inventors is identified as founders of startups, companies that as mostly based in technological breakthroughs. Therefore, these data evidenced that much has to be done to bridge the gender gap and that it must focus on several critical issues such as education, family aid, and policies to instigate women to achieve their place in the innovative world. They also provide evidence that promoting information dissemination about intellectual property related to the knowledge of women in their environments is an efficient mechanism to provide gender equity and equal collaboration in a country's economic and social development.

If women were so encouraged to value their knowledge and protect them as men are, much of the wasted intellectual abilities could be well used to provide direct development, as we can see by considering the relation between patent application by women and their ability to be part of startups, a very risky business, that needs courage and knowledge to be fostered and that can be the driving force to a fast economic development, especially in developing countries.

Data also show that many have improved in the last years, despite the COVID-19 pandemic effect, and women are getting more access to higher education and, therefore, have found working positions similar to men in many places. Women's qualification is thought to be improving which, in addition, may indicate that the path toward equity is being created over secure and consistent strategies of providing as quality education as support to families, in order to promote their effective participation in the labor market in a sustainable way.

It may be too soon to say that the world is coming to equity, and it is still far from the goal to be achieved by 2030, but the intellectual property has proven to be an important driving force to promote education, training, and opportunities for women to be as active as men in the labor market and to incentive women to this endeavor and to be a good indicator to follow the evolvement of such endeavor.

Conflict of interest

The authors declare no conflict of interest.

Author details

Tatiana Ertner*, Diericon Cordeiro, Ramon Miranda and Lucas Aguiar
Chemistry Institute, Federal University of Goias, Goiânia, Brazil

*Address all correspondence to: tatiana@ufg.br

References

[1] Gebru A. The global protection of traditional knowledge: Searching for the minimum consensus. John Marshall Review of Intellectual. Property Law. 2017;**17**:42-91

[2] Dagne T. Protecting traditional knowledge in international intellectual property law: Imperatives for protection and choice of modalities. John Marshall Review of Intellectual Property Law. 2014;**14**:25-49

[3] Gazizova AS. Protection of traditional knowledge: The work and the role of international organisations and conferences. International Journal of Higher Education. 2020;**9**(8):95-99. DOI: 10.5430/ijhe.v9n8p95

[4] Kumar NV. Protection of traditional knowledge: International and National Initiatives and possible ways ahead. SSRN. 2012;**2012**:38. DOI: 10.2139/ssrn.2012724

[5] Hossain K, Ballardini RM. Protecting indigenous traditional knowledge through a holistic principle-based approach. Nordic Journal of Human Rights. 2021;**39**(1):51-72. DOI: 10.1080/18918131.2021.1947449

[6] Porter A. Where are the Women? The Gender Gap within Intellectual Property Allie Porter Texas Intellectual Property Law Journal. 2019;**28**:511-531

[7] Mickelson RA. Why does Jane read and write so well? The anomaly of women's achievement. Sociology of Education. 1989;**62**:47-63

[8] Huyer S. Is the gender gap narrowing in science and engineering?, Chapter 3 in UNESCO Science Report: towards 2030. 2015; chapter 3:85-103. Available from: https://unesdoc.unesco.org/ark:/48223/pf0000235447 [Accessed: December 26, 2022]

[9] Jacobs JA. Gender inequality and higher education. Annual Review of Sociology. 1996;**1996**(22):153-185

[10] Vasconcelos RM. Sui Generis Protection of Traditional Knowledge of Indigenous Peoples of the Amazon. Brisbane, Australia: University of Queensland; 2007

[11] Brazil, Federal Law 13.123/2015 (Biodiversity law)

[12] Hasse G, Bruch K L, Stelzer J. Institutionalizing Biopiracy: Analysis of the Benefit-Sharing Rules in the Brazilian Biodiversity Law. Law, Environment and Development Journal. 2021;17:15. Available from: http://www.lead-journal.org/content/a1707.pdf [Accessed: January 3, 2023]

[13] OseiTutu JJ. Emerging scholars series: A sui generis regime for traditional knowledge: The cultural divide in intellectual property law. Marquette Intellectual Property Law Reviews. 2011;**15**:147-215

[14] Romero TL. Sui generis Systems for the Protection of traditional knowledge. International Law: Revista Colombiana de Derecho Internacional. 2005;**6**:301-339

[15] WIPO/GRTKF/IC/43/INF/7 ORIGINAL: ENGLISH DATE: APRIL 4, 2022 Intergovernmental Committee on Intellectual Property and Genetic Resources, Traditional Knowledge and Folklore Forty-Third Session Geneva, May 30 to June 3, 2022

[16] Kariyawasam K, Guy S. Intellectual property protection of indigenous

knowledge: Implementing initiatives at national and regional levels. Deakin Law Review. 2007;**12**(2):105-127. DOI: /10.21153/dlr2007vol12no2art222

[17] Montanari B, Bergh SI. Why women's traditional knowledge matters in the production processes of natural product development: The case of the Green Morocco Plan. Women's Studies International Forum. 2019;77:102275-10211p. DOI: 10.1016/j.wsif.2019.102275

[18] Convention of Biodiversity. The Role of Indigenous Women In the Transmission of Traditional Knowledge. 2022. Available from: https://www.cbd.int/article/role-indigenous-women-transmission-traditional-knowledge-IDWIP2022 [Accessed: December 18, 2022]

[19] Statement: Indigenous women play a vital role in the preservation and transmission of traditional knowledge. UN Women statement on the occasion of the International Day of the World's Indigenous Peoples, 9 August 2022. Available from: https://www.unwomen.org/en/news-stories/statement/2022/08/statement-indigenous-women-play-a-vital-role-in-the-preservation-and-transmission-of-traditional-knowledge [Accessed: December 26, 2022]

[20] Food and Agriculture Organization of the United Nations. Indigenous women, daughters of Mother Earth. 2020. Available from: https://www.fao.org/3/cb0719en/CB0719EN.pdf [Accessed: December 26, 2022]

[21] UN Women, Turning Promises into Action: Gender Equality in the 2030 Agenda for Sustainable Development. 2018. Available from: https://www.unwomen.org/en/digital-library/publications/2018/2/gender-equality-in-the-2030-agenda-for-sustainable-development-2018 [Accessed: December 26, 2023]

[22] International Labour Organization (ILO). World Employment and Social Outlook: Trends for Women 2018: Global Snapshot. 2018. Available from: http://www.ilo.org/wcmsp5/groups/public/---dgreports/---dcomm/---publ/documents/publication/wcms_619577.pdf

[23] UN Secretary General's High Level Panel on Women's Economic Empowerment, Leave No One Behind: A Call to Action for Gender Equality and Women's Economic Empowerment. 2016. Available from: https://www.empowerwomen.org/-/media/files/un%20women/empowerwomen/resources/hlp%20briefs/unhlp%20full%20report.pdf?la=en

[24] World Bank. Women, Business and the Law 2018. 2018. Available from: http://wbl.worldbank.org/

[25] Lioudis, N. The Collapse of Lehman Brothers: A Case Study Investopedia. 2021. Available from: https://www.investopedia.com/articles/economics/09/lehman-brothers-collapse.asp [Accessed: January 9, 2023]

[26] Chadha P. What Caused the Failure of Lehman Brothers? Could it have been Prevented? How? Recommendations for Going Forward. International Journal of Accounting Research. 2016;**2016**:S1-S5. DOI: 10.4172/2472-114X.S1-002

[27] Fleming MJ, Sarkar A. The failure resolution of Lehman Brothers. FRBNY Economic Policy Review. 2014;**20**:175-206

[28] Mawutor JKM. The Failure of Lehman Brothers: Causes, Preventive Measures and Recommendations. Research Journal of Finance and Accounting. 2014;**5**:85-91

[29] Brenke K. Growing Importance of Women in the German Labor Market. DIW Bulletin. 2015;**5**:51-61

[30] Caki E. The plight of female employment in Germany under school-related COVID-19 control measures. Working paper No. 3. CoronaNet Research Project. Available from: https://econpapers.repec.org/RePEc:ayl:wpaper:202204 [Accessed: January 9, 2023]

[31] ECLAC The COVID-19 Pandemic Has Caused a Setback of over a Decade in Labor Market Participation for Women in the Region. 2021. Available from: https://www.cepal.org/pt-br/comunicados/pandemia-covid-19-gerou-retrocesso-mais-decada-niveis-participacao-mercado-trabalho [Accessed: January 9, 2023].

[32] ECLAC_United Nations. The economic autonomy of women in a sustainable recovery with equality. 2021. Available from: https://www.cepal.org/en/publications/46634-economic-autonomy-women-sustainable-recovery-equality [Accessed: January 9, 2023]

[33] OECD Statistics. Available from: https://stats.oecd.org/viewhtml.aspx?datasetcode=LFS_SEXAGE_I_R&lang=en# [Accessed: January 6, 2023]

[34] Yellen J L. The history of women's work and wages and how it has created success for us all. The Brooking Gender Equality Series. 2020 .Available from: https://www.brookings.edu/essay/the-history-of-womens-work-and-wages-and-how-it-has-created-success-for-us-all [Accessed: January 9, 2023]

[35] U.S. CENSUS. Aging Boomers Solve a Labor Market Puzzle. 2021. Available from: https://www.census.gov/library/stories/2021/06/why-did-labor-force-participation-rate-decline-when-economy-was-good.html [Accessed: January 9, 2023]

[36] WIPO Patent Information Services for Developing Countries. WIPO Publication No. 493(E) ISBN 92-805-1085-9. Available from: https://www.wipo.int/edocs/pubdocs/en/wipo_pub_493.pdf [Accessed: January 9, 2023]

[37] The World Bank and it is available under Creative Commons license (CC. BY.4.0), from the WIPO Patent Report: Statistics on Worldwide Patent Activity Available from: https://data.worldbank.org/indicator/IP.PAT.RESD [Accessed: December 12, 2022]

[38] Status of Women in the States. State Data. 2018. Available from: https://statusofwomendata.org/explore-the-data/state-data/united-states/ [Accessed: December 27, 2022]

[39] Kumar D, Ruby. Women Workers in the Unorganized Sector. International Journal of Research and Analytical Reviews. 2021;**3**:5-10

[40] Martin H. Stagnating female employment rates in France after several decades of growth. Population and Societies. 2022;**606**:4. DOI: 10.3917/popsoc.606.0001

[41] Martin H. 2022, changes in labor force participation and employment rates across successive cohorts in France. Population. 2022;**77**(1):137-154. DOI: /10.3917/popu.2201.0141

[42] KOLMAR. Average Paid Maternity Leave In The US [2022]: US Maternity Leave Statistics. Published in: 2022-09-12. Available from: https://www.zippia.com/advice/average-paid-maternity-leave/ [Accessed: January 17, 2023]

[43] Think Tank. Maternity and Paternity Leave in the EU | Think Tank | European

Parliament. 2022. Available from: https://www.europarl.europa.eu/thinktank/en/document/EPRS_ATA(2022)698892 [Accessed: January 9, 2023]

[44] Donnelly D. Quick Guide to Parental Leave in Asia. Horizons. Published in: 2022-08-08. Available from: https://nhglobalpartners.com/parental-leave-in-asia/. [Accessed: January 9, 2023]

[45] Data provided by WIPO Intellectual property data center available from: https://www3.wipo.int/ipstats/pmhindex.htm?tab=pct [Accessed: January 12, 2023]

[46] WIPO. Women's participation in international patent applications in 2021. Available from: http://www.wipo.int/women-and-ip [Accessed: January 10, 2023]

[47] WIPO. PCT Yearly Review from 2011 until 2022. Available from: https://www.wipo.int/pct/en/activity/index.html [Accessed: January 10, 2023]

[48] Global Startup Ecosystem Report 2020 of the Global Entrepreneurship Network – Genome Startup. 2020. Available from: https://startupgenome.com/reports/gser2020 [Accessed: January 10, 2023]

[49] Data collected from several sources, as listed: Data sources and accessed in 2023-01-10; https://www.enterprisenation.com/learn-something/record-proportion-uk-start-ups-created-by-women/; https://www.moneycontrol.com/news/business/startup/india-has-50000-recognised-startups-45-have-women-entrepreneurs-6984031.htm;l https://www.crunchbase.com/hub/canada-startups-female-founders; https://www.demandsage.com/startup-statistics/; https://abstartups.com.br/onde-estao-as-mulheres-do-ecossistema-de-startups/; https://novobrief.com/spanish-startup-founders/7311/; https://novobrief.com/startups-founded-by-women-attracted-only-1-8-of-the-investment-in-europe/9706/#:~:text=According%20to%20data%20from%20the,6%25%20are%20founded%20by%20women; https://www.statista.com/topics/7033/startups-in-france/#topicOverview; https://www.startbase.com/downloads/female-founder-report/2021/female-founder-report.min.pdf; https://theproductguy.co/number-of-indonesian-startup-founded-by-women/; https://startupmuster.com/reports/Startup-Muster-2018-Report.pdf?key=e0e49024981e6d12568d946c8ba01658e625eb3fdf2989108740b5f452217d89 https://www.crunchbase.com/hub/china-startups-female-founders

[50] Simpson CK. What caused the failure of Lehman brothers? Could it have been prevented? How? Recommendations for going forward. International Journal of Research and Review. 2016;**3**(11):16-31

Chapter 10

New IP and Standardization Practices in China's Data-Centric Digital Economy

Yu Uny Cao and Hu Wang

Abstract

China's digital economy accounts for almost half of its GDP and recent national planning aims to grow it by leveraging data as a key factor of production. To facilitate this, government agencies, enterprises, and service providers are creating rules and piloting new ideas such as Data Intellectual Property and Data Factorization. They are also developing IP registry standards and providing incentives and regulations for data factorization, data intellectual property, data assets, and other data-related components of the digital economy. Since 2019 the activities have picked up paces with multiple provinces and cities competing for first-in-the-nation statuses. It appears China is leading the world in a number of innovations in the coming data-centric economy.

Keywords: digital economy, data as a factor of production, data assets, data intellectual property, data-centric digital economy

1. Introduction

On January 1, 2023, Zhejiang Province in eastern China implemented the *Zhejiang Province Intellectual Property Protection and Promotion Regulation*, a landmark law that is widely watched by practitioners in governments and industries because of its first-in-the-nation provisions regarding "data intellectual property." The *Regulation* defines "data intellectual property" as "data after certain algorithmic processing, possessing both practical value and intellectual achievement attributes, which can be protected in a pan-intellectual-property manner via methods including evidence preservation, and registration." The *Regulation* also requires provincial agencies to make concrete progress by mid-2023 in scaling up existing technology platforms for data intellectual property's evidence preservation and creating an official registrar for data intellectual property.

That is just one activity among the numerous initiatives in new rules, trials and practices in the areas of intellectual property, standards, IP financing, and data transactions that are being carried out by government agencies, service providers, and enterprises, in the drive to building a data-centric digital economy, where data are elevated as a key factor of production.

2. Digital economy features prominently in China's economy

2.1 A large and vibrant digital economy in China

Since the 18th National Congress of the Communist Party in 2012, China has attached great importance to the development of its digital economy and has raised it to the level of a national strategy. In the past decade, China's digital economy achieved remarkable results and attracted global attention. According to the *Report on the Development of the Digital Economy* submitted by the National Development and Reform Commission to the National People's Congress in October 2022, China has made great strides in "digital industrialization" and "digitization of many industries," and the nation has promoted the vigorous development of the digital economy, realized the leapfrog development of digital infrastructure, accelerated the improvement of digital industry's innovation capacity, accelerated transformation in digitization of industries, deepened the digitalization of public services, and continuously improved the level of network security and digital economy's governance, laying a solid foundation for digital economic international cooperation in digital economy.

China's digital economy has been the world's second largest for many years. According to China Academy of Information and Communications Technology [1], from 2012 to 2021 China's digital economy grew from 1.1 trillion to more than 4.5 trillion yuan, and the proportion of digital economy to GDP increased from 21.6 to 39.8%. The size of digital industrialization has reached 8.4 trillion yuan, and the development of digitization of industries has entered an accelerated track, arriving at 37.2 trillion yuan.

A digital economy requires computing power as a key foundation, and the scale of China's computing power industry has grown rapidly in the past 5 years, with an average annual growth rate of more than 30%. At the end of June 2022, China's total computing power exceeded 15,000 gigaflops per second, ranking second in the world. In February 2022, China's "Digital Eastern and Computing Western" project (namely, eastern China focuses on all things digital, and western China on computing power) was officially launched and became a "numeric artery" to link economic and social development in the east and west.

To help frame the understanding of China's digital economy, China Academy of Information and Communications Technology proposed that a digital economy consists of four parts [1]: (1) digital industrialization; (2) digitization of industries; (3) digital governance; and (4) data valorization. The Academy in its report further illuminated the following:

1. Digital industrialization continues to strengthen. In 2021, China's digital industrialization reached 8.4 trillion yuan, which increased by 11.9% year-on-year, accounting for 7.3% of the GDP. Among its components, ICT (Information and Communications Technology) services further consolidated its leading position in digital industrialization, and the software industry and Internet industry continued to increase their proportions.

2. Digitization of industries has entered an accelerated track. In 2021, China's digitization of industries reached 37.2 trillion yuan, a year-on-year nominal increase of 17.2%, and a proportion of 32.5% of the GDP. Industries have fully recognized the importance of developing digital economy, and Industry Internet in particular has become the core methodology of manufacturing digital transformation,

service industry digital transformation continues to be active, and agricultural digital transformation has achieved initial results.

3. Digital governance is being built up. China's digital governance is undergoing a profound transformation from governing using digital technology to governing digital technology and further onto constructing a governance system for the digital economy. Digital government construction is accelerating, and the construction of new smart cities is progressing steadily.

4. Data valorization sees deepening exploration of data's value. The process of data resourceization based on the life-cycle value management chain of data collection, labeling, analysis, and storage, is continuously advancing. The exploration of data assetization is gradually deepening, the question of data right is progressing in the top-level planning, and data pricing, transaction, circulation, and other issues are being explored.

2.2 Digital economy empowers other parts of the economy

As observed everywhere else, digital economy in China is enhancing other aspects of the general economy. This is unsurprising, since digital economy and many other aspects of the economy are knowledge-intensive, and the endogenous economic growth theory proposed by Paul Romer [2] and other scholars explains this well.

Taking green economy as an example, we can observe how digital economy is beneficial and understand the importance of having a well-developed digital economy.

It can be seen that the development of China's green economy in recent years has benefited from the digital economy, and practices in digitization of industries, data valorization, and digital governance have added to the green economy. Studies have shown that, on the one hand, the development indicators of digital economy and green economy are highly coupled [3], and on the other hand, the promotion of digital governance to green economy development can be verified by statistical models.

Research also shows that the mechanisms of digital economy empowering the green economy can be divided into the direct and indirect effects: (1) the direct effect mechanism: Digital economy connects the whole process of production, distribution, exchange, and consumption in tandem, which reduces transaction costs and information search costs, and therefore, enhances the efficiency of the green economy; (2) the indirect effect mechanism: By optimizing the upgrading of existing green industrial structure, improving the level of technological innovation, and raising the extent of free market, digital economy enhances the efficiency of the green economy [4].

Is the empowerment observable? The answer from academia is affirmative. For example, using statistical methods, a series of robustness tests were conducted and the conclusion was drawn [4], that digital economy had significantly promoted the efficiency of green economy; furthermore, through the regression statistical method of different dimensions, it was concluded that between digitization of industries and digital industrialization, the latter had a stronger promotion effect on the efficiency of green economy.

There are many cases in which digital industrialization empowers green economy, leading to energy saving and emission reduction in complex scenarios in carbon-peak/carbon-neutral efforts [5]. An ideal energy network has multiple demands, features multiple sources of energy, and requires orderly configuration to form a smart energy system; it is precisely in this field that the achievements of digital industry are remarkable in directly benefiting the green economy; for example, Yitong Group, the first company in China to promote digital energy-saving services, deployed a complete "Building Equipment Monitoring and Energy Management System" at the high-speed rail station in the new city of Xiong'an, connecting hundreds of sensors, thousands pieces of equipment and various information systems, storing and analyzing more than 3 billion pieces of data annually, and achieving more than 20% energy efficiency.

3. A recent national strategy: building a digital economy "with data as the key factor"

China appears to have the first-mover advantage to build "a digital economy with data as the key factor of production."

A decade ago, a comprehensive report [6] by World Bank and China's top planners outlined number factors of production, and ways to improving them, in order for furthering the Chinese economy.

In October 2019, the *Decision of the Fourth Plenary Session of the 19th Central Committee of the Communist Party of China* added "data" as a factor of production, reflecting the increasingly prominent role of data in improving production efficiency as the digital transformation of economic activities accelerates [7]. In 2020, a top national planning document [8] lists data, as a factor of production, alongside the more traditional four factors (land, labor, capital, technology), while promoting a market-driving mechanism for allocating these five factors.

Under the umbrella of "a digital economy with data as the key factor," China's digital economy is shifting from the traditional elements such as digital industrialization and digital governance to the emerging elements such as data factorization, data intellectual property, and so on. And looking around the world, China is among the earliest, if not the earliest, in deploying data factorization, data intellectual property, and data supervision, in light of the shift.

3.1 Progress in data factorization

Mei Hong, a prominent computer scientist and university administer, proposed that [9] "data factorization is the process of establishing data as an important productive factor and making it participate in social production and operation activities through various means."

We, in the context of the continuous development of the concept of data factorization, from the point of view of data factor's utility, propose that data factorization contains at least the following: (1) producing data with compliance; (2) creating data intellectual property; (3) pricing and trading of data.

Once data are considered as a factor of production, a series of problems need to be solved, solidifying the connotation of the concept of data factorization. Mei Hong proposed the following as core of data factorization: (1) data resourceization, (2) data assetization, and (3) capitalization of data. On the same topic, Qiao Han and Huang Chaochun proposed [6] that (1) to strengthen the supply of high-quality data elements, (2) to accelerate the market circulation of data elements, and (3) to innovate the development and utilization mechanism of data elements. China Academy of Information and Communications Technology proposed [10] solving four existing problems: (1) The ownership of data rights is difficult to define, (2) there is no easy basis for data valuation and pricing, (3) the regulations and rules for data circulation are not perfect, and (4) the technology for data circulation is still immature. WeBank proposed [11] that for data to qualify was a factor of production, it also needs to meet the four basic conditions that are shared by the traditional four factors of production, the four conditions being the following: a property that can be defined, its value can be evaluated, the value can be circulated, and the value can be stored.

3.2 Trading of data factor: China among the world's earliest

We believe that in a data-centric digital economy which elevates data to a factor of production, the trading of data factor reflects the sophistication of the said digital economy. In this regard, China has acted early and done many pilot projects, and is leading the world in experience. Since 2014, China has built many "Big Data" exchanges (exemplified by the Guiyang Big Data Exchange), and over time, newer exchanges have shifted into "Data" exchange (exemplified by the Shanghai Data Exchange). According to information collected by the authors, which might be less than 100% complete, as of October 2022, a total of 46 data exchanges (centers) have been established or are planned to be established across China, see **Table 1**.

Among the newer ones, the Shanghai Data Exchange represents the latest trend. On November 25, 2021, the Shanghai Data Exchange was established, as an important measure to promote the circulation of data factor, release digital dividends, and promote the development of the digital economy. According to Zhang Qi, Chair of the company, the development of data assets is the path to maximize the value of the digital economy and achieve the optimal allocation of data resources. Shanghai Data Exchange actively promotes the leap from data resources to assets.

Shanghai Data Exchange is committed to creating a new data business model that is composed of technology and service providers in the data circulation process, connecting more than 500 data merchants, including data compliance assessment service providers, data quality assessment service providers, data asset assessment service providers, data delivery service providers, data classification, and rating service providers,

No.	Date of Establishment	Name	Location
1	2014	Zhongguancun Shuhai Big Date Trading Service Platform	Beijing
2		Beijing Big Data Traffic Service Platform	Beijing
3		Hong Kong Big Data Exchange	Hongkong
4	2015	Guiyang Big Data Exchange	Guiyang, Guizhou
5		East China Jiangsu Big Data Trading Center	Yancheng
6		Wuhan East Lake Big Data Trading Center	Wuhan, Hubei
7		Wuhan Yangtze River Big Data Trading Center	Wuhan, Hubei
8		Central China Big Data Exchange	Wuhan, Hubei
9		Chongqing Big Data Trading Platform	Chongqing
10		Xixian New District Big Data Exchange	Xi;'an, Shaanxi
11		Traffic Big Data Trading Platform	Shenzhen, Guangdong
12		Hebei Big Data Trading Center	Chengde, Hebei
13		Hangzhou Qiantang Big Data Trading Center	Hangzhou, Zhejiang

No.	Date of Establishment	Name	Location
14	2016	Shanghai Data Trading Center	Shanghai
15		Zhejiang Big Data Trading Center	Hangzhou, Zhejiang
16		Harbin Data Trading Center	Harbin, Heilongjiang
17		Silk Road Brilliance Big Data Trading Center	Lanzhou, Gansu
18		Guangzhou Data Trading Service Platform	Guangzhou, Guangdong
19		Asia-Europe Big Data Trading Center	Urumqi, Xinjiang
20		Southern Big Data Trading Center	Shenzhen, Guangdong
21	2017	Qingdao Big Data Trading Center	Qingdao, Shandong
22		Henan Plains Big Data Trading Center	Xinxiang, Henan
23		Henan Zhongyuan Big Data Trading Center	Zhengzhou, Henan
24	2018	Northeast Asia Big Data Transaction Service Center	Changchun, Jilin
25	2019	Shandong Data Trading Platform	Jinan, Shandong
26	2020	Anhui Big Data Trading Center	Huainan, Anhui
27		Beibu Gulf Big Data Trading Center	Nanning, Guangxi
28		Shanxi Data Trading Platform	Taiyuan, Shanxi
29		Zhongguancun Medical and Health Big Data Trading Platform	Beijing
30	2021	Beijing International Big Data Exchange	Beijing
31		Guizhou Province Data Circulation Transaction Service Center	Guiyang, Guizhou
32		Northern Big Data Trading Center	Tianjin
33		Shanghai Data Exchange	Shanghai
34		South China International Data Trading Company	Foshan, Guangdong
35		Western Data Trading Center	Chongqing
36		Shenzhen Data Exchange	Shenzhen, Guangdong
37		Hefei Data Factor Circulation Platform	Hefei, Anhui
38		Deyang Data Trading Center	Deyang, Sichuan
39		Yangtze River Delta Data Factor Circulation Service Platform	Suzhou, Jiangsu
40		Hainan Data Product Supermarket	Haikou, Hainan
41	2022	Hunan Big Data Exchange	Changsha, Hunan
42		Wuxi Big Data Trading Platform	Wuxi, Jiangsu
43		Fujian Big Data Exchange	Fuzhou, Fujian
44		Guangdong Data Exchange	Guangzhou, Guangdong
45		Qingdao Ocean Data Trading Platform	Qingdao, Shandong
46		Zhengzhou Data Trading Center	Zhengzhou, Henan

Table 1.
As of October 2022, as many as 46 data exchanges (centers) have been established or are planned to be established across the country.

data security service providers, data consulting service providers, data governance service providers, and data intermediary service providers.

3.3 China leading the world in experimenting "data intellectual property"

The World Intellectual Property Organization (WIPO) in 2019 launched a conference series, *WIPO Conversation on Intellectual Property (IP) and Frontier Technologies*, which is to be held two to three times a year. The original idea is that cutting-edge technologies offer opportunities for economic growth, and in order for all to seize these opportunities, there is the need to ensure that the IP system continues to foster innovation and creativity, and to ensure that the system of IP administration continues to evolve.

While the first three sessions all talked about the relationship between intellectual property and artificial intelligence (AI), the fourth session (held in September 2021) changed to Data: *Data: Beyond AI in a fully interconnected world*. In his opening remarks, the Director General emphasized that frontier technologies currently represent a $350 billion market that could become a $3.2 trillion market as soon as 2025, and specifically, if digitalization is the engine of the future economy, then data are its fuel. More than 1000 experts from 113 countries discussed a wide range of topics over the 2 days of the Conversation, with two major topics: (1) What are data and why are they so important in the digital economy to build awareness and understanding; and (2) How do data fit into the current global intellectual property system and whether these current rules are sufficient. During the dialog, experts noted that the IP framework is based on social policies that encourage creativity and compensate for the investment required to produce inventions, that under the current IP framework, patents protect useful innovations with industrial applications, that trademarks are the backbone of branding, and that copyright protects the original expression of an idea, not the idea itself; and all three can be applied to data.

While WIPO in September 2021 conducted a conversation on "Data and Intellectual Property," China's development of a system of "Data Intellectual Property" was clarified in State Council's October 2021 *"14th Five-Year Period" National Intellectual Property Protection and Utilization Plan*.

Since the Plan, implementation trials have been carried out in Zhejiang province, Shanghai, and Shenzhen. In Zhejiang province, from September 2021 to 2022, "data intellectual property pledge" in IP financing, and "data intellectual property trading" were piloted in the city of Hangzhou.

3.4 Data supervision and enterprises' data resourceization

At present, new business models with data as a core production factor continue to emerge, and more and more industries are collecting, generating, and using data at all times. The generation of massive amounts of data is becoming an important strategic resource for the future development of enterprises. At the same time, the regulation and compliance review on data are also getting more and more attention. It can be said that data have stepped into the era of strong governmental supervision.

In recent years, the Standing Committee of the National People's Congress has enacted relevant laws and regulations. Among them,

- The *Cybersecurity Law of the People's Republic of China*, which came into force on June 1, 2017, is a comprehensive legislation to protect network security, safeguard the sovereignty of cyberspace and national security, and social public interests, protect the legitimate rights and interests of citizens, legal persons, and other organizations, and promote the healthy development of economic and social informatization. The law's Chapter 4 "Network Information Security" from Article 40 through Article 50 regulates the activities of network operators in terms of data collection, processing, and use, as well as the corresponding obligations and responsibilities they should assume.

- January 1, 2019 saw the implementation of the *Electronic Commerce Law*, as a special legislation to regulate e-commerce activities. The law includes Article 23 that specifically provides that "e-commerce operators collect and use the personal information of its users, shall comply with the laws and administrative regulations on the protection of personal information provisions."

- The *Data Security Law*, which took effect on September 1, 2021, is a fundamental law in the field of data security in China. The law specifies the rules of data processing activities and data security protection obligations, which will strongly enhance the national data security protection capability and the governance capability of the digital economy.

- The *Personal Information Protection Law*, which went into effect November 1, 2021, is a special legislation that serves as the overall leading law in the protection of personal information. The law has established a system framework of clear rights and responsibilities, effective protection, and standardized use of personal information processing and protection, providing a clear legal basis for personal information processing activities and ample protection for the protection of personal information rights and interests.

In the context of strong regulation of data security, enterprise data compliance is also facing stricter requirements, so that more and more companies are subject to various types of punishment for data non-compliance. As of June 1, 2022, the Ministry of Industry and Information Technology had issued a total of 24 batches of "notifications on apps in infringement of user rights and interests," targeting (mobile) apps that have done irregular collection, misuse of user personal information, and even harassment of users, and thousands of such apps were demanded to be rectified. Notably, apps from major companies, such as WeChat, Douyin, Kuaishou, and C-trip were all found to have done illegal or irregular collection of users' personal information, and the administration continues to maintain high pressure to deter data violations. Large fines for non-compliant management of corporate data, such as the 8.026 billion yuan administrative penalty imposed on DiDi Rideshare by the State Internet Information Office, are ringing alarm bells. Enterprises who have been enjoying the dividends brought by data resources may find themselves looking at data as liabilities.

In these stricter regulatory situations, enterprises much do a god job in data risk identification and prevention before they can gain by data resourceization.

4. A four-part framework for understanding the data-centric digital economy

At a time when the digital economy is turning into a "digital economy with data as the key factor," it is the right time to further clarify the enablement mechanism of the

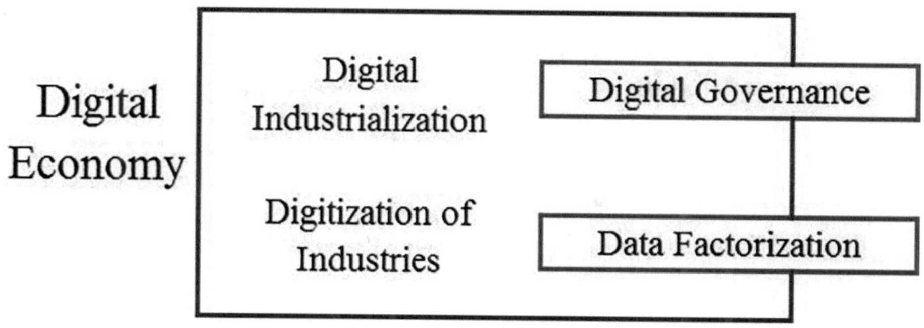

Figure 1.
A four-part framework for a data-centric digital economy.

digital economy for the development other parts of the economy, in order to achieve a new round of more effective empowerment.

We start with a framework [1] proposed by the China Academy of Information and Communications Technology: The "four-part framework" of the digital economy provides a useful overview of the main components of the digital economy: (1) Digital industrialization, which includes ICT services, the software industry, and the Internet industry; (2) Digitization of industries, which uses digital technology to achieve digital transformation of manufacturing, services, agriculture, and deeper digital governance; (4) Data valorization, which involves creating resources from data (data resourceization), data assetization, data identification, as well as data pricing, trading, and circulation downstream.

The Academy further points out that data valorization continues to deepen in various aspects. The process of data resourceization based on the life cycle value management chain of data collection, labeling, analysis, and storage is deepening. The exploration of data assetization is gradually deepening, data rights are orderly promoted in the top-level planning, and the exploration of data pricing and transaction flow is restarted, ushering in a new round of construction boom.

We argue that now that the digital economy has turned to the new stage of "data as the key factor of production," it is time to replace data valorization "data factorization." thus a updated four-part framework befitting the new landscape, see **Figure 1**.

5. Policies, practices, and innovations in data, IP, and standardization

5.1 IP securitization empowers high-tech enterprises

Intellectual Property Asset-backed Securities (ABS) is aimed at high-tech enterprises who own high-value intellectual property rights, which can turn the intangible assets of enterprises into visible capital to feed enterprises' R&D.

For example, in September 2022, the third intellectual property securitization product in Foshan City, Guangdong Province, the "*Xingye Yuanrong – Foshan Yaoda Patent License 3 Asset Support Special Plan*" was successfully issued with an issue amount of 367 million RMB, AAA debt rating, and an issue interest rate of 2.9%, which was a historical low for IPR ABS issue rate of similar terms in China. Foshan's intellectual property securitization products have benefited a dozen enterprises; for example, Guangdong Yin Yang Environmental Protection Company, an environmental protection chemical manufacturing company with good technologies, faces rapid product iteration and high product R&D costs, participated in Foshan's intellectual property securitization products twice in 2021 and 2022, raising RMB 20 million and RMB 12 million, respectively.

Over the years, governments at all levels have promoted intellectual property finance, in which intellectual property securitization has increasingly been recognized and achieved considerable growth. According to the Economic Daily [12], as of late August 2022, Shanghai and Shenzhen Stock Exchanges had successfully issued 65 intellectual property securitization products with an issue size of 15.8 billion yuan, further enriching intellectual property financing channels. Products have been issued in many cities, including Guangzhou, Shenzhen, Shanghai, Beijing, Hangzhou, Zhejiang province, and Changsha, Hunan province.

Intellectual property securitization is designed by financial institutions, in collaboration with industry experts, to turn specific assets of a company into securities. The outstanding advantage of intellectual property securitization is the larger scale of financing. One important type of intellectual property securitization is patent securitization, which is highly suitable for the characteristics of hard-tech enterprises. China's first "pure patent" securitization product was issued on the Shenzhen Stock Exchange in September 2019, providing a total of $301 million in financing for 11 high-tech private enterprises in the Guangzhou Development Zone, and the product was successfully closed in August 2022 and thus fully validated.

The outstanding difficulty of patent securitization is the poor stability of the predictable cash income flow of the patent as the underlying asset. During the years of successful practices, China's intellectual property finance industry has developed effective tools such as "patent twice-licensing model," "formation of intellectual property portfolio, risk reduction," and establishment of project managers for intellectual property securitization projects.

5.2 Data intellectual property pledge empowers enterprises

In September 2021, China's first data intellectual property pledge was completed in Hangzhou, Zhejiang Province. Led by the local Market Supervision and Intellectual Property Bureau, the pilot gathered multiple parties including government agencies, banks, insurance institutions, data companies, etc. Using big data, blockchain, and other technical means, the pilot collected all kinds of data in the production and operation chain of enterprises, and the blockchain evidence-preservation platform issued evidence-preservation certificates to turn the data into data intellectual property rights that can be issued, and finally, based on the data intellectual property rights, the enterprises received bank credits.

Two companies benefited from this first-in-the-nation pilot. One of them is UEFL (Zhejiang) Technology Company, which provides environmental measurement data generated from garbage classification activities. The data's credit is enhanced by Hangzhou High-Tech Financing Guarantee Co., Ltd. and the company was finally granted a credit of 5 million yuan by the Science and Technology Sub-Branch of Bank of Hangzhou.

The pilot in data IP pledge was executed in the following main steps: (1) Receiving the data. The public evidence-preservation platform of Zhejiang IP blockchain receives the data and synchronizes it to Zhejiang Intellectual Property Research and Service Center, the provincial Market Supervision Bureau, Hangzhou Internet Notary Office, and Hangzhou Internet Court; (2) Hosting the data. It is hosted by the big

DOI: http://dx.doi.org/10.5772/intechopen.1001432

data center of Hangzhou Ace Information Technology Co., Ltd.; (3) Confirm the data chain. Zhejiang Intellectual Property Research and Service Center confirms the data chain verification results and issues the "Data Intellectual Property Public Evidence-Preservation Certificate"; (4) Credit granting. Banks and other institution issue credits to the enterprises after receiving the "Data Intellectual Property Public Evidence-Preservation Certificate " as part of the loan condition.

The participants released a Group Standard "*Data Intellectual Property Pledge Service* Protocol" in March 2022, and months later an upgraded version, "*Data Intellectual Property Pledge Operations Specifications*" was drafted in October 2022 as a local standard by Zhejiang province.

5.3 State council and pilot cities fostering data factor markets and opening of public data

At the end of 2021, the State Council issued the "*Opinions on Piloting Innovation in Business Environment*" (State Council Office [2021] No. 24), deploying six cities to carry out piloting innovation in business environment. The *Opinions* consists of 101 reform initiatives in 10 areas; among the "key tasks," the cities are required to "better support the innovative development of market subjects: improve the innovative resource allocation and management mechanisms, explore the access criteria to meet the needs of the development of new business models, and enhance the innovative power of market subjects, ..., and improve the market-oriented pricing and trading mechanism of intellectual property rights, and carry out pilot securitization of intellectual property rights".

The six cities have proceeded in implementing the initiatives, and many are conductive to the buy-and-sell of data factor, including pricing and exchange of data intellectual property, setting up data factor markets, opening government-owned data.

5.4 Standardization enhances digital economy

In October 2022, a set of projects in standardization attracted a lot of competition in Zhejiang Province and around the country, due to both the size (7 projects, each 3 million yuan, to be won) and the content (22 categories in digital economy). Eventually 38 consortia submitted their bids, and the eventual 7 winners were well-deserved the wins.

The winning teams were asked to spend 2–3 years, effectively support the development of industrial innovation standards system, and strive to lead the development of a number of international standards, national standards, industry standards, and group standards.

Some of the 22 candidate categories were high-efficiency crystalline silicon solar cells, flexible thin-film solar cells, smart photovoltaic modules, etc., smart inverters, controllers, high-efficiency power electronics and other key devices, photovoltaic intelligent control platform, energy management, intelligent operation and maintenance, microgrid trading, and other services.

6. Conclusion

Data play an increasingly central role in digital economy around the world, and China has mobilized government agencies and enterprises to elevate data as a key factor of production, emphasizing its economic role. On the road to turning data into a production factor, namely data factorization, its connotation needs to solidify, so that data ownership is easier to establish, data valuation is carried out, data values can be stored, and data transactions are facilitated. To that end, China is implementing a range of initiatives, starting with newly created registry of data intellectual property, new data exchanges, plus numerous rules, trials and practices in the areas of intellectual property, standards, intellectual property financing, and data transactions. With these experiments gaining insights and experiences, a new economic norm that is a data-centric digital economy would emerge.

Author details

Yu Uny Cao[1*] and Hu Wang[2]

1 Zhejiang Intellectual Property Exchange Center Ltd., Hangzhou, China

2 Guangzhou Wosiang Intellectual Property Services Ltd., Guangzhou, China

*Address all correspondence to: caoyu@zjipx.com

References

[1] China Academy of Information and Communications Technology. China Digital Economy Development Report. 2022

[2] Romer PM. Endogenous technological change. Journal of Political Economy. 1990;**98**(5, Part 2):S71-S102

[3] He XJ. The coordinated development of digital economy and green economy under the background of low-carbon transformation. Statistics of China's Foreign Economic Relations. 2021;**151**(4):28-37

[4] Liu Q, Ma YR, Xu SX. Does the development of digital economy improve the green economic efficiency of China? China Population, Resources and Environment. 2022;**32**(03):72-85

[5] Jiang X. Playing the role of platform enterprises to promote the rapid development of the digital economy. Outlook Weekly. 2023;**2**

[6] Mundial B. China 2030: Building a Modern, Harmonious, and Creative High-Income Society. Washington DC: World Bank. Development Research Center of the State Council PRC; 2012

[7] Qiao H, Huang C. Building a digital economy with data as the key factor. People's Daily. 23 Jun 2022

[8] State Council of China. On Improving the Systems and Mechanisms for Market-Based Allocation of Factors of Production. Beijing. 2020

[9] Mei H. Taking a crucial step of data factorization. Economic Daily. 3 Jan 2023

[10] China Academy of Information and Communications Technology. A White Paper on Data Factor (2022). 2023

[11] WeBank. The 2020 Data New Infrastructure White Paper. 2020

[12] She Y. Intellectual property boosts the development of innovative economy. Economic Daily. 25 Aug 2022

Chapter 11

Intellectual Property and the Blockchain Sector, a World of Potential Economic Growth and Conflict

Eva R. Porras

Abstract

This chapter reviews intellectual property (IP) concepts and developments whose outcomes impact the intellectual ownership of key aspects of blockchain technology. The players include governments, legislators, and law makers attempting to make sense of an opaque, impenetrable, and baffling technological and social environment where myth and reality blend. The interested parties are, on the one hand, the IP owners of blockchain-related technological developments and, on the other hand, late comers hoping to deny these rights to use the technology for free. At stake, there are billions of US dollars and the real capacity for a new industrial revolution. In the background, there is a world of spectators with an extremely unequal understanding of the technology. The chapter covers three general areas: an overview of blockchain technology, the use of blockchain technology for the management of IP rights and other intellectual property, and the situation of Intellectual Property rights in the blockchain sector. Focusing on specific developments, the author delves in what is at stake and its economic implications.

Keywords: blockchain, intellectual property, distributed ledger technology, digital right management, patents, copyrights, economic development, ethics, conflict, cryptocurrencies

1. Introduction

1.1 A looming crisis for a brand-new economy

Web3 [1] represents a new generation of the World Wide Web. It is an umbrella term covering the technological and commercial innovations derived from blockchain. Web3 represents a paradigm shift that will revolutionize commerce with as much impact as the internet had itself. But, with great change comes great risk. Hence, Web3's potential for disruption in several domains including the area of intellectual property (IP) rights covered in this chapter.

IP rights are proven by patents or demonstrations of intimate subject knowledge only the creator would have. But contrary to what happens in traditional industrial settings, this is a viewpoint not respected in the current Web3 environment. Thus, rights and protections that are usually expected in other realms of the economy do not exist for Web3, turning this domain of "rights" into a territory for future conflict.

In this chapter, after a brief history and explanation of blockchain technology development, we give an overview of its current developmental stage and warn that the lack of awareness about IP protection in blockchain technologies bodes ill for this nascent industry.

1.2 A brief history of blockchain development

The first successful implementation of the blockchain was the *bitcoin blockchain* whose protocol was presented by its inventor, the pseudonymous Satoshi Nakamoto, in his momentous 2008 white paper: "Bitcoin: A Peer-to-Peer Electronic Cash System" [2]. The purpose of this blockchain was to initiate a peer-to-peer electronic cash transaction system that would allow for transfers of electronic cash representing nanopayments. These payments would support asset exchanges, say for example purchases, "bitcoin" being the currency (or "cryptocurrency") and Bitcoin the underlying blockchain structure.

Bitcoin was designed on the back of failed attempts at creating electronic cash [3, 4] as well earlier blockchain versions [5–9] and multiple other developments [10] in the areas of cryptography and digital signatures. Thus, the enduring success of bitcoin attests to its efficacy: Nakamoto got the design right by making choices that would protect the integrity of the blockchain and would allow it to scale.

Following this accomplishment, many "copycat" cryptocurrencies were launched by making large or small variations on the original bitcoin design. In addition to those, others pretended to have equivalent or comparable constructs, while there were just merely empty shells. However, since these slow and tentative beginnings, a strong and burgeoning multibillion market has grown around these protocols. Clearly, despite the well-known volatility of cryptocurrency prices, blockchain technology itself is here to stay. And this evidence leads to two observations:

a. the successful industrial or business use of blockchain technology is not understood nor valued correctly by the exchange markets, and

b. prices at these exchanges do not reflect the potential for value creation of the various blockchain technologies; rather, these prices result from speculative activities of various parties.

However, even if the specialized press approaches volatility at crypto exchanges with regular financial markets lingo, and even though the average investor cannot tell apart the relevance of the workings of critical components within the blockchains, key actors do understand there lies a world of intellectual property rights underlying the technical trading jargon and personal alignment with logos and cryptospace personalities. Thus, it is informative to review some key aspects of how the technology works, especially its lesser publicly known and most value-adding underappreciated features. Hence, in the next section, we provide a brief explanation using bitcoin as the primary exemplar.

1.3 Overview of blockchain technology

Rather than "electronic cash" a better (though still imperfect) analogy for bitcoin is "electronic gold." Like gold, bitcoin's value is not underpinned by a central authority such as a central bank. Also, like gold bitcoin has a fixed supply of 21,000,000 and needs work (mining) to extract it. The meaning of this is that to access and use the "specific" coins, work needs to be performed. In this later pursuit, Bitcoin is maintained by a network of independent, self-interested node operators that can join or leave the network at any time, without affecting its operation.

Node operators that contribute directly to the network's security and integrity (known as "miners") are incentivized to deploy their processing power via rewards paid in bitcoins. To earn these rewards, miners need to validate proposed transactions and then win a competition against other miners for the right to add a block containing transactions to the end of the blockchain. The miners compete in a sort of "mathematical lottery" in which their chance of winning (and hence their long-term income) is roughly proportional to their processing power. This is the proof of work (PoW).

The "mining" feature of bitcoin has been much maligned because of the amounts of electricity it consumes. This has led to some inaccurate and misguided conclusions, as well as to blockchains naively modifying or eliminating mining as a feature of their system. However, what is poorly understood in general is that mining is intrinsic to bitcoin's viability. Consider when bitcoin was first created its value was negligible and it remained low for a long period. Those were the days when enthusiasts could run bitcoin mining operations on their laptop computers. It is no coincidence that mining bitcoin is now costly and its value high. These two factors are not exactly time-correlated, but they are interdependent: mining operations are expensive *because* bitcoin's value is high and to a certain extent the reverse is also true: the high cost of mining imbues bitcoin with value.

Furthermore, it is precisely the high cost of mining that provides bitcoin's security. These aspects (or rather their *lack* in other blockchains) explain why many other cryptocurrencies have been successfully attacked [11]. A second matter usually ignored is that blockchain will replace a large portion of a much more energy-consuming legacy technology. That is the reason block size and the ability to scale are keys to blockchain technology: the energy needed per transaction decreases exponentially with block size.

The industrial value of bitcoin depends on its ability to perform its function as described in the protocol. Given PoW is a cornerstone of the mechanism that ensures the blockchain's integrity, the consequences of tampering with the mining feature of blockchains exposes the danger of allowing lax protection within the industry. A "free-for-all environment" facilitates slipshod practices and causes severe damage, such as financial losses and lack of trust in the sector. Though this is true in any unprotected industry, it would be exacerbated for blockchain because delivering on its promises (immutability of the records, etc.) is the key of its survival.

Bitcoin has been called "programmable money" due to its inbuilt programming language (bitcoin script or BScript). One can only imagine the havoc a naïve development community could wreak with such powerful but narrowly understood tools at their disposal. On the other hand, the owners of blockchain IP, who have expended effort on R&D and gained unique expertise, are the best placed to fruitfully and safely utilize its deep potential.

2. Intellectual property and the blockchain

Intellectual property (IP) refers to creations of the mind which include a wide range of activities such as:

a. *Industrial property* which encompasses patents for inventions, industrial designs, trademarks, and geographical indications, and

b. *Copyright and related rights* which include literary, artistic, and scientific works.

IP rights are proven by patents or demonstrations of intimate subject knowledge only the creator would have. Legally, a patent, a type of document and a form of intellectual property right [12], allows its owner to exclude others from commercially profiting from the protected invention in the region protected by the patent for a given period (usually 20 years). The rights covered by IP laws help owners benefit from their "intellectual property' giving them income over the use of their patented products, as well as some control over how their property is used. Given the well-being of humanity depends on its capacity to better its condition, technological progress requires these creative actions, their development, and their use. Thus, using intellectual property right laws which shelter these efforts is vital for growth.

2.1 The use of blockchain in the IP enforcement sector

A blockchain such as Bitcoin functions as a database that keeps unaltered records of data in "distributed digital ledgers." This means that the data lodged in the blocks cannot be changed or eliminated, and that the databases are duplicated *n*-times to be distributed among the *n*-nodes in the given network.

Given the transactions are verified and validated by as many computers as they volunteer to be in the network at any given time, this crowdsourcing oversight contributes to the integrity of the ledger and replaces the need for any central authority. In other words, in this type of "public" blockchain, and considering the PoW threshold, no cyberattack could strike all copies of the ledger simultaneously to replace the true ledger.

A consequence of having the information distributed is that there is not "single point of failure," meaning that a hacker could not bring down the network by attacking a single point. The lack of a "central storage" is a key valuable differentiator from legacy systems and the reason why distributed ledger technology (DLT) offers many advantages for IP registration, protection, and as evidence at a registry or in a court-of-law.

A helpful representation of the blockchain can be to think of it as a series of consecutive boxes containing the information of a "system" and the "service" that such system provides [13]. The operations compiled within the blocks could be orders to transfer bitcoins, or "smart contracts": application and execution orders. The blockchain grows joining blocks of successive data, representing later evidence. Thus, for instance, to reverse an action, a new action in the opposite direction would have to be initiated and, to reflect this latter change, all nodes have to be updated. Hence, the length of the chain is determined by the successive blocks added after the network running a consensus protocol certifies the validity of the transactions in the said blocks.

The process that ensures the functionality of the blockchain is material because this innovation is solely endorsed by its real-life use cases, such as the protection of

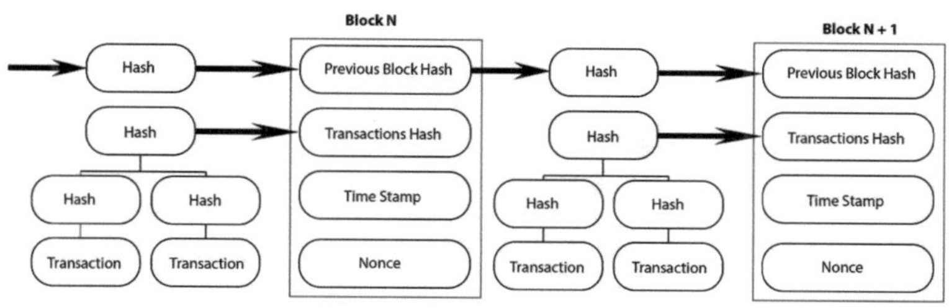

Figure 1.
Time stamp and blockchain structure. Source: The author.

intellectual property. **Figure 1** shows the Bitcoin time-stamping process. This process attests to a time when an event happened, which defines its capacity to be effective in protecting intellectual property rights [14, 15].

This figure shows the process transactions follow in the Bitcoin protocol. Here, we can see how the hash of each event (the transaction) is included in each block. The block of these hashes also includes a stamp, attesting to the timing when an event happened. Given the transaction can represent any event, say when a brand was first publicly used, this time stamp is instrumental in effectively protecting intellectual property rights.

Since DLT creates a secure, time-stamped, immutable chain of information, it is perfectly fit to applications in tracing of processes. This fact has not gone unnoticed, and different governmental agencies and IP registries such as the European Union Intellectual Property Office (EUIPO) are looking into the blockchain as a potential tool for IP management. The idea would be to turn IP offices into "smart IP registrars" so that these offices become accountable as an authority that creates "immutable records" of the events in the life of registered IP rights. For instance, they would be responsible for registering the first time a trademark is applied for, when it was first used in trade, and so on.

Documenting IP rights in a distributed ledger instead of the legacy database would ease IP identification, storage, and evidence furnishing. And the capacity to trail the entire life cycle of a right would provide numerous additional benefits, such as the ability to provide better services, the ease of audits, the simplification of due diligence processes, improved confidentiality, and so on.

With respect to use cases, the potential to use blockchain technology for the management of IP rights is vast as the use of blockchain technology in IP management would greatly improve efficiencies and effectiveness in numerous areas. Here, we review the key categories:

2.1.1 Evidence of creatorship/proof-of-ownership

The growth of the digitalization industry and 4.0 technologies demands a system for providing proof of ownership of intellectual assets. And Blockchain could be just the right technology for registering and verifying the ownership of IP works. **Figure 2** summarizes three aspects of proof of ownership IP.

With respect to patents, if the creator and owner of an invention wishes to secure her rights, she can go to a patent office and register her IP. Nonetheless, if it is a copyright, the creator would have to generate its own evidence as the weight of proof of ownership in this scenario falls on her. In this internet era, anyone can download already created content and use it; thus, exercising the copyright has become very

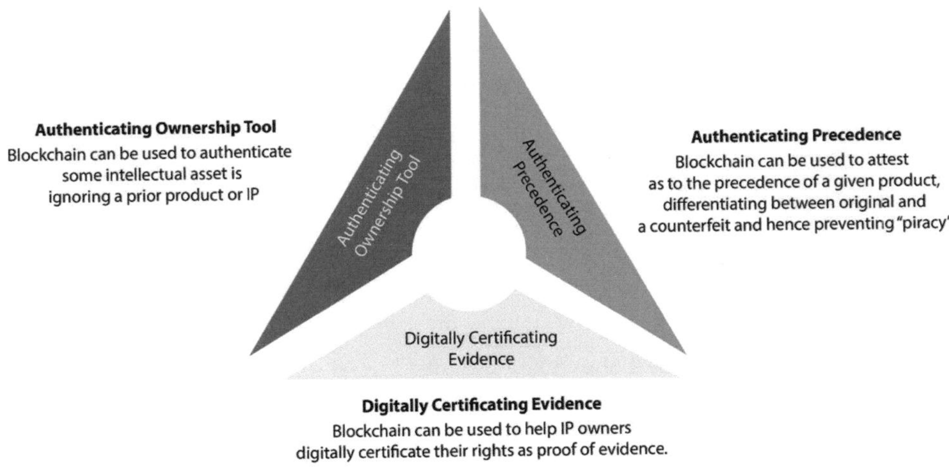

Figure 2.
Three Aspects of Proof of Ownership IP. Source: The author.

challenging. This observation finds a clear example in the current legal dispute between Craig S. Wright, alias Satoshi Nakamoto the inventor of Bitcoin, and the Crypto Open Patent Alliance (COPA), a US-based group of software developers which took his original Bitcoin protocol and modified it while keeping the brand name. We cover some aspects of this dispute in the next section.

The Bitcoin protocol can be used to assess IP ownership. This figure covers three aspects of proof of ownership. Clockwise, the first on the right refers to the antecedents of the asset. Given the blockchain provides an indelible record, it can be used to list "original" products so they can be differentiated from counterfeit ones. The second refers to using the blockchain to certificate IP ownership. For example, by hashing an event such as the patent. The last refers to using blockchain technology to dispute a later claim. This can be done by showing the time stamp of an earlier claim.

Using the blockchain in the proof of owners is already happening as some companies have begun to develop a system that provides blockchain-based time-stamping and validation for the safeguarding of digital assets [16].

2.1.2 Enabling the IP marketplace

Blockchain can be adopted as an IP marketplace where creators list their inventions as ledgers with brief descriptions. This marketplace could then be used to find potential licensees for related know-how of the inventions. For an illustration; see **Figure 3**.

This figure explains how blockchain technology can be used to enable the IP market place.

2.1.3 Evidence of use of IP rights

Given the realities of a globalizing economy to procure protection, IP law and practice has to involve national and international laws. Patent data are publicly accessible through the patenting process. Nonetheless, these data are distributed through the pertinent national and international authorities which operate at varying degrees of efficiency following different policies. Thus, working with global patent data is

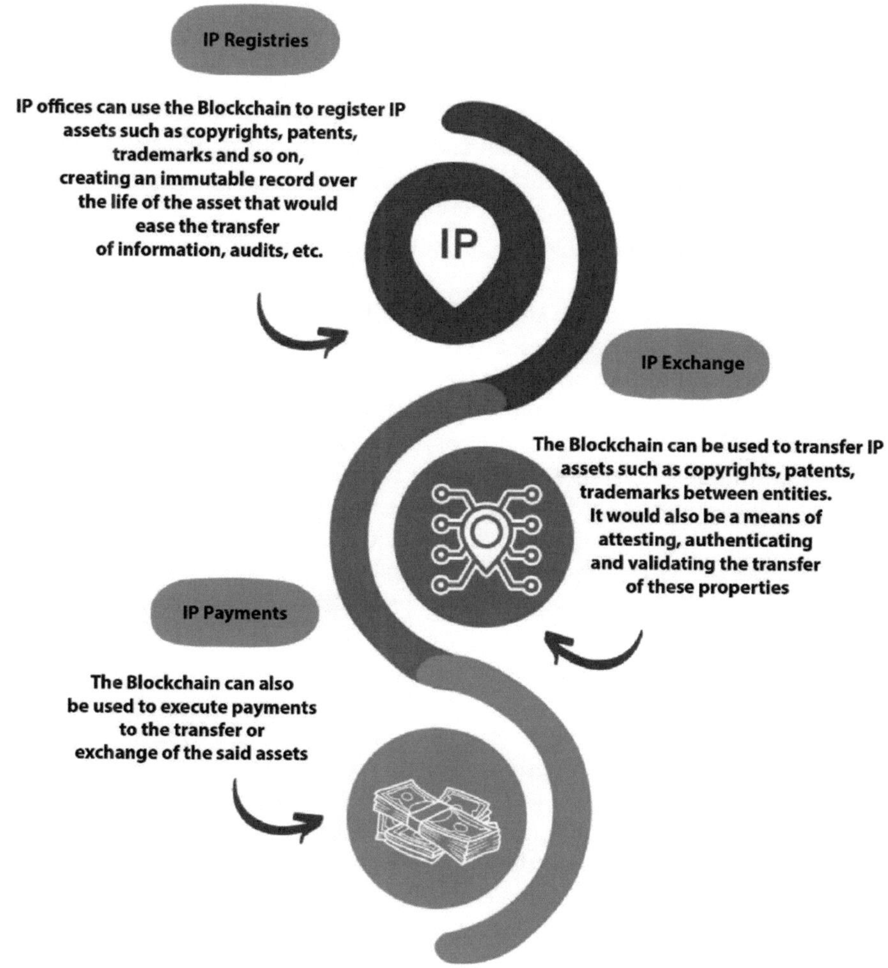

Figure 3.
Enabling the IP Marketplace. Source: The author.

cumbersome and intricate. This is one of the reasons that the blockchain is proposed as an ideal technology to ease the creation of an ownership record that would be used to track ownership status and the use of rights.

In this case, one single ownership record would help IP right owners assess the extent to which their rights are used. For instance, each time a trademark is used, this action could be registered in the blockchain to notify in real time the responsible IP office. This is efficient and reliable process, and the record generated by it would provide solid, time-stamped evidence of the usage of the trademark throughout its whole life.

2.1.4 Provenance, anti-counterfeiting, and enforcement of IP rights

Ledger technology could also help assess provenance authentication by using the blockchain records containing authorized licensee and ownership data, given these record "objectively verifiable details" about the products. Hence, everyone in the supply chain, including consumers and customs, could substantiate a genuine product and differentiate it from a fake one.

2.1.5 Supply chain management

Relatedly, tracking goods on an immutable blockchain can assist brand owners to enforce their contractual rights as well as help identify parallel imports or gray-market activity. This would be of particular relevance in the distribution of products that need to meet regulatory requirements, such as in the pharmaceutical industry.

2.1.6 Smart contracts and digital rights management

In the context of blockchain, a smart contract is a computer program that gets executed automatically whenever a set of predetermined conditions is met. Thus, in the process to secure IP rights, these contracts could facilitate the execution of different actions such as checking the assignment and validity of a patent, negotiating an agreement, executing and paying for a transaction, and informing all interested parties of such transaction. Hence, in IP rights management, smart contracts could be used to establish and enforce private IP agreements such as licenses, the automatic start of contracts including contents such as music and pictures, and to ease and speed the transfer of payments to IP owners. These aspects are shown in **Figure 4**.

This figure shows different uses of smart contracts in the IP space.

2.1.7 Blockchain for version-control in IP of the assets

As patents, copyrights, etc., evolve throughout their lifetime, digital assets produce multiple versions of themselves. Therefore, another use of blockchain technology is to link these versions in a sort of "end-to-end" life cycle maintenance of the asset. For instance, currently defensive publications are used to set a precedent and prevent the patenting of innovations by publicly disclosing the asset at an earlier date. The Blockchain could serve the same function by giving each file a unique fingerprint, removing duplications, versioning each upload, and indexing, so the information is easily tractable.

2.1.8 Blockchain for unifying global patent/IP system

In the IP sector, another major function for the Blockchain is to unify the patent system across different geographical areas. This could vastly improve the effectiveness of IP management, speed up the innovation process in companies, and champion the distribution of information via the ledger.

In this path, some legislations and patent offices started to accept the blockchain as "admissible evidence." Below, there is a partial list of scenarios where courts and jurisdictions have considered blockchain as a "proof of evidence under electronic evidences" and where the legislative has ruled to include the technology as valid part of contractual processes.

- Vermont, USA (2016)

  In 2016, Vermont passed legislation declaring that blockchain receipts accompanied by a written declaration of a person attesting to the details of the transaction are admissible. Under 12 V.S.A. §1913, blockchain receipts are also presumed to be authentic pursuant to Vermont Rules of Evidence [17, 18]. This law has already made use of the technology by making blockchain records admissible in court.

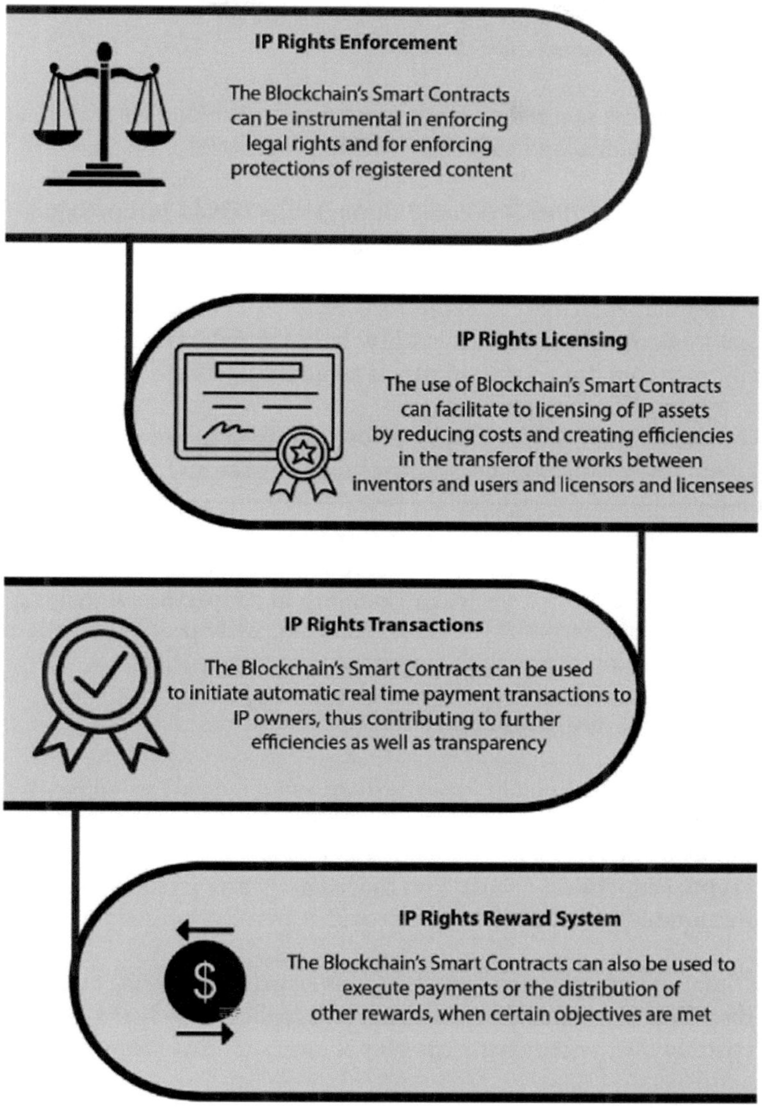

Figure 4.
Smart contracts in the IP space. Source: The author.

- Delaware, USA (2017).

  Delaware General Corporation Law (DGCL) §224 was amended to allow organizations to maintain business records using "distributed electronic networks or databases." [19, 20].

- Arizona, USA (2018)

  Arizona HB 2417 amended its Electronic Transaction Act to include blockchain records, signatures, and smart contracts, which "may not be denied legal effect, validity or enforceability [21]."

quote

44-7061. Signatures and records secured through blockchain technology; smart contracts; ownership of information; definitions.

A. A signature that is secured through blockchain technology is considered to be in an electronic form and to be an electronic signature.

B. A record or contract that is secured through blockchain technology is considered to be in an electronic form and to be an electronic record.

C. Smart contracts may exist in commerce. A contract relating to a transaction may not be denied legal effect, validity, or enforceability solely because that contract contains a smart contract term.

D. Notwithstanding any other law, a person that, in or affecting interstate or foreign commerce, uses blockchain technology to secure information that the person owns or has the right to use retains the same rights of ownership or use with respect to that information as before the person secured the information using blockchain technology. This subsection does not apply to the use of blockchain technology to secure information in connection with a transaction to the extent that the terms of the transaction expressly provide for the transfer of rights of ownership or use with respect to that information.

E. For the purposes of this section:

1. "Blockchain technology" means distributed ledger technology that uses a distributed, decentralized, shared, and replicated ledger, which may be public or private, permissioned or permissionless, or driven by tokenized crypto economics. The data on the ledger is protected with cryptography, is immutable and auditable, and provides an uncensored truth.

2. "Smart contract" means an event-driven program, with state, that runs on a distributed, decentralized, shared, and replicated ledger and that can take custody over and instruct transfer of assets on that ledger.

Unquote
These actions were followed by equivalent changes in Ohio:

- Ohio, USA (2018)

  Ohio, (2018) passed equivalent legislation [22] when the SB300 amended sections of the Uniform Electronic Transactions Act (UETA) were made effective to include blockchain records and smart contracts as electronic records. This change implied the recognition of smart contracts and records stored on blockchain electronic records. The bill also allowed for smart contracts to be as legally enforceable as just any other contract would be, removing doubts as to the enforceability of electronic signatures, records, and contracts that are secured through blockchain technology.

  In addition to establishing the legal equivalence of electronic signatures and records with those manually signed and with paper records, UETA's removed barriers to electronic commerce and technological advances in the use of electronic records, contracts, and signatures. Under UETA Section 1306.01, an electronic signature is an electronic process logically associated with a record that is executed or adopted with an intent to sign. The amendment: *"A signature that is secured through blockchain technology is considered to be in an electronic form and to be an electronic signature."* UETA also requires an electronic record be shareable and retrievable and spells out that blockchain technology can be such an electronic record: *"A record or contract that is secured through blockchain technology is considered to be in an electronic form and to be an electronic record."*

The above steps were taken as the Franklin County Auditor's Office planned to be the first to use blockchain technology to transfer property deeds [23]. That is, to transfer all property records via the blockchain in a digitalized process where all the parties interact remotely, and buyer, seller, bank, appraiser, and title company complete the sale of a home.

- Wyoming, USA (2018)

  In 2018, Wyoming state legislature cleared House Bill 70 (HB 70 [24]) to provide guidelines on how to account for utility tokens used in the exchanged for goods and services and which had not been promoted earlier as investments. HB 70 recognized utility tokens (also called "open blockchain token") as a distinct asset class different from a security and money if these conditions are met:

  1. The protocol developers have not promoted the token as an investment opportunity.

  2. The token can be used to exchange goods or services.

  3. The protocol developer has not entered into a repurchase agreement or has agreed to locate buyers for the token.

  4. People who facilitate their exchange are not the usual broker-dealers of securities.

But HB 70 was just one among four other blockchain-related bills: HB 19, HB 101, HB 126, and SF 111:

1. HB 19 [25] exempted various types of crypto assets from the Wyoming Money Transmitter Act. This is meaningful as a 2015 interpretation of this Act by the Wyoming Division of Banking had made it impractical for cryptocurrency exchange markets to operate in the state.

2. HB 101 [26], the "blockchain filings bill," updated the Wyoming's Business Corporations Act to authorize corporations to create and use blockchains to store and maintain records, to use an databases or electronic network address to identify a corporation's shareholder, and to accept shareholder votes signed by network signatures if tied to a given data address. In essence, this bill specified the requirements for corporations using electronic networks or blockchain databases.

3. HB 126 [27] authorized limited liability companies (LLCs) to establishing a series of provisions that resulted in a structure favorable to decentralized protocols.

This is because it enabled LLCs to establish a compartmentalized series of members/managers, specifying powers, and transferable interests or assets, and distributions to members while providing for limitations on liabilities, and so on.

4. SF 111 [28] exempted cryptocurrencies from property taxes creating a crypto-friendly environment [29].

- Vermont, USA (2018)

  In 2018, Vermont also passed a law establishing "blockchain-based limited liability companies" and "a personal information protection company." The former type of entity was geared to entrepreneurs and companies that wished to prioritize governance structures tailored to the technology [30]. The latter was tasked with guarding consumers' data, in contrast to selling or sharing it as is the case in many social media companies and websites.

- California, USA (2018)

  In 2018, California passed AB2658 [31], an Act to add and repeal Sections 11546.8 and 11546.9 of the Government Code, relating to blockchain technology. The key intent was to modify the aspect of the "Uniform Electronic Transactions Act" which denied "legal effect or enforceability" to an agreement, contract, or record in electronic format or because an "electronic record was used in its formation." Among other things, the Act provides that if a law requires a record to be in writing, or if a law requires a signature, an electronic record or signature satisfies the law.

- Hangzhou, China (2018)

  In 2018, the Internet Court in China accepted "blockchain-authenticated evidence" in a case in which the litigant hired a third-party blockchain deposition service to retrieve evidence for the copyright infringement case being heard [32]. The plaintiff hired a firm named Baoquan.com to capture the evidence and then photographed the defendant's webpages to demonstrate copyright infringement. The court was able to confirm the file downloaded from Baoquan.com was intact. This judgment relied on a process that used data received from the platform: the pictures, source code of the webpage, invocation log, all were obtained and packed in a "package file," and its hash value was obtained and uploaded to the blockchain. This showed the original package file was not compromised as the hash of the downloaded package file could be contrasted with the one stored on the blockchain.

  This rule was confirmed and expanded to all Internet courts by September, after the publication of the Article 11, Paragraph 2 of the *Provisions of the Supreme People's Court on Several Issues Concerning the Trial of Cases by Internet Courts*. This text confirms that.

  Quote

  [] provided the right procedures have been followed: if collected through electronic signature, trusted time-stamping, hash value verification, blockchain, and other evidence collection, and verified with retention and tamper-proof technical means or via the electronic forensics and deposit platform, which are able to prove its authenticity [] the Court will corroborate this authenticity.

Unquote

An interesting aspect of this ruling is that it compels to realize a global analysis of the blockchain evidence, with emphasis on the source.

- Supreme Court, India (2018)

In India, the Supreme Court clarified its position with respect to "enforcement and jurisdiction" in relation to transactions over a blockchain network. Here, Section 65B (Admissibility of electronic records) of the Indian Evidence Act, 1872 [33] was reviewed, and a number of considerations were highlighted of vital importance [34]. Its conclusions cleared the air with respect to admissibility of evidence by way of electronic record under the Evidence Act, both in the context of criminal and civil cases.

2.2 Regulatory challenges of blockchain applications in the IP ecosystem

The key characteristics of standard the blockchain may secure a significant role for this technology when considering its use in the field of IP protection. Accountability, security, transparency, decentralization, and the immutable nature of Blockchain are all essential and complementary to other features such as tokenization, smart contracts, automation and Self-Sovereign Identity (SSI). However, the Blockchain is still at the stage of technological development, and this may announce more evolved applications in the future. For now, there are also multiple challenges with respect to blockchain applications in the IP ecosystem, in particular regulatory uncertainty.

For instance, there are no single straight answers about the regulation of some features and applications of blockchain technology that are new to the legal system. In addition, there is no unification of criteria across the multi-jurisdictional character of blockchain networks. Furthermore, legal uncertainty is multidimensional because many aspects are governed by a plethora of fields (data protection, of contract law, procedural law, law enforcement, etc.) rather than just IP-related legislation. Examples of legal uncertainty include issues related to pseudonymity/anonymity, the absence of a central authority, data protection, valuation, or smart contracts and tokens.

In addition, legal uncertainty has important implications for the development and adoption of the technology. An obvious one is that public authorities might be reluctant to promote blockchain solutions. Also, entrepreneurs might hold back from starting blockchain projects. Last, promoters can encounter multiple obstacles when designing their solutions, particularly when these become connected to the multidimensional geographically diversified legal aspects.

3. Intellectual property and Nakamoto's 2008 protocol, a use case for the blockchain sector

As argued in the previous section, there is a general consensus that IP protection can be improved with the help of blockchain technology. However, even though IP laws protect the interests of the creators and some legal harmonization efforts are taking place, a series of hurdles such as historical lack of adequate information transmission have prevented the development of a more organized legal-enforcement environment.

In time, newly updated IP laws which take into account the specific circumstances of an electronic environment will be perfectly fit to balance out the rights and interests of inventors and users, and of businesses and their competitors. However, until these get sorted out, the historical, technical, and legal complexity of the blockchain sector, will affect its growth and the spectrum of its own applicability. And, these are not the only sources of conflict. In a global digital world that is interconnected in real time, the protection of intellectual property, its management, and monetization is extremely challenging. One key reason is that this type of ownership can be easily copied, stolen, misused, and misappropriated. To resolve these matters is critical because global, worldwide technological progress depends on the protection of intellectual property, and hence the recognition of the competing interests among creators and between the latter and the users.

Specifically, with respect to the distributed ledger, the promise of blockchain technology became a reality following the success of Bitcoin [35]. Thereafter, many creators built upon this protocol to present patent applications for blockchain-related inventions. Some of these later blockchains, claimed methods of improving upon or using the original blockchain, and these activities split the interests of the creators and users between those who do not recognize the property of intellectual rights which protect a number of aspects of Nakamoto's invention, and those who do.

In this context, the resolution of some legal disputes, including one between the inventor of Bitcoin: Dr. Craig S. Wright, alias Satoshi Nakamoto, and a US-based group of software developers organized under the name of the Crypto Open Patent Alliance (COPA), will clarify of the landscape.

3.1 A brief history of the blockchain environment after Bitcoin's 2009 release

In 2008, the bitcoin protocol was made public by Satoshi Nakamoto. Early 2009, the software was released. Thereafter, these documents underwent a series of modifications enabled by the open-source nature of the software. While Bitcoin Satoshi's Vision (*ticker symbol BSV*) maintains the original protocol, the following are some of the modifications developed over time:

3.2 Bitcoin (ticker symbol BTC)

BTC imposed a 1 MB block-size restriction, capping BTC's throughput. An ensuing change was also adopted: Segregated Witness (SegWit); a solution by which transaction data and signatures split making room for more transactions in the small 1 MB block. The limited block capacity resulted in network congestion and impractically high transaction fees, but the throughput limitation was used as an excuse to create "sidechains" for transaction processing (i.e., Lightning [36]), while BTC was kept mainly as the settlement layer. These enumerated here, are a few among other modifications.

3.3 Bitcoin Cash (ticker symbol BCH)

As a response to BTC's block-size limitation, in August 2017, BCH [37] was born to enable some "on-chain" scalability by multiplying the block size by 32.

3.4 Bitcoin Satoshi Vision (ticker symbol BSV)

Later in November 2018, some BCH proponents deleted block size restrictions and created BSV.

This group also reinstated BScript keywords that had been inoperative due to the actions of some BTC core developers and eliminated the ones that replaced these. De facto, these and other adjustments aligned the BSV blockchain with the original 2008 Nakamoto protocol.

The said modifications can be considered "forks": new projects derived from an earlier Bitcoin codebase and blockchain record of transactions. That is, forks occur when a group of individuals chose to establish a new set of rules for, say, Bitcoin. When a group imposes new rules only accepting blocks that follow these, the Bitcoin blockchain (any blockchain) will be split into separate and incompatible projects. Miners and nodes working under the prior governance will only add blocks valid in the earlier framework, ignoring those following the change, while those in accordance with the new rules will accept blocks that follow these. After a fork, what was the one Bitcoin blockchain is now split into two separate and incompatible projects.

In the above-mentioned cases, several facts should be obvious:

1. They all use the Bitcoin name brand to identify themselves

2. The one which acts according to the original protocol is ticker symbol BSV [38]

3. B y forking into subsequent brands the developers responsible for the changes, keep using properties of the earlier ones.

The implication and realization are that the only blockchain working within the 2008 Whitepaper Bitcoin protocol is BSV. The reason is that Nakamoto's white paper: "Bitcoin: A peer to peer electronic cash system [39]" sets a number of conditions the block needs to fulfill:

a. it abides with coin ownership, scarcity, transaction format, script-language execution rules, and double-spend rules, and.

b. it must use the proof-of-work (PoW) consensus algorithm to add blocks to the chain.

The described situation presents a conundrum:

1. Can new projects following different rules (e.g., change in script, block size, consensus algorithm, etc) use the Bitcoin name?

2. Can forks use Bitcoin know-how and patented IP without making due payment or any recognition to the original inventor and/or owner of the patent? Arguably, the "airdrops" by Bitcoin networks generating branches in the blockchain disregard intellectual property rights.

3. How can users distinguish among projects keeping cognate names and properly assess the utility and value of the technology they are buying into?

4. How can IP owners be rewarded for his or her efforts?

These are not trivial questions. Forkdrop.io, a website that focuses "on projects that issue coins via some inheritance of the state of the Bitcoin (BTC) ledger" lists 105 Bitcoin fork projects, and 74 active and 31 no longer in existence [40]. Also, Forkdrop.io accounts for 22 altcoin fork projects that resemble Bitcoin forks, and some which developed from known altcoins. Github.com also provides information on these forks. For a partial list of examples see **Table 1**.

3.5 nChain patents and innovation in the blockchain sector

In an August 2022 publication [41], Dr. Vaughan, the Lead Director of Research for *nChain*, explained how their patent strategy had earned them a recognition as one of the world's top 100 most innovative companies and as a key global blockchain patent maker. nChain's goal is to ease the global adoption of blockchain technology. Hence, to communicate and distribute their wealth of knowledge, this firm joined the IPwe Blockchain Smart Pool, a pool where different companies combine their patents into a single portfolio. For instance, nChain delivered 169 patent families, including 1280 individual patent applications in the cybersecurity, automated contracts, wallets, IoT devices, tokenization, and peer-to-peer communication areas.

At nChain, multiple scientists have contributed over time, but the key to this firm's development capacity and outcomes is Dr. *Craig Wright's historical dedication to these patenting efforts. As a result,* nChain Chief Scientist is an author and co-author in hundreds of patent applications. He is also a part in a series of related disputes including the mentioned COPA's lawsuit. Dr. Wright has co-authored with Dr. Savanah and other scientists countless patents of major relevance. To appreciate the importance of these, we list and briefly describe a few in **Table 2**.

Unfortunately, lack of accountability with respect to mass media communications results in a blurry understanding of the situation. For instance, Nakamoto's request that the white paper is only shared by websites he approves, has been often met with the comment that "sharing the document under the **permissive MIT Software License,** which allows anyone to freely use, modify, copy, distribute, and publish it" [42]. When, in fact, the document was not shared under the MIT Software License [43]. This evidence is intimately related to intellectual property protection.

3.6 Glimpsing at the future

In January 21, 2021, Dr. Craig S. Wright's legal team at Ontier LLP, London, sent copyright infringement notices to five parties hosting the Bitcoin 2008 white paper on their websites. These letters are alike a cease-and-desist request in that they inform a party that court proceedings may be brought against them if they do not stop their infringing actions. Here, Dr. Wright demanded the white paper be removed from their websites. The discrepancy relates the parties' control and operation of bitcoin.org, bitcoin.com, and bitcoincore.org all of which offer "Bitcoin" products (e.g., BTC). That is because, using the 2008 white paper lends credibility to services which follow different protocols. Two of the listed organizations took action to remove the paper. In the third case, Dr. Wright's resolve to enforce his rights was met favorably as the English High Court found in his favor 2 months after filing when bitcoin.org operator "Cøbra" refused to desist [43].

DOI: http://dx.doi.org/10.5772/intechopen.1001882

BITCOIN				**(BBC) Big Bitcoin**
(BICC) BitClassic Coin	**(BTC) Bitcoin**	**(BTC2) Bitcoin 2**	**(XAP) Bitcoin Air**	**(BTALL) Bitcoin All**
(BCA) Bitcoin Atom	(BCB) Bitcoin Boy	(CDY) Bitcoin Candy[3]	(BCH) Bitcoin Cash	(BCP) Bitcoin Cash Plus
(BCZ) BitcoinCash Zero	(BCHC) Bitcoin Classic	(BCS) Bitcoin Class	(BCBC) Bitcoin@CBC	(BCL) BitcoinClean
(BCLD)[2] Bitcoin Cloud	(BTSQ) Bitcoin Community	(BTCO) Bitcoin Coral	(BTCC) Bitcoin Core	(BTD) Bitcoin Dao
(BCD) Bitcoin Diamond	(BTD) Bitcoin Dollar	(BTF) Bitcoin Faith	(BIFI) Bitcoin File	(GOD) Bitcoin God
(BTG) Bitcoin Gold	(BTHOL) Bitcoin Holocaust	(BTH) Bitcoin Hot	(BTCH) Bitcoin Hush	(BCI) Bitcoin interest
(BCK) [1] Bitcoin King	(BTL) Bitcoin Lambo	(BTCM) Bitcoin Metal	(BN) Bitcoin Nano	BTN – Bitcoin New
(BTCO) Bitcoin Oil	(BCO) Bitcoin Ore	(ORI) Bitcoin Origin	(BCP) Bitcoin Parallel	(BTP) Bitcoin Pay
(BPA) Bitcoin Pizza	(BPQ) Bitcoin Post-Quantum	(BTCP) Bitcoin Private	(BPR) Bitcoin Prime	(BTP) Bitcoin Pro
(BRECO) Bitcoin Reference Line	(BCRM) Bitcoin RM	(BCS) Bitcoin Smart	(BTCS) Bitcoin Stake	(BSH) Bitcoin Stash
(BSV) Bitcoin SV	(BTT) Bitcoin Top	(BTV) Bitcoin Vote	(BCW) Bitcoin Wonder	(BTW) Bitcoin World
(BCX) Bitcoin X	(BTX) Bitcore	(BTH) Bithereum	(BTV) BitVote	(CER) Cereneum
CLAM – Clamcoin	(CBTC) ClassicBitcoin	(DLC) Dalilcoin	(FBTC) FastBitcoin	(FBTC) Fox BTC
(HEX) HEX	(LBTC) Lightning Bitcoin	(MBC) Mic roBitcoin	(MWC) MimbleWimbleCoin	(NBTC) NewBitcoin
(NBTC) New Bitcoin	(OBTC) Oil Bitcoin	(QED) Qeditas	(QBTC) Quantum Bitcoin	(B2X) Segwit 2X
(SBC) Smart Bitcoin	(SBTC) Super Bitcoin	(TNET) Title Network	(UBTC) United Bitcoin	(WBTC) World Bitcoin
ALTCOIN			(CLO) Callisto	(DOGX) Dogethereum
(ETC) Ethereum Classic	(ETCV) Ethereum Classic Vision	(CRT) Ethereum Crystal	(ETF) Ethereum Fog	(ETE) Ethereum Emerald
(EMO) Ethereum Modification	(ETG) EtherGold	(ETI) EtherInc	(ETZ) EtherZero	(LCC) Litecoin Cash
(LTCP) Litecoin Private	(LZX) LiteZero	(ONT) Ontology	(CXMR) Monero Cash	(XMC) Monero Classic
(XMZ) Monero 0	(XMO) Monero Original	(XMV) MoneroV	(SAFE) SAFE	(SLTC) Super Litecoin
HISTORIC				(ABTC) ABitchain
(ANON) ANONymous	(BTCV) Bitcoin Blvck	(BEC) Bitcoin Eco	(BTF) Bitcoin Flash	(BLG) Bitcoin Lightning

BITCOIN				**(BBC) Big Bitcoin**
(BICC) BitClassic Coin	**(BTC) Bitcoin**	**(BTC2) Bitcoin 2**	**(XAP) Bitcoin Air**	**(BTALL) Bitcoin All**
(BTCL) Bitcoin Lite	(BCL) Bitcoin Lunar	(BCM) Bitcoin Master	(BTM) Bitcoin Minor	(BNR) Bitcoin Neuro
(BTN) Bitcoin New	Bitcoin Ocho (OCHO)	(BTP) Bitcoin Pieta	(BTP) Bitcoin Platinum	(POINT) Bitcoin Point
(BTCP) Bitcoin Private	(BTR) Bitcoin Rhodium	(BTSI) Bitcoin Silver	(BCS) Bitcoin Star	(SUDU) Bitcoin Sudu
(BTCTI) BitcoinTi	(BTCT) Bitcoin Transfer	(BUM) Bitcoin Uranium	(BZX) BitcoinZero	(BTCX2) Bitcoinx2
(BITE) BitEthereum	(GBYTE) Byteball	(LBTC) Lightning Bitcoin	(SEM) Semux	(XNN) Xenon

Notes
Not a true fork, not claimable at the moment.
The original ticker symbol is BCL, but this is also used by BitcoinClean.
Forked from Bitcoin Cash, not Bitcoin.
Sources: https://forkdrop.io/https://github.com/ymgve/bitcoin_fork_claimer.

Table 1.
Partial list of forks.

Pending and delayed is the Crypto Open Patent Alliance (COPA, a consortium of giant tech and digital asset companies) lawsuit against Dr. Wright [44], as this Alliance requested a new procedural judge, pushing the expected trial date to the first quarter of 2024. Furthermore, significant developments have taken place since April 2021 when they first filed and these will be relevant for future findings. Some of these include Dr. Wrights' recognition by the U.K. High Court as the white paper author, and his victory versus Ira Kleiman. These also include several defamation cases such as the one against blogger Peter McCormack, or his filing against members of COPA Coinbase (NASDAQ: COIN) and Kraken for using the Bitcoin name to sell unrelated projects.

COPA's declared "raison d'être" is: "to encourage the adoption of digital currency and remove patents as a barrier to growth and innovation by obliging its members to refrain from enforcing their patents" [45]. But these declarations of intent are met with some group of counter realities, such as the interesting addition of Mark Zuckerberg's Meta to the Alliance, or the entanglement of rights derived from the forks and airdrops as listed in **Table 1**.

In addition, there is the strange case of COPA founding member Jack Dorsey, Block (NASDAQ: SQ), who has had to recognize and cite in one of his new smart contracts patents the "Registry and Automated Management Method for Blockchain-Enforced Smart Contracts" [46] foundational blockchain patent held by nChain that lists Dr. Wright (together with Dr. Savanah) as its inventor [47]. This is a stimulating development given that COPA's lawsuit is predicated on the belief that Dr. Wright has no claims with the blockchain [48]. As Mr. Dorsey stated to the English High Court "Wright's entire narrative must be tested: in one way this dispute only relates to whether he is or is not the author of the Bitcoin White Paper, but COPA's case is that his entire conduct shows that he is not."

Applied/ Publication February 14, 2017 February 14, 2019	**Inventors: Craig Steven Wright Stephane Savanah**	**Id. # 20190050541**	**Name: A Method And System For Securing Computer Software Using A Distributed Hash Table And A Blockchain**
Description	A computer-implemented method and system for determining a metadata M for securing a controlled digital resource such as computer software using a distributed hash table and a peer-to-peer distributed ledger. This is a blockchain such as the Bitcoin blockchain. The method includes determining a data associated with the computer software and determining a first hash value based on the computer software. A second hash value based on the data and the computer software may be determined. The method further includes sending 140, over a communications network, the data, the first hash value, and the second hash value to an entry for storage in a distributed hash table. The second hash value may be a key of a key-value pair. The data and the first hash value may be a value in the key-value pair. A metadata (M) that is based on the second hash value may be determined for storage on the peer-to-peer distributed ledger.		
Applied/ Publication February 14, 2017 February 14, 2019	**Inventors**: Craig Steven Wright Gavin Allen	**Id. #** 20190052454	**Name**: System And Method For Controlling Asset-Related Actions Via A Block Chain
Description	**Abstract:** According to one perspective, the invention provides a technical arrangement to calculate, register, and/or apportion costs and/or generate income in proportion to the current ownership of an asset. One or more embodiments also comprise a novel technique for generating cryptographic subkeys. Thus, one benefit provided by the invention is that it allows the secure distribution of costs and income for an asset registered and maintained on the Blockchain. In turn, this increases the capability of such assets to meet the real-world needs of various entities such as the asset itself and investing parties.		
Applied/ Publication October 24, 2017 February 7, 2023	**Inventors:** Gavin Allen, Craig Steven Wright	**Id. #** 11574303	**Name:** Blockchain-based method and system for specifying the recipient of an electronic communication
Description	The invention provides a method and corresponding system for controlling a blockchain transaction output and/or specifying the recipient of the output. It also provides a method of controlling and/or generating an electronic communication. The invention is a blockchain-implemented solution, which may or may not be the Bitcoin blockchain. In a preferred embodiment of the invention, the method may comprise the step of sending an electronic notification to a notification address which is provided as metadata within an unlocking script of an input of a transaction (Txi) on a blockchain. The unlocking script is provided in order to spend an output from a further transaction (Tx2) on the blockchain. The input of the transaction (Txi) and/or the output of the further transaction (Tx2) may be associated with a tokenized asset represented on, or referenced via, the blockchain		
Applied/ Publication October 27, 2017 September 12, 2019	**Inventors:** Craig Steven Wright, Pedro Jimenez-Delgado	**Id. #** 20190279197	**Name:** Systems And Methods For Implementing Deterministic Finite Automata (Dfas) Via A Blockchain
Description	The invention relates to a technique for implementing, controlling, and automating a task or process on a blockchain such as, but not limited to, the Bitcoin blockchain. The invention is particularly suited for, but not limited to, automated execution of contracts such as smart contracts for financial agreements. However, other types of tasks and nonfinancial contracts can be implemented. The invention can be viewed as the implementation or incarnation of a state machine or DFA on a blockchain by using		

Applied/ Publication February 14, 2017 February 14, 2019	**Inventors: Craig Steven Wright Stephane Savanah**	**Id. # 20190050541**	**Name: A Method And System For Securing Computer Software Using A Distributed Hash Table And A Blockchain**
	the unspent outputs of blockchain transactions to represent the states of the machine, and spending of those outputs as the transition of the machine from one state to another. The invention provides a technical realization and implementation of a mathematical model of computation conceived as an abstract machine that can be in one of a finite set of states and can change from one state to another (transition) when a triggering event of a finite set (called input) occurs.		
Applied/Publication July 5, 2018 June 18, 2020			**Inventors:** Craig Steven Wright, Stephane Savanah
Id. # 20200195442	**Name:** Method for compiling from a high-level scripting language to a blockchain native scripting language		
Description	The invention provides methods and systems which enable additional functionality to be inserted into blockchain scripts with ease and in an effective and manner. According to one embodiment, the invention provides a blockchain-implemented method comprising the steps of arranging a plurality or selection of scripting language primitives to provide, upon execution, the functionality of a high-level scripting language primitive, wherein the scripting language is associated with a blockchain protocol, inserting the plurality of scripting language primitives at least once into a script, and inserting the script into blockchain transaction (Tx). The high-level scripting language primitive may perform, for example, an arithmetic operation such as multiplication or division. The scripting language primitives may be called op-codes, words or commands, and are native to the scripting language. The scripting language may be Script, and the blockchain protocol may be a version of the Bitcoin protocol.		
Applied/ Publication June 19, 2018 August 16, 2022	**Inventors:** Giuseppe Destefanis, Patrick Motylinski, Stephane Vincent, Craig Steven Wright	**Id. #** 11418590	**Name:** Fast propagation of recent transactions over a blockchain network
Description	A specialized network ("merchant") node to facilitate fast distribution of blockchain transactions over a network of interconnected nodes, as subset of which are merchant nodes interconnected by an overlay network. The merchant node includes a memory storing an assigned portion of a distributed mempool structured as a distributed hash table, the distributed mempool containing pending transactions awaiting confirmation. The merchant node operates by: receiving a transaction, including a transaction identifier; hashing the new transaction identifier to obtain a key; determining, using the key, whether the transaction is stored in the distributed mempool or not and, if not, then storing the transaction in the distributed mempool as a pending transaction; and sending the transaction to a set of nodes other than merchant nodes using peer-to-peer connections. The invention may be used in conjunction with the Bitcoin blockchain or an alternative.		
Applied/ Publication July 26, 2018 July 2, 2020	**Inventors:** Craig Steven Wright, Stephane Savanah	**Id. #** 20200213113	**Name:** Threshold digital signature method and system
Description	A method of sharing a secret value is disclosed. The method comprises distributing respective first shares of a first secret value, known to a first participant (Pi), to a plurality of second participants (Pj?i), wherein said first shares are encrypted by means of at least one private-public key pair comprising a private key and a public key being an elliptic curve generator point multiplied by the private key and wherein a first threshold number of first shares is required in order to enable a second participant to determine the first secret value.		

Applied/ Publication February 14, 2017 February 14, 2019	**Inventors: Craig Steven Wright Stephane Savanah**	**Id. # 20190050541**	**Name: A Method And System For Securing Computer Software Using A Distributed Hash Table And A Blockchain**
Applied/ Publication November 14, 2019 September 15, 2022	**Inventors:** Craig Steven Wright, Jack Owen Davies, Chloe Ceren Tartan, Owen Vaughan	**Id.** #20220294652	**Name:** Systems and methods for efficient and secure processing, accessing and transmission of data via a blockchain network
Description	The invention provides improved methods and corresponding systems for the sharing, storage, creation, and accessing of data stored on a blockchain, e.g., the Bitcoin blockchain. It may form part of a protocol for searching the blockchain for content/data. A method in accordance with the invention may be used for associating or linking data stored within (separate/different) blockchain transactions to enable the identification, retrieval, and/or sharing of data stored therein. Additionally, or alternatively, it facilitates identification of transactions (TX) in a blockchain which store content/data that needs to be shared, transmitted, stored, and/or accessed by a user. Such a method comprises the step of mapping a mnemonic to: (1) a public key (PK) associated with the transaction (TX); and (2) the transaction ID (TXID) of the transaction (TX).		
Applied/ Publication May 15, 2020 September 3, 2020	**Inventors:** Craig Steven Wright, Stephane Savanah	**Id. #** 20200280433	**Name:** Secure multiparty loss resistant storage and transfer of cryptographic keys for blockchain based systems in conjunction with a wallet management system
Description	A solution for controlling access to a resource such as a digital wallet implemented using a blockchain. Use of the invention during setup of the wallet can enable subsequent operations to be handled in a secure manner over an insecure channel. An example method comprises splitting a verification element into multiple shares, determining a common secret at multiple nodes in a network, and using the common secret to transmit a share of the verification element between nodes. The shares can be split such that no share is sufficient to determine the verification element and can be stored at separate locations. Upon share unavailability, the share can be retrieved a location accessibility. For safe transmission of the share(s), the common secret is generated at two different nodes independently and used to generate an encryption key for encrypting at least one share of the verification element to be transmitted securely.		
Applied/ Publication April 28, 2020 July 7, 2022	**Inventors:** Craig Steven Wright, Jack Owen Davies, Alexander Tennyson Mackay, Chloe Ceren Tartan, Wei Zhang	**Id. #** 20220217004	**Name:** Systems and methods for non-parallelized mining on a proof-of-work blockchain network
Description	The present disclosure provides methods and systems for ensuring the security of a blockchain and associated network and for enabling the establishment of consensus regarding the state of the blockchain. A method of the disclosure may be implemented by one or more nodes on a blockchain network, using a nonparallelizable algorithm to calculate an output based on a computational difficulty parameter, a hash of at least one blockchain transaction, and/or a hash of at least one blockchain block header. The nonparallelizable, inherently sequential algorithm comprises at least one of the following operations or a combination thereof: a recursive operation, a modular exponentiation and/or a repeated squaring operation.		
Applied/ Publication March 31, 2021 July 15, 2021	**Inventors:** Craig Steven Wright, Stephane Savanah	**Id. #** 20210216623	**Name:** Blockchain implemented counting system and method for use in secure voting and distribution

Applied/ Publication February 14, 2017 February 14, 2019	**Inventors: Craig Steven Wright Stephane Savanah**	**Id. # 20190050541**	**Name: A Method And System For Securing Computer Software Using A Distributed Hash Table And A Blockchain**
Description	This invention relates generally to blockchain implementations and is suited for, but not limited to, use with the Bitcoin blockchain. It can be used for the implementation of automated processes such as device/system control, process control, distributed computing and storage, and others. The invention provides an event detecting, monitoring, and/or counting mechanism. The event may be, for example, a vote, decision, or selection which is made by a given entity. The invention provides a counting solution in which a computing resource, running simultaneously and in parallel to the blockchain, manages a loop-based operation. The computing resource continuously monitors the state of the blockchain as well as any other off-blockchain input data or source. The execution of the loop is influenced by the state of the blockchain. Each iteration of the loop that is executed by the computing resource is recorded in a transaction that is written to the blockchain. It is stored as a hash within the transaction's metadata.		
Applied/ Publication June 2, 2022 September 15, 2022	**Inventors:** Craig Steven Wright, Stephane Savanah	**Id. #** 20220292471	**Name:** Universal Tokenization System For Blockchain-Based Cryptocurrencies
Description	A method of creating, redeeming, and transferring tokens on a peer-to-peer distributed ledger including generating a blockchain transaction having an output related to a quantity of cryptocurrency and a hash of a redeem script usable for spending the output. The redeem script comprises metadata, which in turn comprises a token representing a tokenized entity. The redeem script additionally comprises at least one public cryptographic key. The metadata is provided in the redeem script at a location designated in the underlying blockchain protocol as a location for a cryptographic key.		

Source:
https://patents.justia.com/inventor/craig-steven-wright.
https://patents.google.com/.
https://patentscope.wipo.int/search/en/search.jsf.
https://patentcenter.uspto.gov/.

Table 2.
Patents of key relevance for the development of Web3.

COPA, the consortium that presents itself against the enforcement of patent intellectual property rights, is the holder of thousands of such rights and growing. These conflicting realities could be interpreted as an attempt to avoid the payment of such rights by some of these members, and a way to crush the competition. Among others, Dr. Wright, Dr. Savanah, and nChain are obvious targets given that they have been building a reservoir of very significant patents for over a decade.

The environment described is one of the arenas where the multibillion-dollar conflicts of interests between major participants of the blockchain sector are being settled. And these events are just the prelude of a combative blockchain-patent-environment. Eventually, the rights of those who have them will have to be recognized and the wrongs of bad actors will have to be discouraged and penalized, just as it happens in any other sector.

4. Conclusion

Due to its technical characteristics, blockchain technology will be at the forefront of the evolution of IP rights protection. In addition, the elucidation of IP rights within that sector itself will help shape the development of this technology. At stake are billions of US dollars, the ability of the industry to grow, and the capacity of economies to benefit from the efficiencies this technology generates. Among the challenges, an unequal understanding of the technology, and the slow evolvement of IP rights management, this chapter has reviewed key developments.

Author details

Eva R. Porras
Blockchain Smart Technologies, Department of Fundamentals of Economic Analysis, Universidad Rey Juan Carlos, Madrid, Spain

*Address all correspondence to: eva_porras@hotmail.com

References

[1] Web3 is also referred to as Web 3.0 and web3

[2] Nakamoto S. "Bitcoin: A Peer-to-Peer Electronic Cash System". 2008. Available from: https://bitcoin.org/bitcoin.pdf [Accessed: March 3, 2023] and Available from: https://www.ussc.gov/sites/default/files/pdf/training/annual-national-training-seminar/2018/Emerging_Tech_Bitcoin_Crypto.pdf [Accessed: March 3, 2023]

[3] Hussey M. "What was DigiCash". 2019. Available from: https://decrypt.co/resources/digicash-what-is-cryptocurrency-explainer [Accessed: March 3, 2023]

[4] Dai W. "B-Money". Weidai; 1998. Available from: http://www.weidai.com/bmoney.txt [Accessed: March 3, 2023]

[5] Chaum D. Dissertation: "Computer Systems Established, Maintained, and Trusted by Mutually Suspicious Groups." Nakamotoinstitute; 1982. Available from: https://nakamotoinstitute.org/static/docs/computer-systems-by-mutually-suspicious-groups.pdf [Accessed: March 3, 2023]

[6] Chaum D. "Blind Signatures for Untraceable payments." 1982. Available from: chrome-extension://efaidnbmnnnibpcajpcglclefindmkaj/ [Accessed: March 3, 2023] and Available from: http://www.hit.bme.hu/~buttyan/courses/BMEVIHIM219/2009/Chaum.BlindSigForPayment.1982.PDF [Accessed: March 3, 2023]

[7] Stornetta WS, Haber S. How to Time-Stamp a Digital Document. Staroceans; 1991. Available from: http://www.staroceans.org/e-book/Haber_Stornetta.pdf [Accessed: March 3, 2023]

[8] Bayer D, Stornetta WS, Haber S. Improving the Efficiency and Reliability of Digital Time-Stamping. Math. columbia; 1992. Available from: https://www.math.columbia.edu/~bayer/papers/Timestamp_BHS93.pdf [Accessed: February 3, 2023]

[9] Stornetta WS, Haber S. Secure Names for Bit-Strings. Nakamotoinstitute; 1997. Available from: https://nakamotoinstitute.org/static/docs/secure-names-bit-strings.pdf [Accessed: January 23, 2023]

[10] Adam B. "Hashcash - A Denial of Service Counter-Measure". Hashcash; 2002. Available from: chrome-extension://efaidnbmnnnibpcajpcglclefindmkaj/ [Accessed: March 3, 2023] and Available from: http://www.hashcash.org/papers/hashcash.pdf [Accessed: March 3, 2023]

[11] Available from: https://cryptoslate.com/prolific-51-attacks-crypto-verge-ethereum-classic-bitcoin-gold-feathercoin-vertcoin [Accessed: March 4, 2023]

[12] Committee on WIPO Standards (CWS). Defined by the World Intellectual Property Organization (WIPO Committee on WIPO Standards (CWS)). Fifth Session. Geneva: World Intellectual Property Organization (WIPO); 2017

[13] Porras ER, Sánchez-Escribano MG. Decentralized blockchain for autobiographical memory in cognitive robotics. AI, Computer Science and Robotics Technology. 2022;**1**:1-19. DOI: 10.5772/acrt.04 [Accessed: March 4, 2023]

[14] Ishmaev G. Blockchain technology as an institution of property. Metaphilosophy. 2017;**48**(5):666-686

[15] Wang et al. A Summary of Research on Blockchain in the Field of Intellectual Property. At the 2018 International Conference on Identification. IIKI: Information and Knowledge in the Internet of the Things. p. 2018

[16] Available from: https://ipwe.com/blockchain-smart-pool/?mod=join-as-a-founder#default-popup; https://www.bernstein.io/; https://www.patentattorneys.ch/en/ [Accessed: March 4, 2023]

[17] Available from: https://www.concordlawschool.edu/blog/news/admissibility-blockchain-digital-evidence/ [Accessed: March 4, 2023]

[18] Available from: https://legislature.vermont.gov/statutes/section/12/081/01913 [Accessed: March 4, 2023]

[19] Available from: https://delcode.delaware.gov/title8/c001/sc07/ [Accessed: February 21, 2023]

[20] Available from: Error! Bookmark not defined. [Accessed: February 21, 2021]

[21] Available from: https://www.azleg.gov/viewdocument/?docName=https://www.azleg.gov/ars/44/07061.htm [Accessed: February 21, 2021]

[22] Available from: https://legiscan.com/OH/text/SB300/id/1795258 [Accessed: February 21, 2023]

[23] Available from: https://eu.dispatch.com/story/news/politics/state/2018/08/23/auditor-set-to-use-blockchain/10899546007/ [Accessed: February 21, 2021]

[24] Available from: https://legiscan.com/WY/bill/HB0070/2018 [Accessed: February 4, 2023]

[25] Available from: https://legiscan.com/WY/bill/HB0019/2018 [Accessed: February 4, 2023]

[26] Available from: https://legiscan.com/WY/bill/HB0101/2018 [Accessed: February 4, 2023]

[27] Available from: https://legiscan.com/WY/bill/HB0126/2018 [Accessed: February 4, 2023]

[28] Available from: https://legiscan.com/WY/bill/SF0111/2018 [Accessed: February 4, 2023]

[29] Available from: https://bitcoinmagazine.com/business/wyoming-house-unanimously-approves-two-pro-blockchain-bills [Accessed: February 4, 2023]

[30] Available from: https://vtdigger.org/2018/08/28/vermont-bullish-blockchain-new-law-takes-effect/ [Accessed: February 4, 2023]

[31] Available from: https://legiscan.com/CA/text/AB2658/id/1821719 [Accessed: February 4, 2023]

[32] Available from: https://www.managingip.com/article/2a5bssmgulfpv353htybk/china-patent-courts-respond-positively-to-blockchain-evidence [Accessed: January 24, 2023]

[33] Available from: https://corporate.cyrilamarchandblogs.com/2020/07/section-65b-of-the-indian-evidence-act-1872-requirements-for-admissibility-of-electronic-evidence-revisited-by-the-supreme-court/ [Accessed: January 24, 2023]

[34] Available from: https://www.mondaq.com/india/fin-tech/975778/a-new-digital-order-unveiling-the-interplay-of-law-blockchain-technology–part-b-blockchain-technology-legal-frame

work-analysing-india39s-blockchain-preparedness [Accessed: January 24, 2023]

[35] Nakamoto 2008. Available from: https://bitcoin.org/bitcoin.pdf [Accessed: January 24, 2023]

[36] Poon J, Dryja T "The Bitcoin Lightning Network: Scalable Off-Chain Instant Payments", chrome-extension://efaidnbmnnnibpcajpcglclefindmkaj/ Available from: https://lightning.network/lightning-network-paper.pdf [Accessed: January 24, 2023]

[37] "Bitcoin cash", Available from: https://bitcoincash.org/ [Accessed: January 24, 2023]

[38] Available from: https://www.bitcoinsv.com/ [Accessed: January 24, 2023]

[39] Available from: https://bitcoin.org/bitcoin.pdf [Accessed: January 24, 2023]

[40] Available from: https://forkdrop.io/ [Accessed: January 24, 2023]

[41] Available from: https://nchain.com/patents-explained-how-nchain-and-ipwe-are-supporting-blockchain-innovation/ [Accessed: January 24, 2023]

[42] Available from: https://protos.com/satoshi-nakamoto-appeals-craig-wright-bitcoin-white-paper-copyright/ [Accessed: January 24, 2023]

[43] Available from: https://coingeek.com/btc-groups-respond-to-bitcoin-white-paper-copyright-claim/ [Accessed: January 24, 2023]

[44] Available from: https://twitter.com/opencryptoorg/status/1381642092624015360?ref_src=twsrc%5Etfw%7Ctwcamp%5Etweetembed%7Ctwterm%5E1381642092624015360%7Ctwgr%5Ee6c5ea4fd17d7238eb83bbf2f0439837d79c042a%7Ctwcon%5Es1_&ref_url=https%3A%2F%2Fwww.coindesk.com%2Fpolicy%2F2021%2F04%2F12%2Fsquare-led-copa-sues-craig-wright-over-bitcoin-white-paper-copyright-claims%2F [Accessed: February 24, 2023]

[45] Available from: https://www.opencrypto.org/about/ [Accessed: February 24, 2023]

[46] Available from: https://patentcenter.uspto.gov/applications/16078605 [Accessed: February 24, 2023]

[47] Available from: US20190057382A1 * 2016-02-23 2019-02-21 nChain Holdings Limited Registry and automated management method for blockchain-enforced smart contracts [Accessed: February 24, 2023]

[48] Available from: https://coingeek.com/copa-block-forced-to-cite-craig-wright-smart-contract-patent/ [Accessed: February 26, 2023]